EFFECTIVE RESEARCH AND REPORT WRITING IN GOVERNMENT

THE McGRAW-HILL SERIES IN PROFESSIONAL COMMUNICATION FOR GOVERNMENT AND INDUSTRY

Consulting Editor
Arthur H. Kuriloff, Management Consultant

Monroe   Effective Research and Report Writing in Government

EFFECTIVE RESEARCH AND REPORT

WRITING IN GOVERNMENT

Jud Monroe
Research Consultant

McGraw-Hill Book Company

New York   St. Louis   San Francisco   Auckland   Bogotá   Hamburg   Johannesburg   London   Madrid
Mexico   Montreal   New Delhi   Panama   Paris   São Paulo   Singapore   Sydney   Tokyo   Toronto

Research is what you do when you need information. It may mean talking to someone on the telephone for twenty minutes or engaging in formal study for six months. Whatever the extent, research always requires a certain kind of hard-headed, systematic, thinking. This thinking process is the subject of this book. Research requires special thinking skills, and it requires changes in the roles played by office staff and management. This book is a guide to behavior that will enable you to do research *and* survive the process professionally.

Library of Congress Cataloging in Publication Data

Monroe, Judson.
    Effective research and report writing in government.

    (The McGraw-Hill series in professional communication for government and industry)
      Includes index.
      1. Government report writing. I. Title.
II. Series: McGraw-Hill series in professional communication for government and industry.
JF1525.R46M65   808'.066'35   79–9279
ISBN 0–07–042784–4

EFFECTIVE RESEARCH AND REPORT WRITING IN GOVERNMENT

1 2 3 4 5 6 7 8 9 0 D O D O 7 8 3 2 1 0 9

This book was set in Melior by Holmes Composition Service. The editors were Robert G. Manley and Donald W. Burden; the designer was Bruce Kortebein; the production supervisor was Richard A. Ausburn.
R. R. Donnelley & Sons Company was printer and binder.

CONTENTS

Preface   vii

Section One: Strategies for Research and Report Writing

Chapter 1: Politics and Government Reports   1
Chapter 2: The Maze of Research and Report Writing: Strategies
*   for Keeping on Track through a Long, Complex Process*   9

Section Two: Brainstorming by Designing the Report

Chapter 3: An Introduction to Brainstorming   19
Chapter 4: Analyzing the Assignment   33
Chapter 5: Analyzing the Audience for the Report   48
Chapter 6: Analyzing the Subject   83
Chapter 7: Assembling an Outline of the Report   99
Section Two Summary and the Answers to Some
*   Questions You May Still Have*   123

Section Three: Planning Research and Collecting Data

Chapter 8: Figuring Out What Data You Need   127
Chapter 9: Finding Data Sources   148
Chapter 10: Planning and Conducting Data Collection   160
Chapter 11: Planning Data Interpretation   182
Section Three Summary and the Answers to Some
*   Questions You May Still Have*   188

Section Four: Analyzing Results

Chapter 12: What Results Mean and What They Don't Mean   193
Chapter 13: What You Can and Cannot Do with Statistics
*   (and Guidelines for Sampling)*   205

Chapter 14: The Cause–Recommendation Problem 218
Section Four Summary and the Answers to Some
   Questions You May Still Have 226

Section Five: Assembling the Final Paper

Chapter 15: Why Writing Is a Problem 229
Chapter 16: Building Sentences and Paragraphs 238
Chapter 17: Editing and Review 249
Section Five Summary and the Answers to Some
   Questions You May Still Have 267

**Section Six: Some Notes on Management Participation
   in Research**

Chapter 18: Staffing and Quality Control in Research 271

The End 280

Bibliography 283

Index 285

PREFACE

There are two certainties in government work—change and reports. Change is inevitable because government involves people. Reports are inevitable because even when people fervently want things to change, they still don't want change for the *worse*. They demand that people in government make the *right* changes, and right changes require careful study and consideration. To make a good decision you need information, which must be gathered, organized, and interpreted, and you need to communicate this information. Thus, research and report writing are inevitable.

As government grows more complex (in response to increasingly complex demands placed on it), the report becomes more and more important. The nice, relatively easy, decisions of one hundred years ago are not so easy any more; decisions, and the reports that explain or lead to them, are being contested more and more frequently by special-interest groups and by the general public. Building a road used to involve only a few reports; now, to satisfy all the people who wish to make sure the decision to build is the *right* decision, it may require dozens of reports. Seemingly simple decisions require extensive study. For example, in 1978 the federal government conducted a study to decide whether to change *stationery size* from 8 x 10½ to standard 8½ x 11. Absurd? Hardly. Consider for a moment the vast quantity of paper used in federal programs. The decision involved millions of dollars and a potential waste of tons of paper. Those who work in government have come to realize that this is the way things are going to be—until the world becomes simpler again.

This increase in paperwork means that every year hundreds of thousands of government employees get involved in at least some phase of the study/report process. Some volunteer; others are summoned to the task. All soon find themselves embroiled in two of the most difficult tasks of all—research and writing.

This is a book about these two tasks, written for people in government who must perform them. It is intended for all those who get

involved in the research and writing processes: the people who request and need the information, those who gather and interpret it,
and those who organize it and report it. This is not a book about how
to do any particular kind of report. It isn't a book about grammar and
style. It's a book about what to *do* when you're faced with an
assignment—a need—to do some research and write up the results.
It's a guide to how to set up a study, think out the research, keep
control over it while it's in progress, make sense out of all the information collected, present it clearly and effectively when the study is
done, and, thus, how to satisfy the many and varied readers of the
report.

The particular study you do doesn't have to be formal research.
Research thinking procedures must be applied to all sorts of tasks,
for example:

  Preparing legislation
  Writing policy and procedure
  Hiring
  Program analysis
  Employee evaluation
  Job description
  Auditing
  Office design
  Workflow analysis
  Office organization
  Planning
  Public relations

Research is very systematic thinking; the "tricks" of research work
any time systematic thinking is in order.

SCOPE

The final draft report is the product of a long series of steps taken
by the researcher/writer. *The quality of the report is as much a
reflection of the quality of the initial thinking that went into the
research as it is a reflection of the writing skills of the researcher/
writer.* Every step, from the initial assignment to the final drafting
and editing process, affects the quality of the final product. Because
all the steps in research and writing are interrelated, this book covers
them all at least briefly. I've tried to identify all the key steps that go
into the whole process of research and report writing and to tie all
these together into one logical, consistent, effective procedure for
getting the report done *properly.*

In building this procedure, I've had a lot of help from people in
government, who have been doing research and writing reports for

many years. They've helped me identify problems, they've taught me the tricks of the trade that really work in government agencies, and they've worked with me in preparing government reports. In short, I've built this book from the suggestions of people in government, as well as from my own experience. I've taken a number of individual suggestions and put them together into a logical, systematic approach to getting reports done.

BASIC APPROACH

This is a "how to" book, and since research and writing are both primarily thinking processes, this is a book filled with practical suggestions about "How to Think." It's about what people do, and can do, to think their way through the whole complex process from assignment to report.

Writing a book about how to think out research and report writing problems involves a lot of digging into peoples' brains to find out what is going on. For example, almost every good report writer I spoke to said that interpreting results was a difficult process they had learned to do over a long period of time. They could show me a collection of information and then tell me what it meant. They had difficulty explaining what went on mentally to enable them to go from raw information to a valid conclusion. After lots of questions and some demonstrations, they could usually explain some of their thinking processes, show me *some* of the steps they had taken to go from one point to the next. If you talk to enough good researchers and writers about how they work, you begin to see similarities in their thinking processes and you begin to fill in gaps. After a few years of donig this, you can begin to put the general steps of thinking down in a rough outline; you can watch people as they go through the steps and tell when they're following the outline and when they're doing somethjng different. In the end, you get a pretty good idea of what thinking processes work in research and writing, of the "best" step-by-step approach to take. You find, too, that what often seems intuitive isn't—it's perfectly logical and orderly thinking. Thinking just happens so quickly that we aren't always aware of what's going on.

There are, then, two kinds of suggestions in this book: first, there are procedural suggestions for handling the day-to-day problems of research and writing (when to review work, when to submit a draft, etc.); second, there are suggestions about how to think through each stage of research and writing. These are the most important parts of the book, because the most impoartant steps in research and writing are mental steps.

CHAPTER CONTENTS

Except for the first two chapters, which set the stage for the rest of the book, each chapter is about a particular stage in the process of going from assignment to report. Each of these chapters is intended to give both a general overview of the particular stage and specific advice about how to get over the hurdles facing you at this point. Each chapter generally contains these sections:

1. Description of the stage, its purposes, its objectives, and its place in the overall research and writing process
2. Analysis of the problems usually encountered during this stage and a brief discussion of their causes
3. Description of a general approach to solving the problems so that the objectives of the stage can be met
4. An outline of specific steps to take to get through the stage—in roughly the order to take them in
5. Examples of these procedures with discussion of each step
6. Rules and guidelines to follow while working
7. Notes to management and staff, explaining he roles they can play during each stage to ensure a good final report
8. Checklists, flowcharts, and other "tools" to refer to while working

When you add all the chapters up, you get a logical, step-by-step guide for moving from the assignment to the report. While many of the steps are not easy, following them carefully does take much of the intuition or guesswork out of research and writing.

HOW TO WORK YOUR WAY THROUGH THIS BOOK

When you look at a tax instruction booklet or an automobile repair manual, you generally give them two readings. First you read quickly, to get an overview; then you read through each portion—*as you work on the tax form or the car.* You look at what the book says you should do, and then you try it. I think that's also the best way to go through this book. Give it a general reading first; then get out a report and work through each stage carefully. Use a report you haven't done yet if possible, or take an old one and work it out from scratch. Experiment with the procedures, techniques, and tools in the book until you've decided which way they work best for you.

As you work through the book, be prepared to find that some stages are easy and some are quite difficult, just as you would find some parts of the Internal Revenue Service Tax Booklet easy and some quite difficult. Even the best scientific researchers don't find research easy, and research into the concerns of people is, and always will be, difficult. But it can be done effectively and systematically by anyone willing to do it carefully.

As a final note, remember that it always takes longer to describe a mental process than it does to do the actual thinking. In some instances, you will find ten or fifteen pages of this book devoted to a single procedure. It may *look* time-consuming. In practice it will only take time to learn the procedure; then the procedure will become a part of your thinking process.

Jud Monroe

STRATEGIES FOR RESEARCH AND REPORT WRITING

The process of research and report writing is complicated. Before jumping into the details of a step-by-step approach, it's a good idea to get an overview of the problems that will be encountered and the general strategies for solving these problems.

The two basic problems that must be overcome are:

1. How to deal with political considerations while doing objective research
2. How to keep control over a very complex process

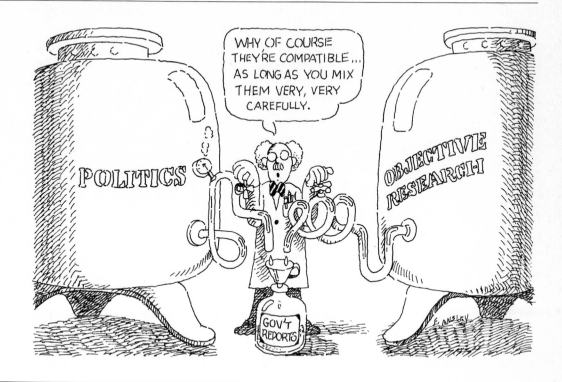

POLITICS AND GOVERNMENT REPORTS

1

Working for the government is different from working in business, in the sciences, or for yourself. When you work in any government agency, you're a part of the political process. What you do has an impact on the quality of political programs and processes. The opposite is also true. In spite of efforts to insulate civil service employees from the political arena, in spite of efforts to separate permanent staff from political changes, every person working in government feels the influence of political decisions—directly or indirectly. This influence is felt very strongly by those involved in decision making, including researchers who gather and interpret the data used in making political decisions.

The political nature of government work affects the research and report writing effort at every stage from assignment to report. The work of government is to make decisions about people and resources in order to answer questions such as:

1. What is the most equitable way to distribute goods and services in society?
2. What is the best balance between the rights of the majority and the rights of the minority?
3. What is the best way to operate to best serve the public?
4. What is the best way to solve social problems?

These are the fundamental questions behind the thousands of detailed questions government employees are asked to answer each day. They aren't usually expressed as dramatically; the first question is more likely to be something quite specific, such as:

> Should we continue the special senior citizen's golf course discount for another year?

Or:

> What would happen if we modified the regulations governing Food Stamp distribution to make it easier for people to get stamps?

These are the questions government employees have to answer.

The purpose of government research is to get information that can be used to help answer such questions. The problem facing the government researcher is that the answers to these questions are ultimately subjective answers. At some point between assignment and report the researcher has to deal with politics, with the controversial nature of any decision that affects people. The researcher can expect to encounter people who will want to twist facts, or ignore some facts altogether. Others will simply draw different conclusions from the same body of facts. To most researchers, who have spent considerable time and energy gathering information and analyzing it carefully, this can make research quite frustrating.

The frustration arises out of the clash between the objective nature of research and the subjective nature of politics. The researcher is committed to objectivity, to finding out what's really happening rather than just what someone thinks is happening. The atmosphere of the office is subjective, political. People in the office are committed to a program, to its goals and to the methods they have worked so hard to implement. The facts the researcher gathers may, at times, upset the routine or even the basic structure of the office. They may, in the hands of the public or of special-interest groups, affect the whole direction of the agency. The researcher gets caught between two worlds. *The problem is how to get the job done, how to maintain the integrity of the research process and the integrity of the political process at the same time.* Both processes are a part of the effort that goes into the final report, but they have to be kept separate to make sure that political considerations don't interfere with the data gathering and that masses of data aren't used to overwhelm the good judgment of those making decisions. It's a hard balance to strike.

The separation between these two processes is evident in many of the public clashes between scientists and politicians. These clashes often sound like this:

Scientist: "It may be concluded from the data collected over the past seven years that continued use of radioactive chemicals in this area will lead to an increase in the incidence of cancer."

Politician: "The use of radioactive chemicals in this area is essential to maintaining production of _____ and thus a healthy economy."

The scientist's factual pronouncement and the politician's generalization about the economy *seem* to be in conflict here, but they aren't. The scientist's statement is apolitical; the politician's is afactual. The scientist appears to be arguing against the use of radioactive chemicals, but actually hasn't said a word about whether they should or should not be used. The politician has not dealt with the fact the scientist has presented. The apparent argument isn't an argument; the two sides are simply living in completely different worlds and ignoring each other.

The effective researcher in government work cannot afford to do either of these things; the report must be factual *and* political. But, there should always be a clear separation between these two parts of the report—and these two parts of the research effort. In short, fact should not be confused with interpretation. There are a number of specific steps that can be taken to keep these two elements of the report separate during research and report writing. These are described in the context of each chapter in this book. The *general strategies* for keeping the two from getting mixed together and confused are outlined below.

STRATEGIES FOR GOVERNMENT RESEARCH AND REPORT WRITING

The basic strategy for effective research and report writing is to take pains to establish your personal credibility, both as a researcher and as a politician. Maintain this credibility at all costs. If you lose it, your ability to get good data will be lost and your ability to defend your political interpretations will also suffer. Establishing and keeping credibility means:

1. *Make sure your data are "clean,"* that they can stand up to close scrutiny. Don't estimate or guess (they're the same thing, after all). Present your data and stand by it, but never try to stretch it too far.

2. *Expect disagreement over your conclusions and recommendations.* As the late Speaker of the House of Representatives, Sam Rayburn, once said, "When two people agree, one of them isn't thinking." When you have made a recommendation, expect people with different points of view to attack it. Give them credit for the integrity of their opinions; in return, demand that they give you the same credit. Never get personal, never take an argument personally.

3. *Make sure you know the politics of a situation before you go out and try to collect data about it.* Knowing what sort of political views you're going to run into will help you keep opinions separated from fact. If you go into a situation "cold," it's easy to get statements of opinion, such as

   Smith says the problem is in the way we're sending out the forms.

confused with fact,

   Thirty-seven percent of the forms we send out go out a month late.

   People are always willing to confuse your research with their half-formed opinions.

4. *Don't start drawing conclusions until you've got all the data you need, all the data you set out to collect.* When you start making preliminary conclusions, your efforts soon become focused on trying to prove these conclusions, rather than on finishing the initial data collection. Every time you adjust your research in midstream, check to make sure you haven't adjusted too much.

5. *Stay out of office politics.* Don't get involved in any of the backstabbing and gossip that goes on. This is probably good general advice, but it's critical to a researcher. One enemy may be able to destroy your credibility at both objective and political levels. If you must climb the office ladder to success, do it openly where all can see.

6. When you finally get into your analysis of results, when you get to the political part of the research and report writing process, *give at least brief coverage of all sides of the argument.* It's fair to spend a lot of time building up your side, to present your conclusions as forcefully and completely as you can, but you need to at least mention the possible opposing views.

7. *Whenever possible, leave decisions to those with the broadest possible political point of view.* If you're a staff analyst in a small office, don't try to make decisions about the future of the whole agency. Explain the options open to the decision makers, explain your point of view, but leave major decisions to those with the overview.

This advice is difficult to follow. It means that you must treat the whole research and report writing process with discipline and care. The most difficult part, though, is the most important and it can probably all be summed up in one simple rule:

KEEP YOUR RESEARCH AND YOUR PERSONAL POLITICAL FEELINGS SEPARATE

Research is a professional activity—keep it that way and you won't have too much trouble with it. If you get personally involved in the outcome of a research project, you'll find research in government terribly frustrating.

A BRIEF ILLUSTRATION

It's probably not a bad idea to look at what this advice means in terms of a simple example. Here's the situation:

> The city council is running a bit short of funds and is looking for ways to cut costs. The Parks and Recreation Department budget is an obvious place to look, they think. They ask you to look at the special reduced fee senior citizens pay for golf at the two city golf courses. Their question is, as usual, a political one: Should we continue to give these senior citizens this special rate?

It's very likely you have some feeling about this sort of question. It's likely to be a political opinion, based on some sense of what's fair and what's not fair. You may think that government shouldn't play favorites; you may think that senior citizens deserve the lower fees. These are political views—save them for after you've developed a research plan and collected your data. Before getting political, find out such things as:

1. How many senior citizens use the courses
2. How many take advantage of the reduced fee
3. How much revenue is lost
4. How many would stop using the course if the fees went up
5. How many feel that a fee increase would be fair
6. How many would be willing to pay extra on a voluntary basis
7. What related programs could be changed to help make up the revenue now being lost

Getting this kind of information *before* making any kind of commitment to a political viewpoint might save you from ever having to take a political stand. You might actually solve the problem without having to get too deeply involved in a political argument. And if you do decide to make a recommendation, at least you'll do so with a full knowledge of the situation you're talking about.

CHAPTER SUMMARY

Any research effort in government is affected by the politics of the situation it involves. You should not ignore political considerations, but you should take pains to deal with the research process objectively and separately from the politics. Get your information, make sure it's reliable, make sure you've got all the data you need, and then interpret. Keep political considerations out of your research until you've got a firm, objectively sound, base to work from. Above all, don't let your personal feelings get in the way of your judgment.

STRATEGIES FOR KEEPING ON TRACK DURING RESEARCH

2

For most people who get involved in government study projects, the initial assignment meeting goes something like this:

1. The person who wants the report explains the problem and the reason for the report.
2. You respond by asking a few questions (not too many, because you don't want the boss to think you're stupid).
3. The boss gives some tentative answers.
4. You talk briefly about how the whole thing can be done.
5. You both agree—with enthusiasm—that the work should start right away.
6. You leave the office wondering what you've really got to do. The boss sits down at the desk wondering whether you can really do it in the time given, maybe even wondering if you really understand what's going on at all.

In the end, you've both embarked on a long and complex project with little more than a vague understanding of where you're supposed to go and how you can get there.

THE PROBLEM

Two major problems have to be solved before you can comfortably do research and prepare a report. They are the vagueness of the whole assignment process and the complexity of the process of research and writing.

Assignments are necessarily vague. The person asking for information cannot be expected to know exactly what information is needed. The boss can be expected to know vaguely what the problem is, but if the exact nature of the information being requested were known, then there would be absolutely no need for research. The boss can only know that information about a certain situation would probably be useful in making a decision about that situation. Assignments, then, will always be vague.

Taking a vague assignment, you also embark on a relatively long and complex process. There are a lot of decisions to be made about what data to collect, where to get it, and how to make sense out of all of it once you've got it. The research process often takes place over weeks and months, not over an afternoon. Day-to-day work is mingled with the research process. Your ability to *remember* the assignment is even a factor. A week after the initial assignment, it's unlikely that either you or the boss will remember a tenth of your discussion. Both of you are also likely to change your minds about what needs to be done over the weeks of research. Given all the little things that can go wrong, a report that turns out exactly as specified during assignment is as rare as an assignment that is really specific.

You start the research and writing process a bit like a traveler in a strange land, knowing you want to get somewhere, but not exactly sure of where you are headed. This puts you in a rather silly situation. You know you have to get going, so you want to start off. But you have no way of knowing whether you're headed in the right direction. Like a traveler without a map, you take a step in one direction, look around to see where you've gone, take another step in another direction, and so on. You readjust your plans as you travel. Your mental wanderings can lead you off track; you have no way of knowing what path you should be following (Figure 2–1).

As any traveler knows, wandering around looking for your destination can be a hit-or-miss affair. It surely takes more time than

FIGURE 2-1/ WHAT YOUR PATH LOOKS LIKE WHEN YOU DON'T KNOW WHERE YOU'RE GOING

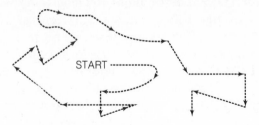

traveling directly from one point to the next. And you also risk running out of gas before you get to your destination—or missing it altogether. *Only if you know exactly where you're going, can you plot an easy, efficient path there* (Figure 2–2).

Nearly everyone who has ever been involved in research has experienced this problem of not knowing exactly where the whole project was going. The last-minute rush, the last-minute changes in the report, are both familiar and frustrating problems.

THE SOLUTION

The obvious solution to this problem of vague assignment and complex process is to sit down and figure out exactly where you're going before you take any steps in researching or writing. In every endeavor, from automobile mechanics to economics, this is the first step. The traveler identifies the destination; the automobile mechanic must know what a well-tuned engine sounds like before starting to work on it; the economist must know what a healthy economy looks like before designing programs to make changes in economic conditions. The researcher must know what the final product of the research will look like before starting to work toward it.

FIGURE 2-2/WHAT YOUR PATH LOOKS LIKE WHEN YOU DO KNOW WHERE YOU'RE GOING

START --------▸ --------▸ --------▸ --------▸ --------▸ --------▸ --------▸ --------▸ FINISH

Since the report is the only tangible final product of the research and writing process, since everything you do contributes to the report, *the report is your destination.* You must know what the report is going to look like before you start the process of going from assignment to report. If you know what the report is going to look like in the end, you can make careful, well-directed decisions about how to get to it—all through the long research process.

If you're asking yourself "How can I know what the report is going to look like until I've done the research?" you've asked the most important question that this book is designed to answer. At this point it's too early to go into details of methods; the general strategies need explaining first.

STRATEGIES FOR DESIGNING THE REPORT BEFORE STARTING RESEARCH

The most important thing you can do to get a concrete idea of what the report is finally going to look like is to start writing things down as soon as you get the assignment. Write down your impression of the assignment, your thoughts about how to do your job, write anything—but start writing. Get your thoughts out of your head and onto paper.

Writing is important because when you write an idea down the idea becomes clearer and more concrete. Almost everyone who has written anything has noticed this phenomenon; as you write your thoughts down in an essay, or on an examination, they slowly become more focused. By the time you've actually written the whole essay, or answered the examination question, you've usually figured out what you wanted to say in the first place. Often, seeing this, students will even try to rewrite—starting from their last paragraph. There isn't anything mysterious or unusual about this; it happens to everyone.

Writing makes thinking clearer because writing forces you to use language in a disciplined manner. Language is systematic; it's a system of symbols and rules for using these symbols. Thinking is random most of the time; your brain wanders from place to place without much direction. By writing, you use language in its most orderly form. By writing your thoughts down, you impose this order, this discipline, on these thoughts. Whatever you decide to write down becomes clearer and more orderly.

At the same time writing helps give order to your thoughts, it also helps you see that order, to look at what your thoughts really are.

When you just sit and think, you often find that your thinking isn't very good. You come up with what seems like a great idea, run off to tell someone about it, and realize just how weak the idea was when you start putting it into words and are forced to argue about it. The process of turning the idea into words gives you a chance to pick the idea apart, to look at it critically. When you explain the idea to someone else, you give this person a chance to find the weaknesses in it. When you write it down, you give yourself the same chance to look at it. You can examine it carefully, pick it apart, play with it. Writing thus gives you something to work on.

Although it's always best to be organized, you can get some advantages from the writing process if all you do is take good clear notes about the assignment or jot down your thoughts about it after you leave the office. There are a number of slightly more organized "games" you can play while you think about the report assignment, all of which make your thinking more concrete.

One of the easiest ways to turn thoughts into writing is to jot down the *words* the boss used when giving you the assignment. Ignore prepositions and conjunctions and the like. Just jot down names and things. Don't bother about what order they came in, or about how important they were; just jot down as many as you can. You may end up with as many as several dozen words for even a simple assignment. These words will roughly represent the things the boss is interested in. You can make them more meaningful by trying to order them in terms of priority, in terms of which you think the boss is most interested in. From a random list—and random thoughts—you'll be able to proceed to a tentative idea of what's really important to cover in your study (Figure 2–3).

Organizing and clarifying your thoughts through writing also leads to some ways of getting feedback about your view of the assignment. If, for example, you write out *your* impressions of the assignment, you have something concrete to hand to the boss and to talk about. The boss can see exactly where you're going, can compare this with his or her own thoughts, can criticize and make suggestions. This can happen only if you've written things down. If it isn't written, everything remains vague.

As you're thinking about the assignment and the research you're going to do, the next most important strategy is to make every decision about research in the context of the final report. Every time you have to decide what to do, try to think about how your decision will affect the final report. For example, one of the basic decisions to be made about any report is whether the report is to be made public or kept for office use only. You can argue about this issue for hours and never really get anywhere. The way to resolve the issue is to figure

FIGURE 2-3/A PRIORITY LIST TO HELP FOCUS YOUR THOUGHTS

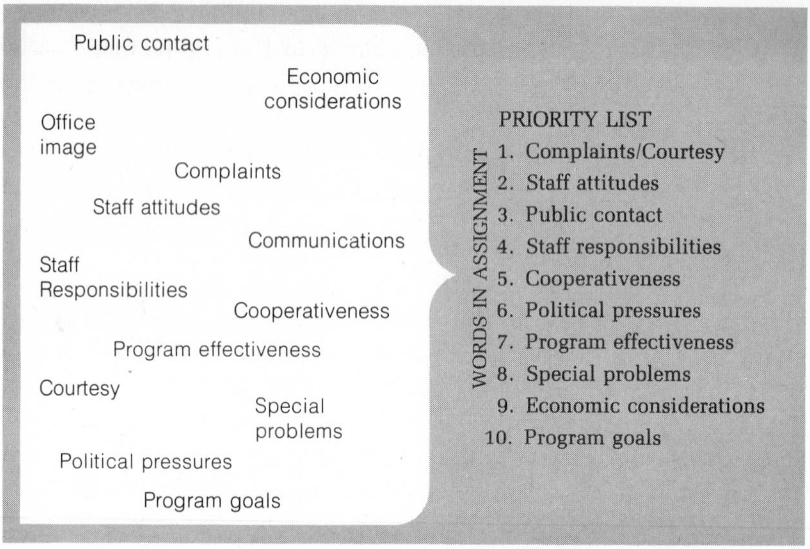

Public contact

Economic
considerations

Office
image

Complaints

Staff attitudes

Communications

Staff
Responsibilities

Cooperativeness

Program effectiveness

Courtesy

Special
problems

Political pressures

Program goals

WORDS IN ASSIGNMENT

PRIORITY LIST

1. Complaints/Courtesy
2. Staff attitudes
3. Public contact
4. Staff responsibilities
5. Cooperativeness
6. Political pressures
7. Program effectiveness
8. Special problems
9. Economic considerations
10. Program goals

ESTABLISHING PRIORITIES CLARIFIES THE ASSIGNMENT, MAKES
ASSIGNMENT GOALS CLEARER AND MORE CONCRETE

out what the decision will mean to the content and tone of the final
report. In a very general way, Figure 2–4 illustrates what you might
end up with. The vague question about whether to prepare a public
or office-only report begins to have concrete meaning only when it's

**FIGURE 2-4/SOME EXAMPLES OF CONCRETE DIFFERENCES
BETWEEN PUBLIC AND IN-HOUSE REPORTS**

PUBLIC REPORTS	IN-HOUSE REPORTS
No jargon	Some jargon OK
Long introduction necessary	Short introduction
Sensitive issues need extensive analysis	Sensitive issues can be handled frankly
No discussion of personnel allowed	Personnel may be discussed with tact

viewed in terms of what the final report will contain. The decision is easier to make and to stick to because its implications for the final report are now clearer.

There are dozens of major decisions that have to be made about even a fairly easy report. Each decision will have an impact on the form and content of the final product. By focusing on what this impact will be as you make the decision, you ensure that the research and the vision you have of the final report are kept consistent.

The *basic strategies* for dealing with a vague assignment and a complex research process are:

1. *Don't just think about things. Write your thoughts down.* Use the writing process to make your thoughts concrete. Use your written notes, assignment analysis, and outlines to get feedback from the person who has assigned the report.
2. *Before you make any decision about your work, think about what the report will look like if you take one direction or the other.* The report is the only concrete product of the entire research effort. The only way to make sure a decision is a good one is to see if it has the right impact on the report.

A BRIEF ILLUSTRATION

In a number of situations, it's important to know whether you're on the offensive or on the defensive. The answer to this basic question influences the nature of the report, the kind of data collected and presented, the scope of the report, and the tone of the writing. The influences are usually difficult to define concretely during the thinking process and don't come out until you get down to writing. Very often, this issue is discussed briefly at the very beginning of the assignment process. The discussion may sound something like this:

Boss: "We just have to remember that this is a touchy situation. When the report comes out, we want to make sure results aren't misinterpreted."

Staff: "Does that mean we should limit our investigation so that we don't get into some of the more political problem areas?"

Boss: "Well, that's not what I had in mind. We're out to do the job right. We just know that this business is going to get looked at carefully by both sides."

Staff: "OK, so we ought to be careful about how we present the data?"

Boss: "Well, not exactly. But we don't want to make it seem like things are wrong when they're really just in need of improvement."

This sort of hemming and hawing can be expected to go on whenever the results of research are even vaguely political. Note how it doesn't really get you anywhere; you go on like this for hours and never arrive at a concrete basis for a decision. To get a more concrete idea of what the issue means in terms of the report, it's necessary to think about the report and about how the report would *sound* if you decided to take the offensive or decided to take a defensive stand. (At this point, I would guess that most readers don't really have a clear idea of what *offensive* and *defensive* mean in this context. They're vague terms, like most of the terms that get tossed around during an assignment discussion.)

Perhaps the first step to take when making a decision like this is to focus immediately on the report and to try writing a portion of the report as it might sound given either decision. Here's how the report's introductory sentences might look from the two perspectives:

1. *If you take the offensive in looking at a problem:*
   "During the past three months, school staff have been working with county representatives to solve a discipline problem at _____ school. We first recognized this problem during a discussion with several parents who were concerned over the procedure for _____. Recognizing that this procedure might not cover the kind of situation the parents brought to our attention, we formed a study group on _____ to develop a solution to this potential problem."

2. *If you take the defensive in looking at a problem:*
   "According to County Regulation 222-33, the jurisdictional authority of school personnel in this county ends when students have left school grounds, or other school-supervised facilities, after normal activities have been completed. This jurisdictional authority was the subject of discussion at a recent (June 2, 19__) meeting of the School Advisory Council, at which a small group of parents questioned the school's standard procedure for _____. It is our intention to cooperate fully with community groups in solving problems that might affect school personnel or students, even when our legal authority to take unilateral action is limited."

In the first of these passages, note that the people working on solving the problem have admitted the problem exists and attacked it; they almost seem to be interested in doing the job. In the second passage, the people have obviously been dragged into the business kicking and screaming. Looking at these passages, it's possible to begin to think about how you want to attack a problem, how you want to set up research, what the full extent of your effort will be. And you can begin to think about how your reader might respond to each of these approaches. Most importantly, you get an idea of how you want the report to sound; if either doesn't sound right to you at this stage, this is probably a good indication of the way you will view the whole report when it is finally done.

The question answered by looking at these passages is an important one: "What kind of role do we want to play in this project—willing participant or reluctant foot dragger?" You could discuss this for a long time. You get an answer when you ask yourself, "Do I really want to stick my neck out and sound like example one?" Or, "Could I really hedge about this and face having to sound like example two?"

Once you've written something down to give yourself an idea of what the report could sound like in either case, you can do further analysis concerning the effect of choosing either role on the content of the final report. For example, you might discover that taking the offensive will require you to gather far more information about the problem than taking the defensive position. Working from the defensive limits your need to collect data to *only the data you need to cover your legal liability*. Choosing the defensive makes for a shorter research effort, but it may also leave you without a solution to the problem.

People *really do* think about these sorts of issues when they get assignments. They are important issues. But the thinking normally doesn't get very concrete until the report is actually being written and the phrasing process starts to focus attention on the issues. Of course, by then it's too late. The time to think about this sort of issue is at the very beginning of the whole research and writing process, and the way to make thinking about such issues concrete is to focus on the report, to see what the report will sound like if you go one way or another.

CHAPTER SUMMARY

You generally tend to start the long process from assignment to report with only a very vague idea of where you want to go. To sharpen this idea, focus all your thoughts on your final product—the report. Try to figure out what it will look like, what you want to say in it, and what you want it to sound like. Turn any of your thoughts on these subjects into words—write them down. By taking these basic approaches to research and writing, you can make your work more efficient and more concrete. When you have written down your ideas about the assignment and the report, have these initial ideas reviewed, get some feedback so that you know you're going in the right direction.

SECTION TWO:

BRAINSTORMING BY DESIGNING THE REPORT

The report is your destination. To figure out how to get there you have to figure out what the report should cover and how it should cover the subject. Brainstorming is what you do to turn the vague assignment into this picture of the final report, this concrete idea of the destination.

Since brainstorming is a mental process, the chapters in this section of the book are about ways to focus and organize your thoughts about the project you're going to undertake. There are five chapters:

—An Introduction to Brainstorming

—Analyzing the Assignment

—Analyzing the Audience for the Report

—Analyzing the Subject

—Assembling an Outline of the Report

You will often find that brainstorming a report really doesn't take very long. An hour or so is often sufficient for a simple project, an afternoon for a major study. What is important is that you do the brainstorming completely before you go on to your actual research. Once you begin collecting data, it takes days to change momentum when you find you've made a mistake. Better to overplan than to underplan.

In this section, the mental processes of brainstorming are described. They may seem to involve a lot of work. They do, but it goes pretty quickly in practice. Practiced brainstorming, even following a fairly strict procedure, can be quick and exciting. It's the most enjoyable part of the whole research process.

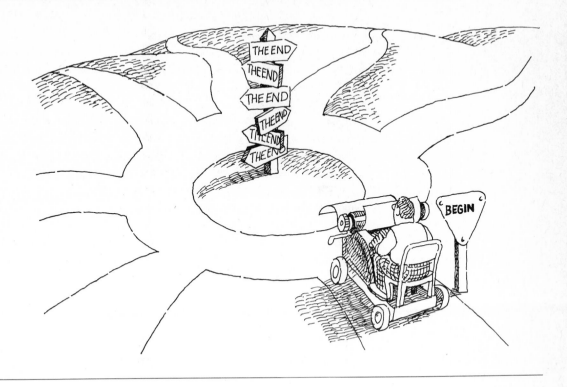

AN INTRODUCTION TO BRAINSTORMING

3

When you walk out of the office with a completely fresh assignment for research and a report, you've usually got a head full of ideas but no real idea of what to do with all of them. You've got some thoughts about the purpose of the report; some thoughts about the scope, the subject, and the focus of the report; some thoughts about the problems you might encounter; some thoughts about who your audience will be when the report will be written; some thoughts about your role in the whole process; some worries about how you're going to get the whole thing done and still do your daily work; perhaps even some thoughts about how the report might sound when you get around to writing it. You've probably also got a head full of questions about these subjects. As you think about them, you shift from one subject to another, your mind wanders from scope of the project, to how much secretarial help you're going to need, and then on to something else.

Even if you've never done a government study and written a government report, you know two things: You have a limited amount of time to get the whole thing done and you have to get the project started as soon as possible. You need to turn the vague thoughts about the project into some form of concrete action or else you'll never get anything done. Knowing this, you take the generally recommended first step for any project—you *brainstorm*.

Brainstorming is simply the process of getting the ideas in your head out of your head and down on paper (or a blackboard) so that you can look at them and sort them out. It's done in a lot of different ways—in groups or alone, by talking about the subject with a group of coworkers, or by sitting down with a blank piece of paper and jotting ideas down silently. However it's done, it has a very important place in the overall research and writing process. If you brainstorm the project well, you get a start in the right direction and establish the right path to follow. If you don't brainstorm the project effectively, you end up redirecting and redirecting and redirecting at each stage of your research and writing.

The *objectives* of this initial brainstorming process encompass more than simply sorting out ideas from the assignment meeting. It is a creative process, designed to start research planning and to generate ideas about how to solve problems. Most importantly, it is also a step designed to permit the researcher to get some concrete feedback from the boss, the person who has assigned the report project. The brainstorming session gets ideas down on paper. These ideas can then be looked at by the researcher and the boss, and the boss can see the thinking that has been done, evaluate it, and make suggestions about the direction the researcher is going in. The brainstorming session is thus almost a part of the assignment process:

1. A vague assignment is given.
2. The researcher brainstorms it and turns it into an *initial project plan or a written statement of the assignment.*
3. The researcher and the boss then review this concrete statement and further refine the assignment.

The end result of brainstorming is, then, a kind of *contract* (Figure 3–1), a simple document that says "This is what the assignment is really all about; this is what is expected in the project; this is what we're going to do."

Turning the initial assignment into a concrete contract for research and a final report makes the whole research and writing process logical and efficient. Both boss and researcher know where the research process is going and both are at least morally bound by the contract process. The contract covers all aspects of the report, in-

FIGURE 3-1/THE CONTRACT PROCESS

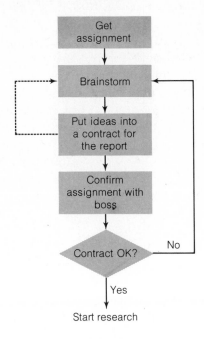

cluding any political considerations that may influence the interpretation of results. If the final report doesn't meet the specifications of the contract, the boss can criticize without fear that the criticism will be misunderstood or taken personally. There is no question of the researcher's not knowing what the assignment was—the contract covers it. And the boss is also aware that the researcher was given opportunity to contribute ideas to the project; the brainstorming is done by the researcher and the contract contains the researcher's ideas as well as those of the boss. At the same time, the contract gives the researcher a sense of job security; if the contract is satisfied, there is very little even the most arbitrary boss can do to say that the report isn't good and that the researcher has done poor work. In short, the contract directs the research and protects both parties to it from arbitrary and after-the-fact criticism.

If the contract is to do all this, it has to be a pretty complete and very concrete document. It is not enough to write a general contract with a lot of vague promises. The report contract must spell out the exact scope of the report (and thus the research effort). All the generalizations of the initial assignment need to be made into specific contract items (Figure 3–2). The brainstorming process is supposed

**FIGURE 3-2/FROM GENERAL ASSIGNMENT TO SPECIFIC
              CONTRACT**

Assignment statement	Contract provisions
The director would like a better picture of how the increase in fees affects those who use the meeting room in the county building.	We will: 1. Identify all major users of the meeting room. 2. Determine what they use the room for. 3. Determine what the fee for this use is. 4. Find out what other meeting rooms are available in the area. 5. Find out why users prefer the county meeting room to the others available. 6. Find out whether the fee increase will cause any users to move their meetings to other facilities. 7. Determine whether this will mean the county will suffer an overall decline in revenue. 8. Determine whether there are ways we can increase use of the meeting room and thus increase revenues.

to lead to the kind of specific contract outlined in the figure between the boss and the researcher.

THE PROBLEM

The brain is a wonderful device. It's a remarkably quick machine and it holds a vast quantity of information. Even a first-time government researcher, a mere novice at the whole process, has enough brain-power to do a first-rate job. The only thing that needs to be done is to use the mental resource logically and coherently. Doing this is the problem, because the brain is also a device prone to wandering, idle thought, and free association. Brainstorming tends to get random and unproductive if the brain is allowed to wander.

Anyone who has been through a group brainstorming session has experienced the frustrations of random process—of the brain's tendency to wander. Such sessions often begin in a reasonably organized manner. Someone usually starts off by saying something like, "OK, the first thing we need to do is define the problem we're working on." Everyone agrees; it is a logical place to start. Members of the group start to do this and soon everyone is getting ideas about what the problem really is. Then the brain's random thinking process takes over. Someone says, "If the problem is _____, then what we have to do is _____." Someone takes issue with this and argues about how to solve the problem. Another brain in the group remembers how the problem was solved two years ago in another agency. Someone else starts fighting about this proposed solution and says that another solution is the only way to solve the problem. All participants start to dig into their memories for facts to support either side of the argument. The facts get disputed, and new facts are introduced. Soon, the meeting breaks down. The collective brain has forgotten that the *problem* still hasn't been identified; it has shifted quickly and randomly to the *solution*.

Imagine for a moment that your task is not storming the brain, but that you are to storm a castle or a fortress. Your object is to get into the fortress, steal the treasure that's inside, and get back out to enjoy the fruits of your labor. You have a large army to do this. You have two ways of accomplishing the goal. First, you can line up all your troops, give them weapons, and tell them to charge the fortress. If you do this, the scene will resemble the war scenes in Hollywood movies—lots of noise, lots of action, and *some* chance of actually getting into the fortress and finding the treasure. Your second option is less exciting, but perhaps a better approach. You can first send in a spy to find out where the treasure is and *what* it is. Then you can organize your troops so that your attack gets you at the treasure as quickly and efficiently as possible—and you don't burn the castle or fortress to the ground in the process. It makes a rotten movie, but you survive the attack.

The same approach can be taken to storming the brain. First, you identify the treasure you're after. Then you break your attack forces into groups—each with a specific task, each designed to get you one step closer to the treasure (the information you need to establish a complete, concrete, contract with the boss). Then you direct your attack, you organize your brainstorming. If you do this, you finish the brainstorming with enough energy to write up the contract and you're able to enjoy the fruits of the brainstorming process.

THE SOLUTION

Organized brainstorming may seem like a contradiction in terms, but it isn't. It can and should be done. It begins by recognizing that there are *three kinds of treasure* you're after when you're brainstorming.

To put together the contract, you need three completely separate kinds of information:

1. *Information about the reasons for the assignment*
2. *Information about the people who will use the final report*
3. *Information about the subject of the final report.*

When you're thinking about the assignment, thoughts about all three of these categories are mixed up together. As you think, they get more mixed up with one another. To get at them in a reasonably efficient manner, it's essential to go after them *one at a time*. If you try to go after all of them at once, you probably won't ever get any one of them completely.

Whether you do it by yourself or in a group, brainstorming is best done in three distinct steps, as shown in Figure 3–3. Although there is a feedback from one step to another, although doing the second step sometimes gives you a few new ideas about what you did in the first step, the emphasis of the brainstorming process ought to be on keeping these searches through the brain separate. To go back to the storming-the-castle metaphor for a moment, the search for the key to the treasure room may lead you right past the room itself. It is perfectly OK to take note of this find, but it shouldn't distract you from the initial search—for the key. In short, do everything in your power to concentrate on one brainstorming step at a time. To the best of your ability, analyze the reasons for the assignment before you go into an analysis of the audience, and make sure you've done both of these steps before you tackle the subject.

AN EXAMPLE

The brainstorming process itself cannot be illustrated here, but you can get an idea of why it's important to separate it into these three subprocesses by looking at the product of brainstorming. First, here's

FIGURE 3-3/THREE BRAINSTORMING STEPS

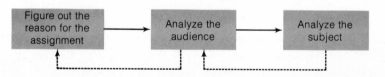

a list of statements about a project—the kind of list that is usually generated by a random brainstorming process:

1. The report is for agency management only—internal report.
2. Question is the efficiency of Internal Audit Section procedures.
3. Data will be used to adjust office procedures.
4. Report is needed because of recent budget cuts.
5. We can consider staff and support budget changes.
6. Audit Division will use report to decide future of the Internal Audit Section.
7. Question to answer is how well we do the job now and how we can do it less expensively.
8. Report will go to Audit Division under boss's signature.
9. Solution to the problem cannot violate job security guidelines.
10. Report will have to cover all phases of audit activity.
11. Boss wants recommendations about personnel and program organization.
12. Problem is that budget has been cut because of questions concerning overall effectiveness.
13. Readers will want to know what the cause of the problem is.
14. Purpose of the report is to reestablish credibility of Internal Audit Section.
15. Cause of the problem is lack of general understanding of the functions of internal audits.
16. Senior staff in Internal Audit Section will respond negatively to most changes suggested that do not ensure integrity of their section.

This kind of list is normal for the average, random, brainstorming session—which usually begins with someone saying, "OK, what *are* we supposed to be doing on this project?" It gives you some idea of what the report is about; it probably reveals enough about the subject to help you figure out some of what's going on. But it is difficult to tell exactly what the report is going to be about because comments about subject, readership, and purpose are all mixed together. It's difficult to get a clear picture of any one of these subjects.

The same statements strike you differently when they are separated into three distinct categories: statements about the reasons for the assignment, statements about the readers/users of the final report, and statements about the subject/scope of the report. It's easier to see contradictions, and it's easier to see how incomplete the list of statements really is:

Statements about the reasons for the assignment

1. Problem is that budget has been cut because of questions concerning overall effectiveness of the Internal Audit Section.
2 Report is needed because of recent budget cuts.
3. Purpose of the report is to reestablish credibility of Internal Audit Section.
4. Data will be used to adjust office procedures.
5. Audit Division will use report to decide future of the Internal Audit Section.

Statements about the readers/users of the final report

1. The report is for agency management only—internal report.
2. Report will go to Audit Division under boss's signature.
3. Readers will want to know what the cause of the problem is.
4. Senior staff in Internal Audit Section will respond negatively to most changes suggested that do not ensure integrity of their section.

Statements about the subject/scope of the report

1. Report will have to cover all phases of audit activity.
2. Question is the efficiency of Internal Audit Section procedures.
3. Boss wants recommendations about personnel and program organization.
4. Question to answer is how well we do the job now and how we can do it less expensively.
5. We can consider staff and support budget changes.
6. Solution to the problem cannot violate job security guidelines.
7. Cause of the problem is lack of general understanding of the functions of internal audits.

Looking at the statements grouped together, it's easier to see the contradictions—the kind of contradictions that often arise in government reports. Most important, it's easier to see just how sketchy this whole concept of the assignment really is. At this point, we really do not know much at all about the reader, and we seem to know even less about the reason for the report. This is easy to see by looking at the statements grouped together. Yet, this is the kind of starting point many researchers end up with when they brainstorm—because they do it randomly.

THE NEXT FOUR CHAPTERS

In the chapters that follow, a complete and systematic brainstorming process is described. The process is designed to help you get a full picture of the final report so that you can prepare a complete contract with the boss. It requires a reasonable amount of effort. Once you learn the procedures, it takes about half a day to think out a report, starting only with a brief assignment. The effort is disciplined; you cannot brainstorm using the methods to be described unless you're willing to discipline yourself. Most important, you must not take the tempting jumps ahead that sometimes present themselves in brainstorming. If you wish to brainstorm systematically, you must make sure that you finish a step before you go on to the next step.

Chapters 4–6 deal with the separate processes of brainstorming—analyzing the assignment, analyzing the audience, and analyzing the subject. Chapter 7 covers the process of assembling the final contract for the boss. It's a long process to read about. Have patience. As you go over the steps, you may find it comforting to know that you will have to do them anyway when you sit down to write. By doing them at the beginning of the project, you're prewriting a part of the report. Your contract with the boss is also an outline for the final report. You spend a bit more time at the beginning, but you make this time up at the end.

NOTES TO MANAGEMENT AND STAFF

To Management

There is much a manager can do to get a project off on the right foot. Here are some suggestions, with brief explanations:

1. *Don't hold anything back during the assignment meeting.* Many managers release information in the office on a need-to-know basis. They tend to hold things back, to carry the burden of problems on their own backs so that staff don't have to worry about them. While this is reasonable in some situations, it is inviting disaster when dealing with any research and writing project. For example, several years ago, I rewrote a report for an agency—a report that was very open and blunt—about the problems facing the agency. The office

To Staff

A manager is someone with twenty or thirty problems to deal with at a time. No manager can be expected to be able to give full time to any one project, nor can a manager be expected to know what information you need for a particular project. Therefore, you must be self-starting when you get an assignment. This means:

1. *Be prepared to ask questions when a project is being assigned.* Don't go into a meeting where you know a report is going to be discussed without a list of questions to ask. Don't just listen to the assignment, make sure you're getting all the information you need.
2. *Restate the assignment before you leave.* End the assignment meeting

To Management (continued)

manager had neglected to tell the researchers that the report was going to go to a State Senator, and they had written the report as if it were for internal use only. For this reason, they had reported only *bad* things they had discovered—all of the good was left out. The report read like a condemnation of the whole agency; it wasn't intended to sound that way—and wouldn't have been a problem if it hadn't been for this one additional reader. The report served its primary audience quite well, pointing out the things that needed change, but would have given its other reader an almost preversely one-sided view of the agency. Fortunately, we rewrote the report to provide a balanced view before it got to the Senator's desk. To avoid problems like this one, make an honest effort to tell the researcher and writer everything you can about the nature of the assignment, the audience, and the subject.

2. *Recognize that the assignment probably is too vague, and institute some form of contract process in the office.* Make a point of having staff bring you some form of contract very soon after the report has been assigned. For short reports, this should be within a few hours or at most a day; for long reports, which may take several months to prepare, allow staff several days to a week for brainstorming. Make sure that you insist on a *written* contract; verbal contracts are always vague and almost always forgotten. And go over the contract with staff in detail, point-by-point. Fight the temptation to skim it and sign off with the intention of looking at it later. Research takes so much time and costs so much money that an hour of contract review is certainly worth the effort.

3. *Give staff information in an orderly manner.* When you're making an assignment, divide your comments into the sections discussed in this chapter.

To Staff (continued)

with a summary restatement of what you see as your job. Then promise to get an outline of the project to the boss for review quickly—be realistic about how long it will take. There is no need to be assertive about this process; be tactful and simply tell the boss that you want the project outline reviewed so that *you* know that your perception of the assignment is reasonably correct. In short, don't attack the boss for being vague or for not having written out the assignment; it really is *your* job to develop the assignment into something concrete. The boss has too many other problems to worry about to do this kind of work.

3. *Don't even think about collecting data until you've got a complete contract for the project. Finish brainstorming before you go out to get information.* It's a real temptation to just jump into a project, to get right out there and start collecting information. Most researchers have felt this almost irresistable urge; they have started designing questionnaires before knowing what they were really after. The result is predictable; a lot of data gets thrown away before the report is finally written. The problem is that research is fun, but brainstorming may not be. Research gets you out of the office, out of the daily routine—brainstorming doesn't. Be patient. Do a complete job of brainstorming. Get a complete picture of what the project will involve, and get this contract approved. Then you can go out in the field and collect your data. Doing this will save you time in the end, time writing and editing the final report, which is the least fun of all the tasks facing you.

4. *Don't narrow the scope of the assignment until you get through with the brainstorming and prepare the contract.* Take a fairly broad contract into the boss for review. Let the boss cut it down to size by eliminating portions of the project. In this way, you make sure you cover the maximum scope; you

To Management (continued)

Talk about the purpose first, then fully describe the audience, then talk about what you see as the subject and scope of the research.

4. *Talk*. Staff will always want to ask questions during assignment meetings, but they won't unless you appear willing to answer them. So, you have to keep the communication channels open; talk about the assignment in an open and relaxed manner. Encourage questions.

To Staff (continued)

don't make any false assumptions about the limits of the project, assumptions that often come back to haunt you at the end of the project.

These suggestions are intended to be quite general at this point. Try to keep them in mind while reading the next four chapters. The brainstorming processes are complex, and keeping these suggestions in mind will keep you focused on the end product of brainstorming—the final contract with the boss.

CHAPTER SUMMARY

For brainstorming to be really useful as a part of the research process, it must be organized, not random. Instead of just talking about

---

FIGURE 3-4/BRAINSTORMING: AN OUTLINE OF BASIC STEPS

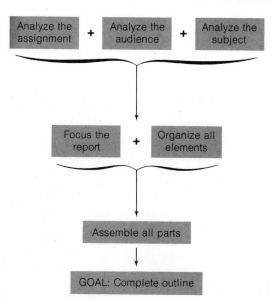

THREE ANALYSIS STEPS: In each of these steps, you will be pulling the elements of the project apart, on paper, so that you can see what you've got to work with.

TWO ORGANIZING STEPS: In these steps, you'll start to give order to everything you've worked out during the three analysis steps

ONE OUTLINE STEP: Here, you put everything together.

FOR EVERY MINUTE SPENT IN BRAINSTORMING, YOU'LL SAVE TEN IN RESEARCH AND WRITING. DON'T TAKE SHORT CUTS. TAKE ONE STEP AT A TIME.

the project casually, you need to focus your thoughts on three essential areas, one at a time:

1. Reasons for the assignment
2. Audience for the report
3. Subjects being covered

Cover each of these areas separately and then assemble the results of your brainstorming into a contract for the report. (Figure 3-4). Once you have a contract, review it in detail with the boss, so that you can see if you are going in exactly the direction you should.

ANALYZING THE ASSIGNMENT

4

If you wanted to, you could expand the scope of a study assignment to cover just about everything that has happened in the history of the world. It doesn't take long to do this, either. A simple assignment to study the causes for one person's problems in fitting into an office atmosphere can grow into a study of office atmospheres in general, can expand to include a study of the office in society, which finally gets you to a study of the evolution of humankind. If you've ever gotten trapped with someone who is interested in these questions in a philosophical way, you know how quickly a narrow, focused, conversation can become a free-wheeling analysis of the world's problems. In short, *every assignment contains the seeds of a major study.* The most obviously elementary assignment may *really* be a request for something quite beyond its stated scope. Conversely, the broadly stated assignment may be far simpler than it looks on the surface.

Whether the boss gives you an hour of discussion or a simple one or two sentence note, the first question you need to answer in brainstorming is, "Just how far am I supposed to carry this assignment?" You need to know where to expand your research and where to limit it. On a practical level, for example, you need to find out whether an assignment to study alternative uses for a park includes uses such as turning it into something other than a park, or whether your alternatives are more limited. You need to analyze the assignment to develop it into an actual statement of what the boss really wants you to do.

PROBLEM

In defining the scope of an assignment, there are two contradictory tendencies. First, you want to cover everything that the boss could want to know about the subject. Second, you don't want to cover unnecessary ground. In thinking about the assignment, you will frequently find yourself jumping back and forth, unable to decide whether to limit the scope or to expand it. This indecision is complicated as you go over the assignment—even if it is a written one—in your head. You end up shifting from one element of the assignment to another, considering whether to expand or contract the scope of the assignment as you do, changing your mind with each shift in thinking.

As this goes on in your head, the clarity of your original understanding of the assignment diminishes; what you *thought* you were going to do gets lost in what you *think you should do*. The sense of direction you got from the original assignment breaks down, and there is nothing to replace it.

SOLUTION

The generally recommended solution to this problem is *to analyze the assignment*. This advice is handed out by just about all research consultants. The only problem is that you need a *method* for analyzing the assignment, a method that will keep you from shifting back and forth from one topic to the next, from one level of the assignment to the next. In short, you need to know what analysis is and how to do it efficiently.

What we commonly call *analysis* is really two separate mental processes; the combination of the two is what leads to an understanding of the subject or problem. A very common example may illustrate them.

During a working day, you often collect a quantity of spare change. If you're one of those people who likes to save this change for a rainy day, you will soon find yourself with a jar or small bank full of coins. *Eventually*, you have to decide what to do with it. You have to convert the coins into usable money. To do this, you have to answer a simple question: "What, or how much, have I got?" To answer this question, you first have to dump the change out on a flat surface and *spread it out*. You have to take the jumbled pile of coins and separate them from one another so that you can see what you've got *one item at a time*. This process of taking a lump sum and breaking it into its individual components is *analysis*, the first step in the overall process that leads to an understanding of what it is you've got. Until you've done this step, you cannot hope to be able to count up all your money.

Once you have all the coins spread out, you then look at them and *sort them into categories*. The categories you choose depend on what you intend to do with the coins. Normally, for instance, if you planned to exchange them at face value for paper money, you would sort them into the five categories: penny, nickel, dime, quarter, half dollar. If you were going to sort them into categories for coin collecting, you would choose dates or condition (or both) as your categories. The point is, you *choose* the categories, and then sort the items into them—*like items with like items*. In going through this category selection and sorting process, you are taking random bits of material and giving them some meaning—you are *synthesizing*. In this synthesizing process, you begin to see what you've really got, what all the pieces add up to.

The assignment can be handled in much the same way. You can begin by breaking it into all its individual parts, and then you can synthesize these parts into a coherent whole—a picture of all the parts in relation to one another. The method I have found most useful for doing this dual process involves two separate analytical steps and one synthetic step.

The First Analytical Step

First you have to see what you've got to deal with. So, think about your assignment and jot down all the words and phrases in the assignment in a list. If the assignment has been given to you in written form, this is particularly important. Here's an example of what you might get:

> *Assignment:* The Board of Supervisors has permitted this department (Parks) to offer senior citizens special reduced-fee recreation permits for a number of activities. Recent budget cuts at the state level have made maintaining these reduced fees a problem. State revenues, which were once used to subsidize these elderly golfers and tennis players, are not available. The Board has asked us for recommendations on this

subject and has suggested that increased fees may be necessary. I'd like you to look into this unfortunate situation and give me a set of recommendations for the Board meeting next month.
Signed: The Boss

From such an assignment, you might get a list that looks like this:

Elements of assignment

–Board of Supervisors	–Permitted
–Parks Department	–Tennis players
–Senior citizens	–Subsidize
–Special reduced fees	–Recommendations
–Budget cuts	–Increased fees
–State revenues	–Necessary
–Problem	–Unfortunate
–Golfers	–Set of recommendations
–Next month	

You could, perhaps, get the same effect by merely underlining the key elements of the assignment, but separating the words from the prose of the paragraph and spreading them out on a piece of paper makes them stand out more clearly. It forces you to look at each piece of the assignment.

The Second Analytical Step

Once you have listed the elements of the assignment, put this list aside and start a new list. Analyze your audience by listing all the possible readers of your report. For the example just presented, you might have a list such as the following:

Readers of report

–Board of Supervisors	–Parks Department
–Golf Association	–Tennis Association
–Senior citizens groups	–County Manager
–County Budget Officer	–Taxpayer groups
–County Planning Department	–County Public Works Department
–your supervisor	

Depending on the nature of your job and on the type of government agency you work for, this kind of list will be shorter or longer. It's important to list *all* probable readers, though, because the final report must be aimed at these readers, and it must be written to cover the subject from their points of view. Some of these people will be more important as readers than others, but all have concerns that need to be dealt with. Some of these will be contradictory concerns, and you should think about these things before you start out on your research.

Using the Lists

Before you begin to synthesize, even before you begin to try to put the assignment elements back together again, you can do some profitable thinking by focusing your attention on each element and thinking about it separately. For example, in the list of elements of the assignment, one of the items was "Problem." If you think about this word being included in the assignment, it gives you some keys to how the Board of Supervisors is thinking about the fee situation. Things aren't "problems" unless the politicians are having a tough time thinking out a solution, unless the alternatives are unpleasant. Otherwise, in this case, the Board would just raise the fees. The fact that the Board has said that this is a problem is an indication that they do not see any easy solutions, which should give you the idea that this report can't be a quick, simplistic job. This impression is reinforced by two other elements—the word "Unfortunate," which the boss has used, and the phrase "Set of recommendations." The boss, too, sees that this report cannot have a single, simple solution and wants you to set forth a number of possible solutions for the Board's consideration. In short, just looking at the elements and thinking about them individually can give you some insight into the nature of the report you have to write.

Looking at each item in the list of *readers* does the same kind of thing. If you consider the differing points of view of those who will be reading the report, you begin to get a picture of the kind of approach you'll have to take. For example, you know that the senior citizens will probably oppose any fee increase and that they are likely to be a hostile audience. You must strongly justify any increase in fee; you have to show them why it is necessary and maybe even how it will eventually benefit them. This means that you may have to do some research to find out their position on this subject. Thinking about each of the readers in this way will lead you to similar plans for research.

The lists are checklists, guides to your thinking at the very beginning of the project. You know from them *what you have to think about* and you can do this thinking one item at a time.

The Synthetic Step

Thinking about the individual elements prepares you to pull everything together into a complete picture of the full assignment. This involves taking your thoughts and organizing them, grouping them together, under a set of headings. A useful way of doing this is to use the thoughts you've generated by thinking about individual items on your lists to answer a set of basic questions about the assignment.

Before you begin any research project, you need clear and complete answers to some very basic questions. You need, first, to know what the report subject is and who is going to look at it. You've got the answers to these questions from the first two analytical steps. Once you know the "What?" and "Who?" you need answers to the "Why?", "How?", "Where?", and "When?" questions. These simple questions can be transformed into a more complete list of questions you need answers to before you can really begin to set up your research:

Questions about assignment

1. Why must this report be developed? What makes it necessary? What will those who have requested it do with the information?
2. What other uses are there for this information? Who else, other than those who requested the report, could use the information and may actually do so?
3. What are the political limits to your study? What attitudes about the subject limit your free exploration? How?
4. What role are you going to play in the development and interpretation of the information you are about to gather? Do you have authority to look at the problem completely? Has anyone already made up his or her mind about the subject? Does this assignment allow you to argue, to present your own point of view—regardless?
5. How does this report fit into the general policy picture in the office?
6. What resources do you have available for this study? How much time, money, staff? What priority does this study have?
7. What are the likely stumbling blocks you'll have to deal with while working on the project?

To answer these questions completely, you need to think about them in terms of the elements of the assignment and in terms of the various audiences for the report. If you focus your attention on answering each question and use the checklists you developed in the previous steps, you will have arrived at a way of putting your thoughts together. Taking the recreation fee assignment as an example once again, here's the kind of thinking you might do while focusing on the first question: "Why must this report be developed?"

Element to think about	Thoughts
Board of Supervisors	The Board has to make up the money the state has taken away from these programs.
Parks Department	The Parks Department is a low-priority item in their view, but it also is a source of fees the Board can use to make up lost income.
Senior citizens	Senior citizens get a lot of benefits from the county's programs, and they don't pay a lot of taxes.
Special reduced fees	They're a group that might be tapped for more funds, especially since they pay less for a lot of services.
Permitted	The Board has permitted them to use park facilities for less in the past because there was always state money to subsidize these facilities. . . .
Subsidize	And so forth, through the checklists.

It would take half a book to recreate the whole thinking process that might take place during this simple analysis and synthesis process. The point is that you use the elements of the assignment list and the reader list to help you think about the answer to each question. You won't find every element helpful for working on every question. But you'll usually find that your thinking about the assignment is far more complete when you set it up in this way.

As you go through these questions, you are doing two things. First, you're focusing your thoughts about the project. Second, you're writing a tentative draft of the introduction to the report. You'll have to edit it, but what you do at this stage to analyze the assignment is exactly what the reader will want to know about at the beginning of the report. So, though assignment analysis may take time, it often saves you equal time later—when you are really pressed for time.

The Pattern of the Questions and the Narrowing of the Project Scope

The pattern of this whole analysis–synthesis procedure is from *general* to *specific*. You begin very generally with a list of all the elements of the assignment and all the readers. If you were simply to look at both of these lists and decide to cover every element completely and every reader's interests completely, you'd be facing a very large research task. As you answer the questions about the assignment, though, you'll find that you are *eliminating* portions of the broad, general assignment. The questions about the reason for the assignment tend to help you eliminate thoughts about just collecting data about the subject in the interests of having the data around; they tend to focus your attention on the practical aspects of the assignment. As you get to questions about the political attitudes of those who have requested the study, you narrow the focus even more. For example, in a very general study of golf course revenues, you might consider alternative ways of raising funds, such as putting in a bar in the clubhouse. There may be political reasons, quite apart from the cost and benefit to be derived from such an action, that make this alternative simply out of the question; it may be against the law, or public sentiment may be so set against drinking on public property that such a suggestion is unthinkable. Knowing this, even thinking about such problems may help you eliminate this as *something to be studied*. The focus of your research is thus narrowed.

The answers to all the questions have this effect, and the scope of the report becomes narrower, more clearly defined, and more focused on practical matters as you work your way through the questions. By the time you've finished, you usually have a clear idea of what the assignment is and you can explain why you took action to focus it the way you did. Schematically, the process looks something like Figure 4–1.

The end result of this analysis and synthesis process is not yet an outline of the final report; it is nothing more or less than a clear statement of the assignment and the things that need to be considered during the next two stages of brainstorming. Such a statement is valuable, even if you take it no further, as a means for getting some feedback about the assignment from those who have requested the report. Particularly if the assignment is for a really major effort, it's useful to go over your analysis with at least one of those in charge of the project.

**FIGURE 4-1/THE NARROWING OF A PROJECT'S FOCUS BY ASKING
ORDERLY QUESTIONS**

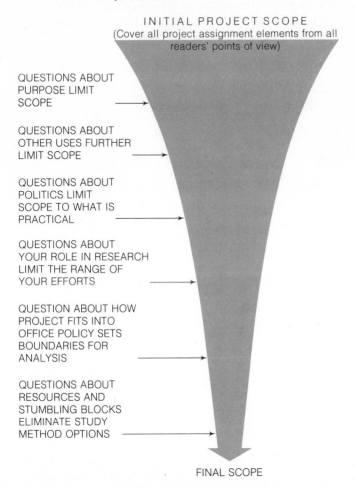

INITIAL PROJECT SCOPE
(Cover all project assignment elements from all
readers' points of view)

QUESTIONS ABOUT
PURPOSE LIMIT
SCOPE

QUESTIONS ABOUT
OTHER USES FURTHER
LIMIT SCOPE

QUESTIONS ABOUT
POLITICS LIMIT
SCOPE TO WHAT IS
PRACTICAL

QUESTIONS ABOUT
YOUR ROLE IN RESEARCH
LIMIT THE RANGE OF
YOUR EFFORTS

QUESTION ABOUT HOW
PROJECT FITS INTO
OFFICE POLICY SETS
BOUNDARIES FOR
ANALYSIS

QUESTIONS ABOUT
RESOURCES AND
STUMBLING BLOCKS
ELIMINATE STUDY
METHOD OPTIONS

FINAL SCOPE

AN EXAMPLE

Since this analysis–synthesis process is a mental one, it's really only
possible to show the products of it in an example, and it isn't practical to illustrate a *complete* assignment analysis. It may be useful,
though, to review this example to see how to go from vague *assignment* to the *two checklists* to the *answer to one of the basic assignment questions*. The example here involves an internal study and
report, the assignment to develop one of those increasingly popular
management information systems.

Assignment: The Operations Division feels that agency managers and supervisors could improve the effectiveness and

efficiency of their planning, and could identify and respond to problems on a more timely basis, if information regarding the performance of their units was available quickly and in usable form. We would like Management Analysis Division to design a system that could provide this information at a minimum cost to the agency.

A note very similar to this one was received by a client of mine at a state agency. Her first impression of the assignment was that it wasn't a very high priority item and that it would be a reasonably easy assignment to complete. She thought that all the Operations Division wanted was a system for collecting information and making it available to the Division's managers and supervisors. The note, after all, is really rather blandly written. A bit of analysis, though, can lead to a better understanding of what was behind the assignment. Thinking about the assignment elements and the readers leads to these lists:

Assignment elements	*Readers*
Operations Division	Operations Division
Managers and supervisors	Managers and supervisors
Improve	Data processing personnel
Effectiveness and efficiency	Agency director
Planning	Planners
Identify/Respond to problems	Personnel Division
Timely basis	Training office
Performance	Budget office
Quickly	Finance Department
Useable form	
Design	
System	
Information	
Minimum cost	

Looking at these elements and thinking a bit about each item leads to a conclusion that this isn't quite as simple an assignment as its seemingly neutral tone might indicate. There are some "loaded" words and phrases in the assignment. Viewing these in the context of the rest of the elements, and without any prior knowledge of this particular office, you might begin to perceive some problems lurking behind this assignment. Here's how these problems might be synthesized in an answer to the first basic question about the assignment: "Why must this report be developed?"

> "Operations Division is requesting this report, this information system, because they are not satisfied with the current planning and response to problems among the managers and supervisors of the agency. They wish to *improve* things, and this implies that things aren't as good as someone thinks they should be. Since they have mentioned information about *performance*, they may be concerned that *they* have no information about how well the agency units are doing or that the data they have doesn't tell them anything and isn't in usable form. While they want this business to be handled in an efficient manner (minimum cost), they have already asked for a complete system for information gathering. They have given Management analysis Division permission to start from scratch—to design a system. This means that they're unhappy enough to make a major effort to improve things. Systems cost money and take lots of time to develop; no budget-conscious administrator is likely to request one unless the present state of affairs is pretty unsatisfactory. The operations people thus want this information so that they can make some fairly important decisions about performance, planning, and how to solve problems. At present, they don't feel they have the information necessary to do this, and they probably feel they don't have adequate control over the managers and supervisors of line units in the agency. They are likely to use this information system to begin to make major changes in the way the agency is run."

If this sounds like an exercise in "reading between the lines," then you have read correctly. That's exactly what this whole assignment analysis process is supposed to permit you to do—in an orderly manner. You don't want to stretch things too far. You would not want to turn this assignment into an examination of everything that's wrong with the agency. But it's almost always valid to read *problem* into the word *improve*, or to read *we aren't satisfied with our overall sense of goals in this agency* into any statement about unsatisfactory *planning*. You often sense these things in the assignment when you're thinking about it, but only when you analyze it in a systematic fashion does this sense turn into something concrete—a statement of the problem you're really being asked to solve.

The person who got the original version of this assignment, by the way, did not sense these things behind the assignment. She designed a system simply to speed up the flow of information, and had to do the whole project over again—to change the emphasis of the project from getting line supervisors data about their day-to-day operations to getting information that could lead to program changes and to changes in the agency's operating procedures.

NOTES TO MANAGEMENT AND STAFF

To Management

In my work as a consultant, one of the complaints I hear most often is that staff do not *anticipate* problems, that they don't see the things an assignment involves and take some sort of planned action to deal with the issues an assignment raises. This is probably a valid complaint, but as a manager, you should remember that you've probably had dozens of years to learn to read between the lines, to understand the workings of government from both political and operational levels. This sort of ability has to be learned.

One thing you can do to encourage this understanding of the complex business of working for the government is to work with staff during the assignment analysis. Give the assignment as clearly as you have time to, but tell staff that you want the whole thing set down in their own words before you give them the go-ahead for actual research. Then, review their perception of the assignment *carefully*. Don't just skim it. Go over it with the idea that you're going to have to live with the report when it is finally produced.

Expending this kind of time on a minor study or a simple assignment to go out and get a few clearly defined pieces of information is probably not a good idea. It will just stretch out the project beyond reason. But on a major report, one requiring several weeks or months of staff work, it is worth the effort. It can frequently save a rewrite of the final report, and almost always saves research time.

Having staff go through such an assignment analysis process in an orderly fashion also allows you to see what reading between the lines they are doing on a project. If they're right, OK. If they haven't read correctly, then you have an opportunity to set them straight quickly. Those who work on a project will always do some reading between the lines. The report will always reflect this interpretation of the assignment. Only if you can see what sort of interpreting they're doing can you see whether they've gone off in the right direction.

To Staff

In many of the research and writing jobs I've worked on, staff have been almost bitter about management's not giving them more to work with on a research project. This bitterness is usually a result of having done some work and then finding out that it wasn't exactly what the boss had in mind—it was either too narrow or too broad. I think the real cause of this problem lies in many staff researchers not knowing what is expected of them. Few realize that they are expected to do more than just what the boss asked for.

Of course, if you do more than the actual assignment calls for, you can get yourself into trouble, because you can seem to overstep your bounds. You thus need to do both—you have to think about the subject independently and you have to make certain you check with the boss frequently to make sure you aren't going too far, to make sure you haven't extended the research beyond what is needed or wanted. Doing this requires some long-range planning.

The first thing you need to do when you find out you're going to be doing research is get organized quickly. Don't wait a week before you do this assignment analysis; if you have to, take it home and work on it. Get it done and get back to the boss with any questions very quickly. In this way you can establish that you're actually doing the job. You can gain some trust, and with it a degree of freedom by establishing your interest in getting the job done. Next, when you do discuss the assignment, remember that the boss is not responsible for giving you all the answers. If the boss had the answers, you wouldn't be doing the research. Understanding this, treat your discussion as a learning experience for yourself—don't preach, ask questions. You will end up introducing new views of the subject to the boss, but you don't want to appear pushy about this. The boss, after all, knows that you probably didn't get an absolutely complete assignment. Do everything you can to get the assignment clarified, but don't rub it in.

To Staff *(continued)*

Perhaps you can get the feedback you want and need by asking for it like this:

> "After we talked about the _____ project yesterday, I worked out a written statement of what I think we ought to consider in setting up the study. I'd appreciate your looking at it and telling me whether I'm going in the right direction."

In short, there is no need to *tell* the boss the assignment was sketchy. Be tactful.

You are likely to find some resistance to this procedure during your first research project for any given supervisor. But, if you're willing to keep at it over a period of months, you can begin to develop some professional credibility. If the boss sees that when you have questions they are *good* questions, important questions, pretty soon you'll find it easier to work out a truly cooperative report effort. The boss will trust you to do the interpreting of the basic assignment, and you'll be able to go to the boss to get feedback.

To establish your credibility over the long run further, you might consider giving the boss frequent, regular progress reports—even if they're not asked for. Don't make a big deal out of them, just get them on the boss's desk at regular intervals. Make them meaty. If you're having a problem, say so. If you are progressing on schedule, say so and summarize the progress. Do this like clockwork.

Your ability to do a research project in government depends on your establishing a clear relationship with the boss. The boss must see that you recognize your responsibility to do most of the *thinking* on the project, as well as most of the leg-work. The boss must also see that you're willing to submit your thinking to scrutiny and that you welcome direction. If you can demonstrate these two things, you can probably establish a good working relationship with the boss and get the feedback you need to do the research effectively.

As you are refining the assignment, note that you are also making an effort to deal with the political questions. You are estab-

To Staff (*continued*)

lishing a clear context for your work, and finding out as much as you can about the politics of the situation that has led to the report request. Thinking about your readers, some of whom are political and some non-political, forces you to take a broad, practical view of what you're doing. You eliminate thoughts about making everyone happy early in the project. You get down to the business of providing information that will lead to sound, politically and administratively reasonable decisions.

CHAPTER SUMMARY

Before you can begin to think about what to do or what data to collect, you have to analyze the assignment and read between the lines to figure out what's really going on. You can do this in three stages, as illustrated in Figure 4–2. Once you've answered the questions about the assignment, you should get the answers reviewed immediately. Do this tactfully.

FIGURE 4-2/A FLOWCHART OF THE ASSIGNMENT ANALYSIS PROCESS

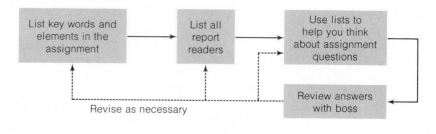

You may wish to use the form shown in Figure 4–3 to help organize your thoughts about the assignment.

FIGURE 4-3/ASSIGNMENT ANALYSIS FORM

Fill out all sections of the form. Have it reviewed and keep the form as a record.

LIST REPORT ELEMENTS HERE	ANSWER REPORT QUESTIONS HERE	MAKE REVIEW COMMENTS HERE
	1. Purpose of report:	
	2. Other uses for report:	
	3. Political limits to report:	
	4. Your role in study process; your limits:	
LIST READERS/USERS HERE	5. Report's relationship to overall office policy:	
	6. Resources available:	
	7. Stumbling blocks:	

5 ANALYZING THE AUDIENCE FOR THE REPORT

To this point, the emphasis of this book has been on preparing yourself to get down to work, on analyzing the assignment, on thinking about what you've been asked to do. The strategic considerations now lead to a step that is relatively easy to take and contributes much to the final design of the research effort and the final report.

In analyzing the assignment, you have written down a list of readers. You have looked at the assignment and decided that these people or groups of people will have some reason to read the final report. Even if they are not primary readers, even if they will only see the report *after* it has been used for its primary purpose, you have decided that they have a legitimate interest in the report and that this interest should be considered. Now, you need to consider the nature of their interest. In doing this—in analyzing your audience—you will arrive at a concrete plan for the final report. And, you will solve many of the problems that frustrate report writers at all levels of government.

PROBLEM

The problem that plagues all researchers and report writers is that few know what they have to *do*, what data they have to gather and how thoroughly they have to explain it, to *satisfy* the readers of the final report. Most reports are written with the expectation that they will have to be rewritten; for some reason, it is almost always assumed that the readers will not be satisfied by the first formal draft of a report and that they will send it back for revision. Many report writers even think that this is a necessary frustration, because it's important to the development of the report to have it criticized and rewritten. This is their way of getting feedback from the boss. They may even assume that the boss enjoys or otherwise encourages this process of redrafting and rethinking. In almost every agency, you'll find people who repeat some version of the cliché, "Don't worry about the first draft; the boss always sends it back anyway."

There is a *real* problem behind this old cliché, and even the office cynics recognize it and take it seriously. The problem is knowing what to do to satisfy the reader. It's a problem because not satisfying the reader means more than just having to rephrase a draft paragraph or two. It often means you have to go out and collect new information. It means you may be wasting time and energy collecting information that isn't really wanted. It means you're working without any real assurance that what you're doing is going to be accepted.

The problem is complicated by the very nature of any research. How can you know what you're going to say about a situation until you've gone out and gotten the needed information about it? How can you be sure you're going in the right direction until you've gotten your results and looked at them carefully?

SOLUTION

Solving this problem begins with the basic brainstorming strategy of separating your thoughts about readers from your thoughts about the subject. Don't worry about the subject. Don't worry about the data you're going to collect or about how you're going to collect it. For a time, put aside your concern for the subject and concentrate your thoughts on the audience for your report.

In thinking about your particular audience, there are some general *principles,* some general characteristics of readers as a group, that you can build on to develop a concrete picture of what it will take to satisfy your particular audience.

Principle 1: The Reader Is a Constant

The person who assigns the report will generally be one of the final readers of the report. Over a period of six months, circumstances may change, the person may age a bit, and there may be slight changes in the way in which the report will be used in the office, but *the person who assigned the report will still be the same person.* The same holds true for the other readers of the report. You can expect them to have the game general interests at the beginning of the research process that they will have at the end of the process, when they read the final report.

In general terms, then, the reader is a constant. Out of an audience of, for example, fifty people, you can expect five or six people to change jobs; you can expect the circumstances of others' jobs to change a bit, but your audience will remain substantially the same from beginning to end of the report. Basic personalities will not change substantially, nor will basic interests.

That your overall audience remains relatively constant doesn't mean that you won't have to adjust your efforts a bit when you do get a change in boss or a change in agency direction. It does mean that you can design your report to meet the needs of your current audience with reasonable assurance that it will still meet the needs of the final audience. Nothing short of a major shift in basic agency policy will invalidate this principle. And if there is a basic shift in agency policy, you're likely to get reassigned as well.

Principle 2: The Situation Determines the Readers' Interests

Everyone reading this book knows that when you switch roles, you also switch interests. Students who were never before concerned with making a good impression suddenly start wearing suits and ties when they start to earn a living. Employees who were only concerned with getting the immediate job done well suddenly begin to think about long-term effectiveness and efficiency when they become supervisors. Couples who never worried about money suddenly become very cost-conscious when they become parents. The interests of a person change when the person changes position or situation.

What this means for the researcher and writer is that the report doesn't have to be designed to meet the needs of individual personalities as much as it has to be designed to meet the needs of people playing particular roles. For example, a report directed to a budget officer should be designed to meet the needs of *any* budget officer—not the particular Jane, John, Mary, or Bill who happens to hold the job at any particular time.

The reasoning behind this is very simple. People are hired to fill positions in government—very seldom is a position created to suit a particular person. The stability of the bureaucracy depends on this ability to interchange one person with a set of skills for another person with an equivalent set of skills. So, the job defines the person who fills it; *any* training officer must be interested in the same sorts of things that *all* training officers are interested in; *any* accountant must be interested in the same things *all* accountants are interested in. In short, there is some reasonable stereotyping that you can do when you're looking at your audience and trying to figure out how to satisfy its members.

Because of this, personnel changes that might tend to make your audience less than constant can be deemphasized. If, for example, your boss transfers to another agency, you may be reasonably comfortable in the knowledge that your new boss will share many of the old boss's professional interests. The two people may be quite unalike personally, but they will both be interested in the things all bosses are interested in, such as getting the work of the office done with a minimum of trouble, keeping staff in positions appropriate to their skill levels, and making sure the office doesn't violate overall agency policy. In short, even when you do have a change in the personnel who make up your audience, your audience remains almost constant.

Principle 3: The Reader Is Someone with Questions

When you get an assignment, your readers are really sending you off to gather information so that they don't have to do it. There are two reasons for this: First, they're ignorant—*they don't know what they're asking you to find out.* Second, they're not able to get the information themselves; either they don't have time or energy or they don't know how to get it. So, you are appointed to go forth and get this information for them.

At a very basic level, the assignment to do a research project is very much like any simple, everyday request for information. For example, you often ask friends to get information for you. They may be going somewhere you haven't been and you request a report from them by asking something like "When you're downtown, check out the sale at Sears for me. The kids need some school clothes." Behind this assignment is a bunch of simple questions: "Do they have the things the kids need?" "In the right sizes and colors?" "How much are they?" "Is it worth getting all the kids into the car and going downtown to get the sale items?" When your friend returns with a report on the sale, you ask these questions. If the answers are "right" you go to the sale; if not, you don't go. *If you don't get answers to all your questions, the report is unsatisfactory,* and you are usually a bit frustrated by your friend's lack of care in research: "Oh, you didn't check prices; well, thanks anyway." The friend can guarantee a satisfactory report, regardless of the actual information brought back, by anticipating and answering all your questions. You may not be happy with the answers, but you'll at least have the information you need to make your decision to go or not to go.

The formal research and reporting project is different from this simple situation only in the number and complexity of questions to be anticipated and answered. The assignment is not usually quite as simple as checking out a sale, and there is a broader audience to satisfy, each segment of which may have different questions about the same subject. *The way to satisfy the audience of your report is to answer all the questions each member has about the particular subject you've been assigned to look into.*

Principle 4: Readers Are Predictable

In any given situation, with any given reader, it is quite easy to predict the questions the reader will want you to answer. To do so, you need only understand the situation and the reader. For example, a few moments of thought is all you need to anticipate the questions behind a request to check out a sale. The questions are obvious—once you start to try to think of them. They aren't even very different from one person to the next, provided the assignment has the same purpose. For each situation and purpose, you get a general list of questions. If your reader's purpose in asking you to check out the sale is to determine whether to go to the sale, you get one set of questions; if the reader is not a buyer but another department store owner who wants to see what the competition is doing, you get another list. Here are some sample questions from each situation and purpose:

Buyer's questions	*Competitor's questions*
Do they have the things I need?	Are the prices low enough to draw our customers away?
Are they cheaper than I would pay here, near home? By how much?	Is their quality the same as ours?

There are a dozen or so more questions you would want to answer for each audience, some general, some specific. And, given an understanding of the reader and of the purpose of the report, these questions would be easily predictable.

Because we are constantly involved in small-scale, everyday assignments to collect information and report back to someone, most people are really quite capable of predicting the questions behind a simple request. And they are thus quite good reporters—they come home with the information they've been (vaguely) asked to get. The trouble is that this sense of what the person asking for information is really after comes with experience; it takes most people a long time to learn what their friends want them to find out about a sale or a product. Through trial and error, the sense of what questions are really behind the request is slowly refined—and it's probably done unconsciously.

The same may be said for the experienced researcher and report writer. Over a long time, some people in an office will learn to cover a certain situation in a certain way, to answer a set of unspoken questions every time they are given a particular kind of assignment. But this learning by trial and error is painful, and it's wholly unnecessary. A little simple analysis can allow you to predict your readers' interests—the questions they want answered—*before* you ever go out to collect data. The analysis begins with the list of readers that you made while you were analyzing the assignment. Starting with this list, you follow a simple procedure:

Procedure for Analyzing the Readers' Interests

1. *Make a list of all your readers—by position rather than by name.*
2. *For each reader or group of readers, jot down what you think they'll use the report for.*
3. *Group readers according to the use they have for the report.* For example, put all readers who will use the report to make a decision about office policy into a single group; put all those involved in regulatory uses of the information into another group; and so forth. Don't worry about having one reader in several groups; this won't affect the outcome of the process.
4. *Jot down the basic professional interests of each group.* Here you have to think about your past experiences; if you think about what you've read about each group, about what people in the office have said about each group, about what you've seen of each group, you will find you really do have a good basis for determining these people's interests.

5. *Given these interests, try to figure out what questions each group would have about the general subject you're working on.* There are two ways of doing this. You can be imaginative, creative, and simply put yourself in the reader's position— and guess. Or, you can actually do some research into your readers. If, for example, you're interested in predicting the questions of members of a committee or board, you might examine the minutes of meetings or records of decisions to get an idea of what questions members ask. In most cases, though, you're going to have to try to put yourself into your readers' situations.

6. *Once you have listed all the questions you can think of, put these in the order in which you think the readers will want them answered.* Here again, you're going to have to do a little guessing. But the order will usually be pretty logical and obvious. For example, if you have a question such as "Which of the three major alternatives should we select?" and another question such as "What are the effects of selecting ＿＿＿ alternative on our budget?", you can easily see that you must answer the first before you attempt the second.

Questions Are an Outline for the Report

After you've gone through this simple process, you'll have a list of questions. The questions represent the readers' interests, what the readers really want to know about your subject. And, since you've got them organized and they're in the order in which the reader wants them answered, all you have to do to prepare the report is get the answers and then write them down—in the order you've established. Here, then, is what your report would look like if you were writing about the sale downtown to a reader interested in buying children's clothes:

Questions

Do they have children's clothes?

Size 10 girls' jeans?

In dark blue and red?

How many pairs were left?

At less than $12?

Was the sale crowded?

Will there be any left by 6:00 when I get there?

The report

They have plenty of children's clothes on sale, including the size 10 girls' jeans in blue and red that you wanted. I saw a whole stack of each size and each color marked down from $18 to $10.99 a pair, but they were going fast so I'd get there before 4:00 if you expect to be able to get several pairs. And traffic was miserable. I'd call before you go and make sure

You went—do you think it was worth your effort?

they'll hold some for you, or else it could be a waste of time.

If the list of questions you develop is complete, there is no need for the report to be revised. It will, by answering all the readers' questions, satisfy your audience. There is no need to answer any other questions either; you can get right to the point without a lot of hemming and hawing.

Question List Defines Research Effort

Knowing the readers' questions gives you both an outline for the report and, consequently, an outline for the research effort. If you know that you're going to have to answer a particular question, you also know that you're going to have to collect the information necessary to do this satisfactorily. If you know in advance what you should be looking for in the way of children's clothes, then you can go immediately to that particular rack in the store and count the number of pairs of jeans and check the prices. If you don't know that your reader wants to know the number of size 10 jeans left and their price, then you could spend weeks gathering completely useless information about every item in the store.

Anticipating the readers' questions helps you focus the research effort. Doing this properly is important. If you leave a question out, then you won't answer it. Thus, you should always try to err on the side of including too many questions, rather than on eliminating important questions. Knowing the range of questions the reader wants answered, of course, depends on your having done a complete job of analyzing the assignment.

EXAMPLES

In practice, anticipating the readers' questions for government reports varies in complexity with the nature of the report. It's relatively easy to do when you have a single readership, when the report is only going to one person or group. It gets difficult when you have to satisfy several groups with a single report. An example of how the process works in each case is in order.

Writing to One Audience

The everyday policy memo provides a good example of anticipating the questions of a single group audience. The audience is easy to discuss and predict because it's narrowly defined—its members will always be employees who are relatively familiar with the subject matter, even if they don't have detailed knowledge.

The purpose of a policy memo is to describe a policy *change*; generally speaking, you don't write a complete memo merely to describe a policy already in effect. Nevertheless, we'll define our purpose in this instance precisely: we're going to deal with policy changes only. Our assignment is to explain a decision to change _____ policy.

The readers of this memo will all be staff of the agency. The policy file is not normally open to other audiences, and thus we can focus on the needs of a limited group of readers. The purpose of the memo is to get those who read it to recognize the change and act accordingly. We're after changing the way in which staff think about a subject and the way in which they do their daily routines. They'll use the information in the memo to guide their actions.

As readers, staff are basically interested in:

1. Doing their jobs with a minimum of effort.
2. Doing their jobs effectively.
3. Making a good impression on the people they serve.
4. Influencing the workings of the agency—they want to have some impact on the world, or else they would not have gone into government. They're dedicated, even though they won't admit it on a bet.

There may be some exceptions to these statements, but since we're writing to a group rather than to individuals, we'll just have to cover all these interests. It may also seem that we're being a bit cynical, but it is honest to say that staff are interested in doing the job with a minimum of effort. This interest is important, because if we don't consider it, we'll find out that we don't really convince staff that the policy change is worth paying attention to.

Considering these interests of staff, we can probably expect them to want the answer to the following questions:

1. What is the new policy and procedure?
2. How is it different from the old policy and procedure?
3. What is the effect of the change on what we'll do?
4. Why did we have to make this change?
5. What was wrong with the way we did things before?
6. How will this work in normal situations?
7. By the way, what *was* the old policy?
8. What will happen under some unusual circumstances?
9. Why didn't you try _____ instead of this change?

10. What do you want me(us) to do about this change? How do you want this change implemented?

To make sure that these are *actually* the questions staff will ask about a policy change, I've done two things. First, I've asked over 200 government workers at all levels to tell me what they want in a policy change memo. Second, I've tested this list by writing memos without answering one or more questions and have found that the answers I've omitted were missed—staff asked for the answers. In short, this list has been tested. But I originally got it by simple analysis. I just put myself in a staff employee's position and thought out the questions.

The questions are, at this stage, disorganized. They really need to be answered in the following order.

1. What was the old policy?
2. What is the new policy and procedure?
3. How is it different from the old policy and procedure?
4. Why did we have to make this change?
5. Why didn't you try (something else) instead of this change?
6. What was wrong with the way we did things before?
7. What is the effect of the change on what we'll do?
8. How will this work in normal situations?
9. What will happen under some unusual circumstances?
10. What do you want me(us) to do about this change? How do you want this change implemented?

A policy change memo that answers these questions will generally answer all of staff's questions. But, more importantly, the question list directs the research that *should* go into the memo. The person who is changing policy should consider all these questions before issuing the memo in the first place. The person who makes the policy change decision should make sure that these questions can be answered satisfactorily before making the decision. In short, by looking at this kind of outline for the report, you get a good idea of what you have to do before you can actually prepare the report itself, before you can write the answers to the questions. The questions define the scope of the research effort and the report.

Writing to a Multiple Audience

For major research and report projects, you're more than likely to be directing your report at answering the questions of a variety of readers. This requires you to carry out your reader analysis for each group of readers and then to assemble the groups of questions into a single, coherent report.

A good example of this kind of report is the increasingly popular *program justification*, which is an analysis of why your particular program should continue to receive funding. This kind of report is quite complex; it must meet the needs of four distinct audiences, each of which will use it for a different purpose:

1. *Agency managers* will use a program justification to help them in their planning for the years to come and to help them make decisions about which portions of their overall program are strongest. They'll use the information in the report to argue for funds and to point out agency accomplishments. Although the report is generally called a program *justification*, it is used often as a source of information for program analysis and redesign.

2. *Finance and accounting agents*, both within and without the agency, will use the report to check the costs of various portions of the program and compare these costs to the benefits identified in the report. Budget decisions will be made on the basis of this cost/benefit analysis.

3. *Agents of the executive and legislative branches* will examine the report to determine whether or not the program is meeting the need identified when it was first set up. This need may be as lofty as "to prevent human suffering" or as down to earth as "to keep constituents in _____ district happy so that _____ can stay in office." Image is very important to this audience, which may have trouble separating fact from illusion—and may not want to do so.

4. *The public* will eventually read elements of the report, either in whole or in part. Special-interest groups will publicize parts; newspapers, radio, and television will carry other portions of the report. These people will be interested in whether the program meets the needs of the public—either of very narrow special interests or of broad social groups.

Meeting the needs of such a diverse audience requires some very careful analysis. It takes several hours of thinking to arrive at a final list of general questions to be answered in order to satisfy all four groups. Since writing out this amount of thinking would require about 500 pages in this book, the end product will have to suffice as an illustration. In the list of questions below, the audience for each answer is indicated in parentheses following the question: M = agency managers, F = finance and accounting agents, EL = executive and legislative readers, P = public and special interests. In looking over this rather long list of questions, note that it contains sections not normally found in the *traditional* program justification. It has this broader scope because the readers of such reports want the questions answered, whether they're traditional or not. Legislative analysts, for example, want questions about the program's future answered, even though this isn't a normal part of a justification for an ongoing program. Note also, that most questions have multiple audiences. This means, of course, that you have to deal with answers at several levels of detail. For example, an answer sufficient for a manager may not be at all sufficient for a budget analyst.

Questions readers want answered when you're

SUMMARY JUSTIFYING A PROGRAM

Long reports have to be summarized because some readers do not have the time to read fifty to one hundred pages of detailed analysis.

1. What is the program and why was it set up? When, how, and by whom? (M,F,EL,P)
2. What are the program's objectives? Who is it supposed to serve and how? (M,F,EL,P)
3. How is the program currently operated? (M,EL,F)
4. How important is the program to those it serves? (EL,P)
5. What is the current cost of the program, and what is the current benefit to the public? (EL,F,P)
6. What is the future of the program? Where should it be going? (EL,P)
7. Should the program be allowed to continue? To receive funding? To be operated by the current agency? (M, F, EL, P)

BODY OF THE REPORT

The body contains sections that correspond to the questions asked in the summary.

Program History

1. What is your program and why was it established? (M,F,EL,P)
   a. Why was it needed? (M,F,EL,P)
   b. What were the original program goals? (M,F,EL,P)
   c. When, how, and by whom was it set up? (M,F,EL,P)
2. What would have happened if your program had not been set up to meet the need? (EL,P)
3. In the history of the program, what have you achieved? What are the most significant milestones? (EL,P)

Program Objectives

1. What are the present program's specific objectives? (M,EL,P)
   a. What are you trying to accomplish on a practical level? (M,EL,P)
   b. Who are you trying to serve and why have you focused on these people? (M,EL,P)
   c. What is your order of priority for these services? (M,EL,P)
2. What support have you received from those affected by your operations? (EL,P)
   a. Do those you're trying to serve concur with your sense of objectives? (EL,P)
   b. Are your priorities in line with those of the people you're trying to serve? (EL,P)

Program Structure and Operations

1. What do you do or produce to meet your objectives? (M,F,EL,P)
   a. What are your major activities? (M,F,EL,P)
   b. What is the magnitude of your activities? (M,F,EL,P)
   c. What is the timetable of your activities? (EL,P)
2. How are you set up to conduct your program and meet your objectives? (M,F,EL)
   a. What is your administrative structure? (M,EL,F)
   b. How are decisions affecting the program made? (M,F,EL)
   c. How do you interact with other agencies serving the same people? (M,F,EL)
   d. How do you review your effectiveness and efficiency? (M,F,EL)

Program Importance

1. How important is the program to those it serves? (EL,P)
   a. What would they do without it? (EL,P)
   b. What other programs would pick up the slack? (EL,P)
2. How strongly do those served by the program feel about it? (EL,P)
   a. What are their positive feelings? (EL,P)
   b. What complaints do they have? (EL,P)
3. What would the public response be to major changes in the program? (EL)
   a. How would the public respond to canceling the program? (EL)
   b. How would the public respond to strengthening the program? (EL)

Program Costs/Benefit Analysis

1. Regardless of your program's public image, what are the concrete benefits the public receives from your program? (EL,F)
   a. What specific services or products do you provide? (EL,F)
   b. What is the direct benefit of these services or products to those who receive them? (EL,F)
   c. What indirect effects does your program have on your client population or on those associated with it? (EL,F)
   d. What do these benefits mean to the health and safety of those you serve and the general public? (EL,F)
2. For each benefit, what are the specific costs involved in production or delivery of the service? (EL,F)
   a. What are the personnel costs per unit of service or product? EL,F)
   b. What are the supplies costs per unit of service or product? (EL,F)
   c. What overhead is attributable to the service or product? (EL,F)
3. Do the benefits received justify the costs? (M,F,EL,P)
   a. Could we do it for less? (M,F,EL,P)
   b. Could someone else do it for less? (M,F,EL,P)
   c. Could we get along without it entirely? (M,F,EL,P)

Note: If the answers to these justification questions are that the program isn't justified, then the report is completed with a simple recommendation to end the current program. If, however, there is some hope for the program—despite its flaws—then the report continues through the two sections outlined below. This issue is raised here because the report may be prepared by someone who feels it is valid to get rid of the program. Agencies have been known to make such recommendations.

The Future of the Program

1. What more must be done to make sure the program achieves its objectives? (M,F,EL,P)
2. What new objectives might be considered for this program? (M,F,EL,P)
   a. What are the problems faced by the people the program is serving? (M,EL,P)
   b. How can the program act to help solve these problems? Why should it do these things? (M,EL,P)
3. To solve these problems, to meet new objectives or better meet old ones, what changes are necessary over the next _____ years? (M,EL)

        a. What do you need to do administratively? (M,F)

        b. What legislative or executive actions would help you solve problems and meet these objectives? (M,EL)

        c. In making changes, how will you ensure that objectives are met? (EL,F)

        d. How will you ensure that present programs aren't harmed as you focus attention on new ones? (EL,F)

4. To meet its objectives, what resources must the program have and from what sources? (EL,F)

        a. What kinds of facilities are necessary? (EL,F)

        b. What kinds and numbers of personnel are necessary? (EL,F)

        c. What kind of support from other agencies is necessary? (M,EL,F,P)

5. How should these resources be provided? (EL,F)

        a. What funding sources are available? (EL,F)

        b. How much support from each source will be necessary? (EL,F)

6. What will you do if you do not get all the funding and support you feel you need? (EL,F,P)

        a. What portions of the program will be cut back? (M,EL,F,P)

        b. Who will be affected by the cutbacks and why? (M,EL,F,P)

Recommendations

In detail, what actions do you recommend to maintain or improve the program? When? How? By whom? (M,EL,F,P)

    Although this list is fairly long (containing over sixty questions), it is still a rather general representation of the interests of the four groups of readers. It's general because many of the specific questions such readers ask are determined by the nature of the program being justified. Nevertheless, it should provide an adequate general framework for your efforts to determine the scope of any particular program justification. In using it (and other question lists like it at the end of this chapter), remember that it should be adapted to your specific needs:

1. You may wish to change the order of some of the sections. Depending on your analysis of your particular audience, you may want to put specific recommendations at the very beginning of the report—as a part of the summary. You might also wish to discuss the future of the program before going into the detail of cost/benefit analysis, provided that there is no question about the general value of the program.

2. You will surely wish to make many additions to this basic list, depending on your program.
3. You may decide not to answer some of the questions. Some are a bit touchy politically and you may avoid them for this reason. You risk disappointing some of your readers if you do so, but you may wish to take this risk.

Uses and Limits of Reader Question Lists

There are two things about this simple process of turning an analysis of your readers into an organized list of questions to answer from your research that make it worthwhile as an early step to take in the brainstorming process. First, you can get a picture of the final report in this way and this enables you to direct your efforts. From such a picture, you can plan out your research. Second, because the general situation determines the general questions that will have to be answered, you can start planning your research before you even know what your subject is. For example, you do not need to know the subject of a policy change memo in order to get a clear, concrete, idea of the scope of the final report. *All* policy change memos should cover the questions set forth on page 57. These two properties give reader question lists a number of uses:

1. *You can use them over and over again, adapting them to specific situations.* Once you have worked out and tested a set of questions in a situation, you can use this same set for other, similar, situations. All you have to do is *generalize* the questions so that they do not refer to any particular situation, and you have a tool that may last you decades. There are a number of such general reader question lists included at the end of this chapter. They provide an overall idea of what kinds of questions you have to deal with in a number of situations you'll find yourself involved in over years of government work—proposal writing, analysis of problems, job description, etc. You can pass lists such as these around an office, getting additional questions from those with different perspectives. You can establish an office standard for various kinds of reports by specifying that all reports of a certain type should cover answers to a particular set of questions. In short, you can use the question lists you generate (and those provided here) to establish some sense of permanency and consistency in the reports you have to write, or if you are a manager, in the reports you want staff to prepare.

2. *You can use the lists to get an idea of how people are going to respond to your work.* When people see a question, they almost automatically think of the kind of answer they might give. This gives them an immediate sense of what the final report might actually look and sound like, and they can then respond to this feeling. For example, if you find that one of your readers can be expected to ask a question like "Why haven't you done a better job of meeting these objectives?", you can pretty quickly see that the answer to such a question doesn't have a chance of being positive in tone. The question is so negative that it will force the report into a negative tone. It may thus be a question you'd be better off avoiding. More importantly, your sensing that the answer will be negative in tone may tip you off to some of the political problems you'll have to face in preparing the report. If you're going to have to answer questions such as this, you're going to have to be ready for a fight.

3. *You can use the question lists as the basis for initial staff assignments.* One of the problems facing *groups* that have been assigned to a research effort is the problem of dividing the effort up so that members aren't always stumbling over each other. Research staff can get a better sense of exactly what they're supposed to do, as well as a sense of how their individual work contributes to the whole project, by having a specific set of questions to work on. A research group leader can divide the research effort among group members by report section, or may select specific questions for each member to get answers to, according to the skills they have or their background knowledge in the agency. Being able to do this early in the research process, before anyone establishes any *research territory,* helps avoid problems when the report is finally prepared. All members of the research team know the *limited* scope of their work and know that their work fits into a whole—it isn't the whole project. The tendency of individuals to overemphasize the work *they've* done at the expense of work done by others can be better controlled. In addition, if the research effort is divided according to the questions to be answered, there is no problem in keeping group members focused on the purpose of the report. The vague, general purpose of the report can be dealt with at the beginning and end of the research and report writing processes; while the research is *in progress,* each group member can concentrate on the narrow-range purpose of answering very specific questions.

4. *You can use the question lists to get some feedback from the boss and to commit the boss to a research direction and scope.* By looking at a list of questions to be answered by a research project report, the boss—the person who has assigned the report—can tell immediately if your concept of the project is consistent with his or her concept of it. If it is, then getting the boss to approve the question list can give you a solid indication of what the boss will accept as a final report. If it isn't, you can adjust it quickly.

There are also several limits to the uses of these question lists. First, the ones presented in this book are general. They thus represent the kind of questions the reader will ask, but they are not exactly phrased to represent the interests of the reader in any particular report. They have to be adapted to your specific needs. Second, when you're designing such a question list yourself, the result is only as good as your analysis of the audience. If you don't include all possible audiences, then your report will not be complete. So, for this process of making your audience's interests into a list of questions for the report to work, you must take time to identify all your report's readers. You must not just assume that the report will be read only by a few people.

NOTES TO MANAGEMENT AND STAFF

If you looked at the questions in the last example carefully, you probably noted that some of them were questions that could be answered by gathering data, while others required interpretation. You may have also noted that they were usually separated quite clearly. In doing this, you ensure a separation of the actual data you collect and the political thinking that goes into analyzing it. In short, it is at this stage that you provide for the separation of the objective research and the political process. You group questions carefully. Then, if your readers want you to change an interpretation, you can do so without ever touching the data you present. The data can stand on its own.

To Management

There is always a strong tendency in research to want to get out into the field to collect data—to get the assignment out of the thinking stages and into the work stages. One of the jobs facing a manager who has asked for a report is to make sure that staff

To Staff

The first time you try this procedure of analyzing the reader to anticipate the reader's questions, you're likely to find it difficult. Most people do, because most people take it very seriously—almost as if it were an academic exercise. The key to the process,

To Management (*continued*)

don't give in to this desire to get going on the data collection until they've thought the whole project out very carefully. If you can encourage staff to do this, you'll find the time spent in review and redrafting at the end of the report can be considerably reduced.

You can help staff resist the urge to collect some data by telling them that you want them to give you an outline of the final report before they do so. Make it a requirement. And then review the outline they give you seriously and carefully. Let them know that you're not impatient, that you realize research takes time, and that it's best done when it's well planned. *It may be reassuring to know that the planning effort, which takes so long to describe, doesn't take more than 4–8 hours once staff get a handle on these procedures.* The mind just works faster than any description of a mental process.

Using a question list as a basic outline form is a good way to get staff working on something concrete. They do not have to know the answers to know what the questions are. As a manager, you can get a very concrete picture of the final report before you authorize extensive work.

To Staff (*continued*)

when you're having trouble with it, is to try to think in the same terms your reader would use. Act out your reader's questions. Pretend that you *are* your reader. If your reader is a taxpayer, pretend you're angry or frustrated. If your reader is a politician, pretend you're very impressed with your own importance. Your actual reader may not be exactly like the stereotype you adopt, but adopting a stereotype will help you think your way through this reader analysis. After all, the stereotype became a stereotype for a reason—it was close enough to the truth to be a useful exaggeration. You can always tone down the questions later.

Another problem you will probably encounter in doing this question anticipation process is that as soon as you get the question worked out clearly, you'll start to try to answer it. That's fine if your report has only one question. But if you have a complex report to do, the tendency to want to answer every question as soon as it is formulated will get in the way of your effort to get all the questions down. Besides, answering the questions is what the research is all about. So, while you're on this brainstorming step, concentrate on it exclusively. Make sure you get all the questions down and organized before you even begin to think about answering them. In short, control your thinking process. Don't let it get random.

After you have designed your question list, put it away for awhile. Take about a half hour to do something else, and then come back to it for a quick review. The break will usually help you fill in any gaps.

Finally, remember that the question list is a prediction of what the reader will want to see in the final report. Treat it as a prediction, and make sure you check the accuracy of your analysis by reviewing the reviewers' comments against your questions—after the whole report is done. If the report ends up being different from what you had originally predicted it would look like, jot down the differences and think about them the next time you start a project. In short, use the question list to help you figure out where you went wrong—if you do go wrong somewhere during the research project.

CHAPTER SUMMARY

The object of the report is to satisfy your readers' needs for information. Your readers are people with questions about a subject. The questions are a function of the situation and the purpose of the readers in wanting the information, as well as a function of the roles the readers are playing. The interests of the readers are predictable and can be expressed in terms of the questions they want answered. A list of these questions, organized in the order they should be answered in the final report, provides the researcher with a concrete picture of what needs to be covered in the final report. It thus acts as a guide to the entire research process. Developing such lists of reader questions involves taking the following steps:

1. *Make a list of all readers—by position, not by name.*
2. *For each reader or group of readers, jot down what you think they'll use the report for.*
3. *Group readers according to the use they have for the report.*
4. *Jot down the basic professional interests of each group.*
5. *Given these interests, try to figure out what questions each group would have about the general subject you're working on.*
6. *Once you have listed all the questions you can think of, put these in the order in which you think readers will want them answered.*

There are two kinds of reader question lists you can generate using this procedure. First, you can make up lists to cover a general situation, such as any policy change or any program justification. Second, you can make the list specific to your own project. The general lists are good guides to follow when you're making up specific lists.

A number of general question lists, covering some of the most frequent kinds of reports written in government, are provided in an appendix to this chapter.

Brainstorming by designing the report

APPENDIX

READER QUESTION LISTS

Here are some general guides to the interests of readers of some familiar kinds of reports. Use them to help you prepare more specific lists of questions. The question lists cover:

1. Giving assignments
2. Responding to complaints
3. Explaining rules
4. Describing jobs
5. Writing recommendations
6. Doing feasibility studies
7. Studying problems
8. Doing environmental impact assessments
9. Writing proposals

Some of these may not *sound* like research projects, but they can all be thought of as requiring research. All require you to gather information in order to answer the readers' questions.

At the beginning of each question list is a brief description of the situation for which the questions are appropriate and of the rationale for the questions.

Remember, if one of these question lists doesn't meet your particular needs, you can prepare one that does in about an hour. You can then add it to these and slowly build up a file to cover most common research and reporting situations.

Questions readers want answered when you're

GIVING AN ASSIGNMENT

Unless the assignment is very simple, people will find it difficult to concentrate on and complete efficiently if all they have been told to do is "Do _____." They *want and need* to understand the assignment. Understanding requires the answers to the following questions:

1. What is it that you want done?
2. What is it that you want me to achieve by doing this? What are your objectives?

3. Why do we have to meet these objectives?
4. How important is this work?
5. How should it be carried out? To the letter, or can I exercise judgment in getting the objective achieved?
6. What is the absolute deadline for it to be done?
7. What help can I have?
8. Are there any problems I'm likely to run into that you can tell me about now—before I start the assignment?

Note that these questions are similar to, but not quite the same as, those included in Chapter 4 (Analyzing the Assignment). Note also that in many cases, answering these questions will require you to do some very simple research.

Questions readers want answered when you're

RESPONDING TO COMPLAINTS

Preparing a response to a complaint really is a research effort, *legal* research in many cases. Complaints imply a hostile readership; to this audience you must explain everything or risk a counter-argument. The response must also satisfy your boss. It must stand on its own as a summary of the complaint and the situation that led to the complaint. Remember, your response may become a legal document.

1. What incident generated the complaint? What happened? When? Where? What does the complainer say was wrong?
2. What are the key elements or issues raised, in order of importance?
3. What does the law, the policy file, or some other source of regulations have to say about such situations?
4. For each key element of the complaint, is there evidence that the law or policy has, indeed, been violated? How did you arrive at these conclusions?
5. What is going to be done about the complaint? Are there any alternatives? Why did you select the action you have?

Of course, the person making the complaint is primarily interested in question 5. The other readers need questions 1–4 so that they know what is going on. And the complainer also *needs* these questions answered to fully understand the final conclusions.

Questions readers want answered when you're

EXPLAINING A RULE

Explaining a rule is another legal research task. To give an adequate explanation, you usually have to gather some background information. It's unlikely that the answers to all the readers' questions will be in your head. This set of questions is based on the questions *judges* habitually answer when explaining rules to juries.

1. What is the intent of the law, rule, or regulation?
2. In simple terms, what does the rule say? What is the basic principle it sets forth?
3. What are the key points in this rule?
4. How does this rule apply in situations such as the one we're involved in now?
5. Are we complying with the rule—letter and intent?
6. If not, what do we have to do?

Note that these questions presume a *practical* reader interest. Unless you're writing to an academic lawyer, you can probably assume your readers will have such an interest—that they're reading the explanation because they're affected by it.

Questions readers want answered when you're

DESCRIBING A JOB

Whether you're announcing a new position or simply trying to clarify the duties of an old one, job descriptions are likely to give you fits. They're difficult because the *tradition* is to write very brief descriptions, and these do not cover the myriad questions readers have about the job. To get the answers to all the following questions into a one-page job description will require you to write very carefully.

1. What is the job title and what department is the job in?
2. What are the goals of the job?
3. How does this job fit into the overall activity of the agency?
4. What is the input for this job? What materials are used and in what form do they arrive in this office?
5. What is the expected output? How fast?
6. How do you go from input to output? Essential steps? Essential interactions with others? Authority and responsibility?

These questions apply even if input and output are nebulous items. For example, if input is *problems* and output is *solutions,* you still have a valid set of answers to these questions.

Questions readers want answered when you're

RECOMMENDING SOMEONE

Most people treat recommending someone for a job or an award as something requiring only very general statements. The readers of such recommendations find them almost useless, because there is no way for the reader to judge the honesty and sincerity behind the general statement. A good recommendation is full of specific data about the person being recommended. To answer the readers' questions may also require some research into the nature of the position or award.

1. Who are you recommending and for what?
2. Who are you and how are you qualified to make this recommendation?
3. Why are you making this recommendation?
4. How much do you know about the person you're recommending?
5. What do you know about what this person has *done* that leads you to believe that he/she is qualified for this position or deserving of this award?
6. If this is a recommendation for a job, how do you think this person will be useful to the new employers?
7. How strongly are you making this recommendation? How does this person compare to others?

Note that you have to establish your own credibility before you can really go into your recommendation. Sometimes this can be done by simply mentioning your title and where you work. At other times, it may require a paragraph of its own.

Questions readers want answered when you're

DOING A FEASIBILITY STUDY

Anytime someone asks you to decide whether or not to do something, they're asking for a feasibility study. The thinking, decision-making process outlined by this question list applies to even the simplest studies of feasibility. For example, you cover all this territory in your *head* even when you're asked something as simple as "Should we move that desk over by the window rather than leave it in front of the door?"

Unlike previous question lists, which have been short and simple, this list contains a number of questions. Your answers will vary in length and depth of analysis, but you should consider answering all questions for any feasibility report.

SUMMARY

1. What proposed action was evaluated? Why is this sort of action needed? What is the goal of the action?
2. Given the present resources available to the agency, can this proposal be implemented?
3. All things considered, is it the best action we can take to achieve the goal—to meet the need?
4. Should we take this action? Will the benefit derived from doing so outweigh the costs involved?

BODY OF THE FEASIBILITY STUDY

The Proposed Action

1. What is the proposed action that is being evaluated?
2. What is the goal of the proposed action?
   a. What is the result desired?
   b. Why is this result important?
   c. Why couldn't things be left alone?
3. What are the key parts to the proposed action, the major elements that will determine its success or failure?
4. What are the major assumptions behind the proposed action?
5. Who might be involved in the change?

Feasibility or Practicality

1. What resources would be needed to implement the proposal?
   a. Money?
   b. Time?
   c. Space?
   d. Materials?
   e. Personnel?

2. Would implementing the proposal require intangible resources such as changes in administrative structure, changes
   in attitude, changes in basic policy?
3. Does the agency have the resources, tangible or intangible, to
   allow the proposal to be implemented?
4. Would the benefit to be derived from implementing the proposal be worth the resources necessary to make it work?
5. Can this proposal be implemented?

Alternatives

1. Are there any other ways of achieving the same goals?
   a. Administrative?
   b. Legislative?
   c. Operational?
2. How should these alternatives be evaluated? What are the
   criteria that should be used to evaluate them?
3. Given these criteria, which of the alternatives looks best?
4. Is this alternative better than the action being proposed?
5. All things considered, which is the best action to take to
   achieve the desired goals?

Recommendations

1. What action should be taken?
2. How should the recommendation be implemented?
   a. When should it go into effect?
   b. Who should be involved in implementing it?
   c. What should the schedule of actions be?
   d. What are the responsibilities of all involved?
   e. How should we make sure the recommended action is
      working as expected? When should we check it out?
3. In the end, what benefit will be derived from taking this
   action?

Even when you're not asked to supply alternatives, you can usually count on your readers' wanting an analysis of them. The
assignment to "Tell me if we can do _____" almost always means
"Tell me if we can do _____, and what else might work better."

There is one section you can add to almost any report as an
appendix—a *methods* section. If you're doing scientific research,
this is always important. The research results are really only as good
as the methods used to get them. A scientific audience will demand
a methods section; the administrative and public audience very frequently doesn't demand one. It's a good idea to supply this section,

though, outside the actual study narrative. In this appendix, cover the following questions:

1. What general approach did you take to your data collection and why?
2. How is this approach valid under the circumstances of your study? How did you make sure your results would be valid?
3. What were the major steps in your research effort?
   a. For each step, what did you use?
   b. For each step, how did you carry out the step?
   c. For each step, what major problems did you encounter?
4. How valid and how accurate are your results?
   a. Are you sure that if you did the same thing over again, you'd get the same results?
   b. Are you sure that your results really represent the way things are?
   c. Can action be based on your results without fear of failure?

Questions Readers Want Answered When You're

STUDYING A PROBLEM

I would make an educated guess that about 40–50 percent of the major research reports done by government employees are studies of a problem. Someone in the office has noticed that something isn't going right and wants staff to figure out what's wrong and what to do about it. This kind of study is so frequent that many agencies offer special *problem identification* training courses to staff.

The problem report requires research into four areas: what the problem is, what caused it, what can be done to solve it, and how this solution can be implemented. You might think of this sort of report as a detective story with a feasibility report attached to it.

SUMMARY

1. What is the problem?
2. Why is it important to solve the problem?
3. What caused it?
4. What alternative solutions are there?
5. Which solution is best to take?
6. What should be done to implement the solution?

BODY OF THE REPORT

Introduction: The Problem and Its History

1. What is the situation that led to this report?
   a. What was happening to make the report necessary?
   b. Who requested the report and why did they want the situation looked into?
2. Things aren't a *problem* unless things aren't going as they *should*. What is the desired state of affairs; what is it that should be happening?
   a. Who should be doing what? When, where, and how?
   b. What product, what result, should be evident if things are going right?
3. What is the history of the problem? When was it first noticed? How long has this been going on?

Effect of The Problem

1. What effect has this problem had on the organization?
   a. On operations?
   b. On morale?
   c. On the organization's image?
   d. On the organization's *ability* to operate?
2. How has the problem affected specific parts of the organization more than others? Where is the effect felt most?
3. What is the overall magnitude of the effect? How much has it affected the organization?
4. Is the organization hindered in achieving any of its basic goals?
5. What will happen if we do not solve this problem?

Cause

1. What are the factors that may have contributed to the problem?
2. Of all these, which are primary factors? Which must take the main share of the blame for the problem?
3. How have these factors worked to cause this problem? What is the mechanism for their action on the organization?

Alternative Solutions

1. In order to be a workable solution, what criteria must an alternative meet? What should we be looking for in examining solutions and why?

2. What are the alternatives—all of them?
3. Which alternatives meet the minimum criteria?
4. Which of the alternatives that meet the minimum criteria is the best, considering all aspects of office operation—money, staff, time, administrative structure, facilities?
5. What are the possible effects of each solution—beneficial and detrimental (side effects)?

Conclusions and Recommendations

1. Which alternative, or alternatives, should we take? Why?
2. What will its effect be—in detail?
3. What problems will we encounter in taking this solution?
4. How will we be able to measure the effect of this solution so that we can make sure it's working?

Plan of Action

1. In chronological order, what should be done to implement this solution?
2. What resources need to be committed to implementation?
3. How should steps be scheduled?
4. Who should be responsible for each part of the implementation?
5. When should we start on the first step?

Note that the questions here suggest a very broad responsibility on the researcher's part. It has been my experience that this is exactly what management expects in this sort of report. The manager doesn't want a simple statement that "There's a problem—this is it." The manager is action-oriented and wants to know exactly what to do about the problem. As a researcher, you may find that some of your research involves working with the manager to work out the answers to the last set of questions—before the report is presented.

Questions readers want answered when you're

DOING ENVIRONMENTAL IMPACT ASSESSMENT

The environmental impact assessment report is one of the most complicated reports *because it must satisfy an extremely diverse audience.* It must satisfy lawyers (for and against the project), engineers, biologists, ecologists, managers, public-interest groups such as the "Friends of _____," regulatory boards, administrators, and legislative bodies (at times). To satisfy all these readers, such a report must really be three or four reports in one and it must be clearly divided according to the kind of audience that will read each sub-report.

While very few government employees will ever *prepare* such a study or write such a report, most will at some time be involved in *analyzing* one. Environmental impact assessment is becoming increasingly important.

The three subreports in these reports are (1) an overview for general audiences, (2) a legal document, and (3) a scientific impact assessment report. There may also be *backup* reports covering each portion of the research that went into the report. In looking at these reports, it's important to realize that impact assessment is an extremely complex and difficult task. The question lists below are nothing more than a logical framework for this analysis; writing out all the questions your audiences will ask will involve your expanding these lists considerably to cover the questions particular to your report subject. Here, then, are the *general* questions:

THE OVERVIEW REPORT FOR THE GENERAL AUDIENCE

1. What is the project? What is the area it's being proposed for? Why is it being proposed? Why is it needed or wanted?
2. What is the value of the area now? What is it used for? What animals and plants that we especially value are there?
3. What do we lose and what do we gain if the project is allowed?
4. Can some compromise be arranged? How?
5. Can we reduce any harmful impact, or make up for it somehow?
6. What do project planners have to say about this? Special-interest groups? Government officials?
7. What do independent, objective, observers think about the planned project?
8. Where do we go from here? What can be done to resolve any issues that haven't been resolved? How? What should we do?

Note that you cannot write this sort of general overview until after all the scientific and legal work has been completed. You must finish the two long reports that follow first.

THE LEGAL DOCUMENT

Case Background

1. What is the history of the area in question? The history of the project in question?

   a. What was the original state of the area in question and
        how has it changed over the years? Why has it changed?
   b. What is the relationship of the limited area being studied
        to the larger environment—physical and social?
2. How does the project fit into the area? What part of the area
   will it occupy? How important is this part?
3. What, in summary form, are the legal issues this project
   raises? Why are they important?

Case Analysis

1. In relation to this kind of project, what are the key points of
   law?
   a. What was the intent of each portion of the law?
   b. What is the letter of the law? What rules are set down to
        ensure that this intent is met?
2. In relation to this particular project, what are the key issues
   in regard to the intent and letter of the law?
3. For each issue you bring up, what is the evidence for the
   project's being within or without the letter and intent of the
   law?
4. Are there any mitigating circumstances that should be taken
   into account before the project is judged within or outside of
   the law?
5. Is the project lawful? Should it be allowed to go ahead?

Summary of Scientific Evidence to Support Case Analysis

1. How will the project alter the environment—both the environment of the immediate area and that of surrounding areas?
   a. What elements of the environment will be most affected
        and how?
   b. What would the environment be like after the project was
        implemented and how would this be different from what
        it is now?
2. What modifications could be made to the project to reduce
   any impact or compensate for it? In your judgment, should
   these be made?

Project Planner's Response

1. Regardless of the legalities of the case, what actions do the
   project planners intend to take to comply with the spirit of
   the law and with the desires of the community?

Note that *one* person is not likely to be able to prepare this whole report. It will take cooperative effort on the part of a good lawyer and a good scientist, each working on his or her own section. Knowing this in advance of the actual research should suggest some staffing requirements for the assessment report group.

THE SCIENTIFIC IMPACT ASSESSMENT REPORT

The Environment

1. What kind of environment are we dealing with?
   a. Where is it—geographically and in terms of populations?
   b. What are its dimensions—size, shape, depth, etc.?
   c. What is its importance to humans? To plants and animals?
2. Is this the kind of environment that is classified as delicate or robust?
3. What is the area used for?
   a. Commercial uses?
   b. Recreational uses?
4. What are the boundaries of the area studied?
   a. How were these boundaries set?
   b. What are the boundary lines?
   c. What are the problems with these boundary lines?
5. How does the environment work?
   a. What are the physical and biological variables that affect the environment?
      (1) When are these variables important?
      (2) How do they affect the environment and by how much?
      (3) What controls these variables (human and natural)?
      (4) Which are the most important to the existence of the environment as a distinct area?
   b. How does the environment fluctuate in response to the things that affect it?
      (1) What are the changes? How big are they?
      (2) What is the frequency of the changes?
   c. What are the major outputs of the environment?
      (1) What are the physical outputs (such as silt, water, air currents, temperature influences)?
      (2) What are the biological outputs (such as number of fish, birds, seeds, plant life)?

The Biology of the Environment

1. What are the permanent, resident, organisms?
   a. Plants?
   b. Animals?
2. What is the structure of the plant/animal community?
   a. How are populations distributed?
   b. What food chains/webs exist?
   c. What are the major intraspecies interactions?
   d. What are the major interspecies interactions?
   e. What are the major pathways for interaction in the community (physical and biological)?
3. What organisms pass through this permanent community?
   a. How do they interact with the community?
   b. What is their influence on the community?
4. How important is it to human populations that this community exist?

The Proposed Project (or Ongoing Project)

1. What is the project that is being proposed?
2. What are the key elements of the project in relation to the environment?
3. What will the project do to change the environment?
   a. How will elements of the project interact with the environment and the community?
   b. How will the elements of the environment respond to this project?

Impact Study Methods

1. Which elements of the environment did you select to study in depth?
   a. Why did you select these and not others?
   b. How are these elements going to allow you to assess the impact of the project on the whole environment?
   c. Are these elements especially valuable in their own right?
2. What method did you use to study each element?
3. How did you conduct your study of each element?
4. How reliable are your results?
5. How did you go about analyzing your results to determine how they indicate the project's impact on the environment?

Results

1. What elements of the environment will be directly affected by the proposed project?

2. What elements will be indirectly affected? How?
3. What will be the result of these effects on each element? Will the project increase or decrease the numbers or nature of each element?

Discussion: Assessment of Impact

1. Given what you have found out, how will the project affect the environment and the organisms in it?
   a. What will the environment look like after the project gets started? What immediate changes will take place?
   b. What long-range changes are likely to take place?
2. Do these changes mean that the impact of the project will be harmful?
   a. From a biological perspective (long and short term)?
   b. From a social perspective (long and short term)?
   c. From an economic perspective (long and short term)?
3. How sure are you that this is true?
4. What is going to be lost if this project is allowed and what is its value?

As I was working on this list of questions with a number of ecologists in government, university, and private research groups, I found all of them quite concerned that these questions would be very difficult to answer. I agree. They are difficult questions. Some of them are almost impossible to answer. But the readers still want them answered. And it is the readers' desires that are represented in all these lists. A qualified answer is better than no answer at all.

Questions readers want answered when you're

WRITING A PROPOSAL

If you want to do something and you have to ask permission, you're involved in making a proposal. In this situation, regardless of the extent of the proposal, the reader has some basic interests that you must deal with. These are *need* and *your credibility.* If you can't establish that there is a need for what you're proposing and that you can actually do the job, you won't get permission or funds for the project.

So much has been written about proposal writing, that this list of questions is very limited. It's an expression of the very general reader interests.

1. Why do we need to do something?   (*Problem*)
2. What do we need to do?   (*Solution*)

3. How do you know *that* will work?
4. OK, what exactly will you be trying to achieve?
5. How do you plan on doing *that*?
6. Has anyone else done anything like this before?
7. OK, what do you need to do this?
8. How come it will cost that much?
9. Can't you contribute something, if it means so much to you?
10. How do I know you're the right person to do it?
    a. What experience have you got?
    b. Who have you got to help you?
    c. How much of this project have you already done?
11. OK, but what do we get out of this if we give you permission to do it? How does this help us or those we're interested in?
12. How do you want to set up the finances, support, for this?
13. How will you let us know about the results?

Within the limits of polite prose, I've tried to phrase these questions as I've often heard them when sitting around evaluating proposals. They should give you a good idea of how a cynical reader looks at proposals—which are almost always designed to do some form of good.

ANALYZING THE SUBJECT

6

Knowing the readers' questions gives you a pretty good starting point for planning your research, but it doesn't yet give you a *complete* picture of your final destination; it doesn't give you a complete outline of the final report. You still need a clear idea of what kind of information you'll have to gather in order to answer the questions. To get this information, you have to analyze the subject. So, you put aside the list of your readers' questions and you begin to look at the *things you have to examine*.

In analyzing the assignment, you've taken the first step in the process of analyzing the subject. You've isolated the key words in the assignment and made a list of them. Since these *words represent the subject you're going to deal with*, they are a pretty good starting point for your analysis. They give you a sort of checklist of things to think about while you're trying to answer the readers' questions.

The connection between the readers' questions and these key words from the assignment analysis is simple. As you try to answer each question, your mind will wander from one part of your subject to the next. If you want to make sure that you cover the whole subject, if you want to make sure that you don't forget anything while you're working, you need only run down your list of key words and ask yourself this question:

> "To answer the readers' question, do I need to get information about this word (subject), or about this word (subject), or about this word (subject) . . . ?"

You look at the question and scan the list of key words to see what it is you have to cover. Since the list of key words covers the whole assignment, you ensure yourself against forgetting anything important by taking this simple step. And you can begin to fill out an outline.

The senior citizen's golf course fee example from Chapter 4 can be used to illustrate this simple process. As you may recall, one of the key words in the assignment was *problem*. Since the person who assigned the project was thinking about the situation as a problem, you would probably save yourself some trouble and use the list of Readers Want Answered When You're Studying a Problem (page 74) as a guide to the scope of the paper. You would pull this list out and sit down with it and with your key word list. On a scratch piece of paper, you would jot down each question and then scan the key word list to see what you might wish to consider in answering this question. You would jot these things down under the question and then go on to the next question. You would slowly build an outline. The process illustrated in Figure 6–1 can be continued until you have a complete outline.

THE PROBLEM

This simple, almost mechanical, process has only one flaw—the key words are almost always pretty broad terms. They represent huge chunks of data, not nice, easy to discuss, bits and pieces. For example, suppose one of your key words is *management*. Suppose also that you're answering the question "What is the problem?" and that you decide that to answer this question you must consider management. You may jot this word down as a subheading, but you may also find yourself faced with a new question, such as "When I'm talking about management in this section of the paper, what do I cover?" You need another checklist, a list of things to consider when you're dealing with the broad concept of management.

FIGURE 6-1/SCANNING THE KEY WORDS

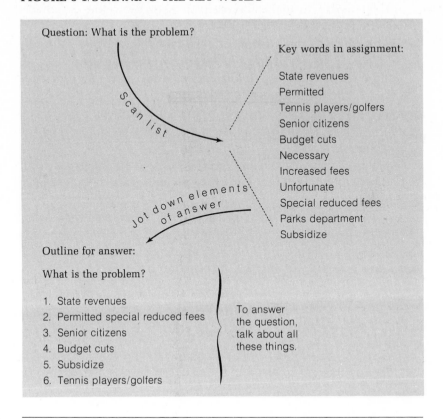

Question: What is the problem?

Key words in assignment:

State revenues
Permitted
Tennis players/golfers
Senior citizens
Budget cuts
Necessary
Increased fees
Unfortunate
Special reduced fees
Parks department
Subsidize

Scan list

Jot down elements of answer

Outline for answer:

What is the problem?

1. State revenues
2. Permitted special reduced fees
3. Senior citizens
4. Budget cuts
5. Subsidize
6. Tennis players/golfers

To answer
the question,
talk about all
these things.

You need to further break down the word (subject) *management* because if you don't, your thinking will not be precise, and this will affect your research and your subsequent writing efforts. You will find it quite difficult to *gather information* about broad concepts, and you will find it even more difficult to interpret information that is collected.

Nowhere is this problem more evident than in politics, where broad concepts are bantered about by both sides and the voter is almost always at a loss to decide who to vote for. Take, for example, the standard talk about "a healthy economy." Everybody is in favor of this; every politician talks about taking action to ensure such an economic state. But if you try to find out what the politicians *mean*, you often find that they themselves don't know. It's only when you can get them to break this concept down into specifics that you can begin to see what they mean. You may find that "healthy" means high interest rates to one person and low ones to another, or that "healthy" means full employment to one and cheap labor to another. When you begin to make this sort of distinction, the differences between politicians can be significant.

Making these broad concepts concrete and specific is quite difficult. There have been dozens of books, for example, that have tried to define just what *management* is. And very sophisticated economists argue about what a "healthy economy" is made of. The problem arises because of the way most people approach the process of *defining* what something is, of determining what a broad concept is all about.

The normal way to go about defining a broad concept is to attempt to *find an equivalent*. Thus, you often see phrases such as "a healthy economy *is* a sound economy" or "management is the art of getting people to do work for you." These sorts of statements make great clichés. But it is as hard to collect data about "a sound economy" as it is to collect data about "a healthy economy." Equivalency definitions also lead to a lot of circular thinking:

Understanding = Comprehension = Knowing = Understanding

You can spend all the time you want trying to make sense out of a concept by trying to find equivalents, and you're just going to end up back where you started—with a vague concept. If you doubt the truth of this statement, just start trying to define *love*. Ten years after you start, you'll be back at the beginning.

A SOLUTION

In order to make any sense out of broad concepts, you have to analyze them, to break them down into their parts, rather than looking for equivalents. It isn't that the process of looking for equivalents is *wrong*, it's just that it doesn't help you think in concrete terms. To make your thoughts concrete, you need to ask a different question:

NOT:	BUT:
What is it?	What is it composed of? What are its *parts*?

This is a scientific question. In asking it, you are saying that you can understand something by looking at all of its parts.

To see where asking this basic scientific question leads you, consider the example of *management*. Almost every manager I've met has at one time or another talked about the difficulty of managing and of figuring out just what to tell people when they ask "What do you do?" Their answer almost always is vague: "I'm a manager; I manage." "Oh," is the usual response, and the subject is dropped. What *should* the answer be? Well, it should sound like this: "I'm a manager; I do _____, and _____, and _____, and _____; and these things all add up to managing." The job, the whole business of management, becomes the sum of a bunch of parts rather than a mystery. Explaining the parts and how they fit together allows you to define the vague term.

What are those parts? What does such a sum-of-parts definition look like? An abbreviated definition of all the things that go into management looks like the chart in Figure 6–2. This definition was constructed by a group of managers in state and local government during a 3-hour seminar. Their combined experience totaled more

FIGURE 6-2/COMPONENTS OF MANAGEMENT

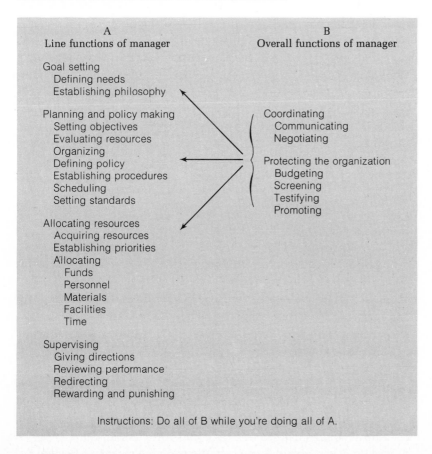

A
Line functions of manager

B
Overall functions of manager

Goal setting
　Defining needs
　Establishing philosophy

Planning and policy making
　Setting objectives
　Evaluating resources
　Organizing
　Defining policy
　Establishing procedures
　Scheduling
　Setting standards

Allocating resources
　Acquiring resources
　Establishing priorities
　Allocating
　　Funds
　　Personnel
　　Materials
　　Facilities
　　Time

Supervising
　Giving directions
　Reviewing performance
　Redirecting
　Rewarding and punishing

Coordinating
　Communicating
　Negotiating

Protecting the organization
　Budgeting
　Screening
　Testifying
　Promoting

Instructions: Do all of B while you're doing all of A.

than 1000 years of managing. After this definition had been developed, all pretty much agreed that "Yes, this is what I mean when I say I'm a manager; I do all these steps; I consider all these parts; they add up to management." Most of the managers also agreed that at any given time in their careers, different parts seemed more important than they did now, and that their emphasis on each management function changed as the office atmosphere changed. Nevertheless, this *set of elements* gave them something concrete to think about when they thought about their jobs.

What does this kind of sum-of-parts definition mean to the research effort? How do you use it? If you were interested in collecting data about management, you would use this definition to set up your data collection. You can collect data about how, when, why, under what conditions, and where *goals are set*. You can collect data about who is involved in this *goal setting*. And, knowing what other people have discovered about the importance of the goal-setting process, you can draw conclusions about the effectiveness of management—in this *one* area. You can do the same kind of data collection and interpretation about each of the other components of the definition. The result is that you can say something concrete about the vague concept of *management*.

The importance of taking this subject analysis step cannot be overstated. You can't do research effectively without taking this step, because you can't study broad concepts. You have to turn concepts into something concrete or else you can't gather information about them; you can collect *opinions* about concepts, but not factual data. The difference between these—opinion and data—is critical. You can ask employees if they think the manager is a good manager; you'll get an opinion in return. You can ask them if they are included in the goal-setting process at the beginning of a project or whether the goals are set before they are introduced to the project; you'll get facts from these questions. You won't get facts unless the questions are specific. The questions can't be specific until you've broken the concept into its parts.

I ran across an example of this problem while I was writing this book. A sociologist published an article about how much people "knew" about modern contraceptives. He had phrased his question to his subjects roughly:

> "Do you know about (*the pill, vasectomies, etc.*)?"

He found, for example, that most people *knew about* the pill. But what does this mean? Did they know its chemical composition? Did they know how to use it? Did they know about its side effects? He could not answer any of these specific questions, because he had not broken the conceptual term *know* into specific elements.

As you're looking at your list of key words from the assignment analysis, you should look at all of them in terms of what their parts are. You should take out a few pieces of paper and jot down sum-of-parts definitions for all the broad terms you've taken out of the assignment. You'll find this difficult, but there are some tricks to doing it quickly and completely.

1. *Take the words one at a time.* It's hard enough to work out a sum-of-parts definition for a single word. Putting two or three together will make it almost impossible. So, even if you usually see words in a phrase associated with one another, break the phrase down. Examples of such phrases include: *criminal negligence, planning and development, program analysis,* and *management by objectives.* For such phrases, deal with each word, with each part of the subject as a separate entity.

2. *Don't think about your particular project while you're doing the sum-of-parts definition.* Thoughts about your project will tend to make your definition very narrow. Try to avoid this and work toward very general definitions. If you're defining a word such as *design,* make your definition include the elements that make up *any design.* If you're analyzing a word such as *job,* jot down the elements of *any job,* not your particular job. In focusing on the word(subject) in a general sense, rather than dealing with particulars of the subject at hand, you develop a kind of *conceptual view of the subject.* This allows you to view the particular subject from a firm base.

   Suppose, for example, that you were preparing to do some research to *design a new procedure for office mail receiving.* One of the words you'd want to look at and define would be the word *design.* If you look at this only in terms of office mail receiving, you're going to get a very narrow view of what design is all about. If you look at the word independently, you might arrive at a general list of the components of any design process. It would look like this:

   Design

   1. Need—problem to be solved
   2. Identification of problem cause
   3. Establish parameters of solution
   4. Determine what resources are available
   5. Collect data about alternative solutions
   6. Evaluate alternatives
   7. Select methods and components

8. Put methods and components together
9. Test against parameters of solution

Whenever you design anything, from an office system to a car, you go through these design steps. And, when you start to do research leading to a design—of anything—this definition will give you an outline of the research process. It tells you that you have to start your design by finding out why it's needed. Next, it tells you to find the cause of the problem (so your design will solve the problem, instead of just glossing over it). Then it reminds you not to look for solutions until you've decided what qualities you want the solution to have. And so on. You use the general definition to guide you through the research into a specific problem.

3. *Don't eliminate components just because they don't seem to fit into your project.* Frequently, people will go through this sum-of-parts definition process as though they were already half through the research process and knew what had to be studied. They think of a component and immediately eliminate it from consideration because they think it won't apply or that it's silly to write something down that is obvious. Yet it is frequently these very obvious points that your reader will be thinking about when you're answering a question. Of course, the first step in any design process is to establish a need. Of course, you have to cover this in your research. Of course, you have to talk about it in the final report—because however elementary it may be, the reader won't understand the design without it. In short, the obvious is something you should expect to have to deal with.

An example of how the obvious can be important, and of why you shouldn't eliminate elements just because you don't think they will apply to your situation, occurred some time ago when I was working with a biologist for a state fish and game department. The biologist had been asked to estimate the impact a new regulation would have on a "fishery," an area heavily used by anglers. The biologist had defined the term *fishery* very carefully from a biological perspective, but had left out an obvious part—a fishery isn't a fishery unless someone fishes there. Anglers had been left out of the study, because the biologist had thought this too elementary to consider. The boss, however, proved very interested in the elementary, very interested in the impact of the regulation on the anglers who used the area. When we included this element in the final research plan, it made the biological study *also* a practical study. In short, you're doing this analysis of the subject to help you set up the research; don't eliminate anything from your definitions until you've looked at it seriously. Sometimes the obvious will also be the most important part of the study.

4. *Keep your thinking simple. Think out your definitions in terms of common, everyday, situations.* People tend to imagine that the thinking that goes into research must be terribly sophisticated. The opposite is often true. The really good thinker often thinks very plainly and can explain the most complicated things in simple terms. When you're looking at a broad concept word (subject), this simple, down-to-earth approach is critical in getting a usable definition.

   Some of the broad concept terms that are frequently a part of government research and reporting projects are *efficiency, decision making,* and *program.* Discussion of these terms and of what they mean can get pretty weighty—if you let it. But if you think about efficiency in terms of something mundane such as gasoline mileage, you realize that it's really a very simple term describing the ratio between input and output. When you think of decision making in terms of the hundreds of decisions you make during a day (decisions to buy a bottle of wine, to watch a television show, to get out of bed), you will find it a much less imposing task to discover the simple steps that are the components of this process. And, rather than thinking of programs in terms of massive government bureaus, you can get a good definition by thinking about them in terms of radio and television programs, which have all the elements of the formal government type of program.

   When you're looking at a word (subject), then, try to think of it in terms of something familiar. Then examine your thoughts to determine the elements of the familiar thing you're thinking about. Later, apply your definition to the more complex subject at hand.

5. *Test your definition on something simple.* After you've worked out a definition you think is good, try it out on something. For example, if you have a definition of what a design involves, see if that definition actually covers an everyday design process—run through it, acting out the steps as you go along. If it works for something simple, it's probably going to work for something complicated.

6. *Have a little faith.* If you want to get water out of a pump, you've got to prime the pump; you've got to put a bit of water into it to get things started. If you want to get anything out of

this sum-of-parts definition process, you've got to do it with a certain amount of energy. You have to start out, work through the process, even though you may not see where it's leading you at all times.

After you've done this sort of thinking for a few reports, you'll begin to see that it *does* get you to the point of being able to do research. You'll begin to see that the things you do research on need to be broken down before they're understandable. And you'll begin to enjoy this process. Until then, put some energy into it.

7. *If you can, work cooperatively.* This process requires thinking, which is always done best by two or more brains.

8. *Keep the definitions you get.* Once you have spent the time to go through this analysis of the subject, keep a file of the results. Odds are you will someday use these definitions again, and then you won't have to redefine. Since the definitions tend to be general lists of the components of any broad concept word (subject), you can use them again and again. For example, the definition of *management* in Figure 6–2 should give you an idea of what you're dealing with whenever you have to think about this complex subject.

AN EXAMPLE

To see how going through this process can turn a normally careless research and reporting effort into a systematic operation, consider one of the simplest, shortest, reports you will ever have to write—the simple cover letter for your resume.

This cover letter, or *job letter*, as it is often called, deserves a lot more careful consideration than it usually gets. To write a good one, you really need to do some research. What do you need to study? To find out, take a look at the key words in the "assignment": *job* and *letter*. From definitions of these words, you can develop a plan for research.

First, what is a job? What elements go into a job? Everyone is familiar with this word, but few people have ever bothered to analyze it. If you begin to think about your own job and then examine your thoughts, you'll probably find that you have come up with all the following elements:

1. Objectives: short-term and long-term
2. Tasks: inputs, outputs, processes, schedules

3. Rewards: money, benefits, personal and social rewards
4. Resources: money, people, facilities, materials, systems
5. A context: a physical environment; a social, religious, political, traditional (customs), and psychological context
6. A history: a series of chronological changes

This is a summarized outline of what you think about when you think about any job.

Once you have this definition, what do you do with it? First, since you would not be writing a cover letter to your resume unless you were looking for a job, you use this definition as a checklist for your research. When you find a position that looks good, on the surface at least, you start to collect information about it. You collect information about each of the categories and items on the definition list. The more information you can get, the more likely it is that you can make an intelligent decision to apply or not to apply for the job. And, every element can be important. For example, you may very much like the work, but the *schedule* for doing it may not be to your liking. You may find the social context to your liking, but you may not like the weather in the area where the job is located. The job may pay well, but you may not wish to do meaningless work—regardless of the pay. In short, all the elements need to be researched if you expect to get information that will allow you to understand the job being offered.

The second use for this definition is as an outline. You can use the headings as outline headings for your research, jotting down material you find (as you find it randomly) under the appropriate heading.

The third use comes when you actually begin to write the job letter. One of the questions your reader will ask is "What can you do for the company (me)?" In answering this, you may wish to refer to any number of elements from this definition; you might want to talk about how you are particularly suited to the job because of your experience dealing with the inputs required, or how your objectives are consistent with those of the company. Whatever, you can help yourself think about this by referring to the checklist. And, now that you have the checklist, you don't ever have to do it again. Whenever you're looking for a job, you've got a general outline for your research.

We have not yet defined the word *letter* and it is, too, a subject for some minor research. Its components are:

1. Paper
2. Type
3. Ink

4. A form
5. An envelope
6. A return address
7. A stamp

It may well seem silly to even mention this definition, but if you think for a moment, this too is something you should probably collect some data on. One of your questions is "How do I impress the reader?" Every item above has some influence on the impression you give the reader. For example, many personnel consultants suggest that the paper you use should be nothing less than 25 percent cotton bond. If you have a letterhead of your own, so much the better. Type? Elite looks more professional than pica or any of the special types except Letter Gothic. Ink? Black, of course, and a carbon ribbon will make an even better impression. Form? As of 1978, modified block was in general favor and will probably remain so. Envelope? You may think this is going too far, but it does make the *first* impression. It should probably be of the same paper as your stationery. Consistency and attention to detail often pay off. The return address and stamp aren't critical factors in making a good impression, as long as the return address on the envelope is the same as on your stationery and there is adequate postage. (Be careful about being scornful of this advice; a three-page resume can mean you need *two* stamps.)

These comments about the job *letter* are based on several long talks I've had with placement agency managers who have actually *done research* on these subjects. With good candidates abounding, the little touches can make a difference.

This example was not intended to get you thinking about leaving your present job; rather, it was designed to show how even the most mundane subject—when dealt with systematically—can yield interesting research material. The process of defining the parts of a word (subject) often seems to be extravagant. You may get the impression that the components you generate just can't be important. But if you think about how you can use them to help you think about how to answer the readers' questions, you will almost always find this a useful process. It will make your thinking complete.

NOTES TO MANAGEMENT AND STAFF

To Management

If you want things researched well, you should do everthing in your power to encourage staff to work out such sum-of-parts

To Staff

One of the things staff gets criticized for most is not thinking completely. It's difficult to think completely without having all the

To Management (*continued*)

definitions of the key words in the assign-ment you make. For self-starters on your staff, this won't be necessary. For those who haven't made a habit of getting going on their own, you may wish to have this sort of analysis done in small groups, where the group dynamics can help carry them through the difficulties of doing this detailed analysis of the subject.

One of the best ways of doing this is to take a few moments with staff to review their analysis. Look over the definitions. Talk about which components in each you think will be particularly important for them to study in this particular situation. Help them refine their thinking about the research on the basis of this kind of analysis. Then they may begin to see that it is a practical way to define what has to be covered to answer your and the other readers' questions.

You can also act as a librarian. You can set up an agency file of such definitions (so that whenever someone has to do an *efficiency* study you can show them quickly what this term means and how it's used in the office). In doing so, you'll slowly build up a kind of policy file, and a good record of the thinking that has gone into other agency reports. With each definition, you might ask the originator to supply a few paragraphs explaining how it was used in the research. After doing this for several years, you'll have some materials that will make your office's research much more efficient.

To Staff (*continued*)

things you need to think about spread out in front of you. If you define the important words in the assignment, all the words that describe your subject, then you build a nearly complete list of the things you should consider as you answer the readers' ques-tions. Then, as you scan this expanded checklist, you're almost sure of being able to see what you have to study.

You may find that this isn't an easy think-ing process. It takes some imagination and creativity to break down the more imposing governmental terms into simple component parts. If you can, then, get a group together to do it. It's much more fun done with a work group, and this usually helps you loosen up for thinking.

To give yourself an idea of the kinds of definitions you're shooting for, look over those given at the end of this chapter. I've tried to pick terms that are frequently used in government work. The definitions in this section have proved useful in a number of situations.

CHAPTER SUMMARY

The key words you isolate from the assignment provide you with a general checklist of things to cover while you're trying to answer the readers' questions. To get a precise, specific checklist you should take each of these key words and analyze it—break it into its parts. These sum-of-parts definitions give you a good idea of what specific subjects you may have to do research on. Once you have these defi-nitions spread out before you, you can see all the bits and pieces of your research, and you can then begin to put the readers' questions and these pieces into a coherent outline of the final report. From this outline, you can then work efficiently to conduct research and get the information the readers need from your report.

APPENDIX

SAMPLE SUM-OF-PARTS DEFINITIONS

Here are several useful sum-of-parts definitions you may find useful as checklists for many government research projects. All those you find here have been developed and used by people working in government agencies, people I've worked with on research and reporting projects.

Note that some definitions are organized as flowcharts—this is because the word being defined describes a process and the parts of the process are *steps*. There are other forms that have been applied to the elements of these definitions; there's a logical reason for each. The reasons are explained in Chapter 7, on assembling the final outline.

With each definition, there's a brief note about how to use it, because there are many uses for each.

Note, as you look at these definitions, that they can probably be used for all equivalent terms, too. For example, the definition for *procedure* also covers *process*. The definition for *effect* will do for *impact* or *consequence*. The definition for *audit* will do for *examination*, *evaluation*, *study*, and *investigation*, although this last contains a few more components in legal cases.

1. Procedure: A procedure always has all the following parts:

A goal → A starting point → An ending point

—Steps to get from one point to the next
—People responsible for doing the steps
—Resources for getting the steps done
—A schedule for getting the steps done

Using this Definition: These are pretty obvious components. But how many procedure manuals cover all of them in describing the procedure? Not many. If you are asked to write a procedure for the office, you should use this list of components as a guide; you'll find that if you cover all these elements—in your research and in your report or manual—your readers will be satisfied with your description. If you're trying to find out what a procedure is, if you're doing research, you might try asking questions about each of these components.

2. Efficiency: Efficiency is a comparative term. Its components
   are:

Using this Definition: When you're talking about efficiency,
you're *summing up the relationship* between input and output. Low input (cheapness) is not efficiency. You must establish the ratio of input to output in order to talk about efficiency. The lowest overall *ratio* describes the most efficient
situation. So, when you speak of efficiency, always express it
in this way; discuss both input and output.

3. Effect: To discuss effects (or impacts), you have to cover:
   —Initial situation
   —Input (either an input of energy, ideas, money, num-
      bers, mass, or a change in organization)
   —Change in situation
   —Result

Using this Definition: In discussing effects, most people tend
to leave out any discussion of the initial situation and the
result. These two elements are essential to the readers'
understanding of effect. Without a knowledge of the first, the
reader can't make the comparison and can't see the change
easily. Without a discussion of the end result of all the
changes in the situation, the reader can't understand what
the changes *mean*. Thus, it's important to collect data about
all components whenever you're looking at an assignment
asking you to measure effect. You can't measure it without
firmly establishing what the initial situation was and what
the end result is.

4. Audit: An audit is a comparative *process* with the following
   steps:

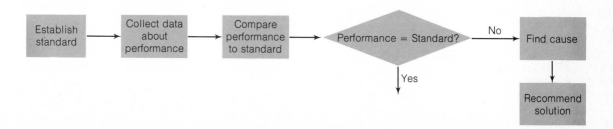

Using this Definition: An audit supervisor and I worked up
this little flowchart to stress the importance of conducting an

audit in an orderly manner—starting with a complete under-standing of the regulations (the standard). We then included a step in the office procedure to ensure that auditors re-viewed the standards before they went into the field. This little definition also provided us with general subject head-ings for an office policy and procedure manual, a set of guidelines for conducting an audit. For each of these head-ings, we then use subheadings, which we got from the defini-tions of policy and procedure.

5. Program:

—A purpose or purposes (a need and a desire to meet the need)
—Policies (rules, limits, definitions of the way the pro-gram meets the need, achieves the purpose)
—Resources (money, people, facilities, organization)
—Procedures for achieving the purposes:

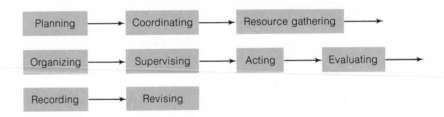

Using this Definition: When you're studying a program, you're usually evaluating it, trying to find out if it's working. In doing this, you should begin broadly by considering its purposes and whether or not the need for the program still exists. Then you should look at the basic policies of the pro-gram and evaluate them. Then you can look at whether the program has the resources necessary. And then you can look at the actual operations of the program, at how each of the basic procedures (see the definition of procedure on page 96 for subheadings) fits into the effort to achieve the purposes of the program. In short, this definition provides you with the logical *method* for evaluating a program.

It also is a good outline, a good set of headings, for the *results* portion of your report. When you're answering the question "What is the cause of the problem?" you'll want to talk about which of these elements is and which isn't the cause—and this will require you to gather data about all the elements.

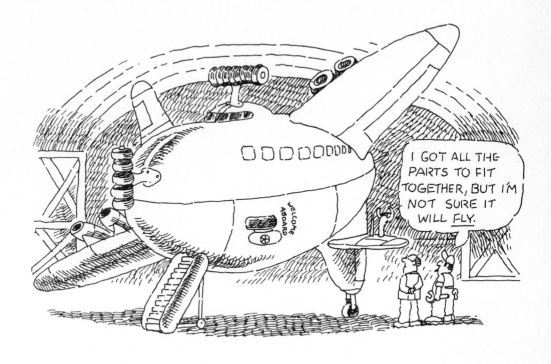

ASSEMBLING AN OUTLINE OF THE REPORT

7

At this point, you're about three hours into a good brainstorming session; for really major reports you may have taken as much as 5 or 6 hours. You have the assignment figured out. You have a list of questions the reader wants you to answer. You may even have had the opportunity to confirm the assignment and to have the boss check your list of questions over. You have the major key words from the assignment defined in terms of component parts; you've analyzed the subject and know what each key word means, what each key word is made up of. And you have all this spread out in front of you *on paper* on a work table. *The brainstorming is about over.*

To get a complete outline of the final paper—the purpose of this whole brainstorming process—you have only two more steps. You need to pull all the bits and pieces together to make them coherent. To do this, you have to decide what the true *focus* of your research is going to be, and you have to decide how to *organize* the elements.

THE PROBLEMS

Both of these steps are problems. Both are difficult because they're *conceptual*. How do you *focus* ideas? How do you *organize* ideas? Much has been said about both of these processes, but they are, for the most part, treated as *arts*. They're a bit mysterious. It is, indeed, difficult to define clearly what it is you *mean* by these terms. Everyone uses them, and everyone tells you to do these things in every report you write. But they're vague.

The problem, then, is to find some way of making these vague processes—focusing and organizing—less vague. In doing so, it will be necessary to discuss them in terms that will permit you to produce an outline that is appropriate. The questions then become "How do you arrive at the *right* focus for the whole paper?" and "How do you make sure that every time you organize, you're doing it *right*?" These are not questions to be answered lightly. But they need to be answered.

THE SOLUTION TO THE FOCUS PROBLEM

Some of the techniques of the sum-of-parts definition process can be used to lead to a better understanding of what people mean when they say "focus the paper," or "the paper lacks focus." If you think of focusing in terms of the ordinary meaning, in photographic work, the term becomes clearer. In photography, you achieve focus when the things you've selected as the key elements in your photograph are clear. If you're doing a portrait, the person must be clearly visible; the foreground may be hazy and the background may be blurred, but the person should be distinctly visible. This is exactly what *focus* means in writing and in research. *The key element of your work must stand out from all the background and foreground details.*

Think for a moment about the key words in your assignment. You brought these into better focus as you underlined them or wrote them down separately on a scratch pad (or the assignment form at the end of Chapter 4). You brought them into focus by pulling them out of the background material of the assignment.

Now, you have a group of key words. To focus your thoughts about the assignment, you have to select one of these key words as your focal point and establish a subordinate relationship between this word and the rest of the key words. In doing this, you'll do exactly what the photographer does—you'll draw your own eye, and later the reader's, to exactly the point you want. This is theory. The practice is really quite simple.

To focus your thoughts about your research and your paper, we'll go back to the basic brainstorming principle and design another portion of the paper. This time, we'll work on the title. The title is important because it must fit the paper. Usually, people write their titles after they've done the work; they struggle to find a title that exactly covers what they've said in the paper. As they find one, they often also find that it helps them understand what they've just done. This is because in writing a title, they're pulling key elements of the paper out of the background of hundreds of words and thus focusing their thoughts. If you write the title *first*, you begin the whole research process with a clear focus. You then fit the paper to the title.

A title is built from the key word list in a few simple steps. Notice, as you work through these steps, how the disjointed list of key words becomes a coherent idea, and the most important elements of the idea become clearer. For this process we'll start with the simple list of key words given in Step 1 below.

Step 1: Jot down key words from assignment

Management	Personnel
Critique	Analysis
Audit	Efficiency
Office	Data processing
Effectiveness	

Step 2: Give each a high or low priority in terms of how important the term would be to explaining the subject to someone.

High	Low
Management	Office
Data processing	Analysis
Effectiveness	Critique
Efficiency	Personnel
Department of _____	Audit

Step 3: Put the high-priority words in the order in which they might appear in a title:

Management, Data processing, Department of _____, Effectiveness, Efficiency

Step 4: By adding connective words and phrases, and by changing the form of the key words if necessary, try out some titles.

1. Management of Data Processing in Department of
   _____: Effectiveness and Efficiency
2. Management for Data Processing in Department of
   _____: Effectiveness and Efficiency
3. Management for Data Processing Effectiveness and
   Efficiency in Department of _____.
4. Management in Department of _____: Data Processing Effectiveness and Efficiency
5. Effect of Management on Data Processing Effectiveness and Efficiency in Department of _____.
6. Managing Department of _____'s Data Processing
   for Effectiveness and Efficiency.
7. Department of _____'s Data Processing Management: Effectiveness and Efficiency

Step 5: Select a title that *exactly* expresses the paper you have
in your mind.

Managing Department of _____'s Data Processing for
Effectiveness and Efficiency

In working through this simple process, and in finally selecting
this title, I have exactly focused thoughts about this subject which
was, at first, nothing more than a jumble of key words. Each of the
titles was different in significant ways from the final choice. Some
suggested a broader scope than I was willing to deal with (Management in Department of _____: Data Processing Effectiveness and
Efficiency). The final selection is far narrower.

If I had not had a really clear idea of what I wanted from this
report, I might have taken the title list to the boss—and had the boss
select the title that most closely expressed his or her interests and
focus. Whoever selects the title, the important thing is that once you
have a title you can see what the focal point of the research is going
to be and what the connection between this focal point and all the
subelements of the paper is. In this case, the focal point is the first
word—managing. That's what this paper is going to be about—the
process of managing. It will be a "How To" paper, setting forth the
methods the Department of _____ can use to make data processing
effective and efficient. With this title, I can even begin to see how the
actual paper might sound:

"To achieve effective and efficient data processing, the first
thing to consider is . . ."

In short, from the title, I can tell what it is I'm trying to *do* in the paper.

Using the Title

Selecting a title can make you conscious of your own thoughts and can help make your thoughts concrete. You have to pay some attention to the title if you expect to be able to use it to help you focus your thoughts. It's important, for instance, to look at the *form* of the words and think about what this form *means*. You will probably select a title without doing this consciously; you'll select a title with *managing* rather than *management*, for example. In doing so, you're giving yourself a concrete indication of how you're thinking. In this case, your selection is an indication that you're thinking about your subject *as a process*, rather than as a *thing*. What this means is that you're focusing your thoughts on the steps taken in the process of managing rather than focusing on the results of these steps. It also indicates a practical approach rather than a theoretical approach. In short, you make your title selection, and then you look at the title to see what it was about this particular title you liked so much.

Think about Differences between Titles. To help yourself see what your selection of title indicates about your thinking, look very carefully at the differences between titles. For example, analyze the differences between these two titles from the previous example:

Management in Department of _____: Data Processing Effectiveness and Efficiency

Managing Department of _____'s Data Processing for Effectiveness and Efficiency

These titles both contain the same words and they cover the same subjects. But their focus is different. The first suggests a look at all management functions in the department, with data processing being only a subheading. The second places far greater emphasis on the data processing. The first would produce a rather large, theoretical report; the second a report focused tightly on a single function. Neither is necessarily *right*. You could prepare a report from either. But they are significantly different, and your choice of one focus over the other will be based on your perception of these differences and your understanding of the assignment. You put all this understanding in a nutshell when you express it in terms of a title.

Look at the Forms of the Words in the Title. You can take the same subject matter and deal with it in a number of different ways. These are often indicated by the form of the word you use to describe the subject in the title. For example, you can look at a word such as *effectiveness* from a number of different perspectives:

Word form	Perspective
Effectiveness	You're looking at performance, at action leading to achieving a goal.
Effect	You're looking at the way in which one thing changes another.
Effectively	You're looking at the agent of the change and the actions that can be taken to achieve the goal.
Effecting	You're looking at the actions that generate the change.
Effective	You're evaluating the way in which the agent of change is acting.

The word form indicates the way in which you're thinking about the subject. When you select the title, you probably make this sort of distinction unconsciously; looking at the form you select tells you what you were thinking about.

Look for the Nouns in the Title. The nouns in the title give you a clue to your overall organization, to the way in which you'll set up your analysis and discussion. The main noun in the title

Managing Department of _____'s Data Processing for Effectiveness and Efficiency

is *Data processing.* It's the *focus* of this study. So, you might find it useful to set up the paper so that every section of your analysis has this focus. To do this, you first have to deal with data processing; you have to have a sum-of-parts definition. Here's a good general one:

Data processing

1. Goal
2. Data needs (what you need to achieve the goal)
3. Sources for data
4. Collection procedure
5. Processor (usually a computer, but could be a person)
6. Program (a way of organizing the data into useful form)
7. Conversion process (for getting the data into a form usable by the processor—*coding* in computer terms)
8. Input process (for getting data into the processor)
9. Time and energy to run the data through the program

10. Output
11. Use of the output to achieve the goal

Anyone familiar with data processing knows that you can't do it unless you have all these components. Leave any one of them out and you don't get data processed.

What do you do with this definition, knowing that it represents the components of the focal point in your title? You use its components as the subheadings for the paper. Under each subheading, you discuss what a manager can do to contribute to the efficiency and effectiveness of this portion of the data processing: What can the manager do about goal setting that will make data processing effective and efficient? What can the manager do about establishing which data are needed to make data processing effective and efficient? What can the manager do to find data sources to make data processing effective and efficient? And so on through the whole set of eleven components.

How does this outline of subheadings relate to the *overall* outline of reader questions? In the midst of every list of reader questions is a series of questions about the subject. There are introductory questions, there are questions about methods, there are questions about conclusions—and there are questions about the subject. The sum-of-parts definition of the main noun in the title gives you the subheadings for the detailed answer to the questions about the subject. Schematically, an outline for the paper thus looks like this:

1. Questions about the purpose, scope, and background to the study
2. Questions about the way in which the study was done
3. Questions about the subject—results of research
   a.
   b.
   c.   Sub-headings from sum-of-parts
   d.   definition of main key word in
   e.   the title.
   f.
4. Questions about the meaning of the results
5. Questions about what to do about this

And so forth. If you go back to some of the checklists of the readers' questions in Chapter 5, you'll see that most of them break very neatly into such groupings.

The component parts of the other key words give you the subheadings for *other parts of the outline.*

SUMMARY

By establishing a clear focus for you, the title helps you assemble the final outline of the report. It helps you decide what your research is really about, what it is you're really studying. By analyzing the title you select, you also establish subheadings for the main portion of your report—your results.

THE SOLUTION TO THE ORGANIZING PROBLEM

If you have tried any of these processes, you will have noticed that the questions you generate in analyzing the reader and the components of your sum-of-parts definitions don't come out of your head in an organized fashion. Your brain works by free association most of the time, and so you're stuck with question lists that aren't coherent and sum-of-parts lists that don't show you how all the parts fit together. And, as you try to put these two parts of the report together, you will find that they *have to be organized* before you can proceed.

IF YOU'VE DONE ALL THE STEPS TO THIS POINT, YOU HAVE ALL THE PIECES OF YOUR PROJECT SPREAD OUT BEFORE YOU. ORGANIZE EACH, AND YOU CAN THEN ASSEMBLE THEM INTO AN OUTLINE, USING THE TITLE AS YOUR GUIDE TO THE FOCUS OF THE WHOLE REPORT.

What it Means to Organize

Organizing is a process everyone does everyday, a process with two basic components: pieces of data (things) and a system for placing the pieces in some relationship to one another. So far, we've dealt with the pieces. We've talked about breaking audience interests into individual questions and about breaking the key words in the assignment into individual components. We now have to put them together so that the interrelationships among them are clear.

Repairing an automobile engine gives us a good, common example of organizing. The first step in repair is to take everything apart—so that you can look at it, measure things, and see what's worn out. Then, you replace the worn out items; you buy parts. Then you have to put the whole engine back together again—that's organizing (reorganizing in this case). There is no absolute *right* way of doing this. You could, for instance, throw all the parts in the back seat and have the car towed—that's one way of organizing. You could weld all the parts together and make a statue with the largest and heaviest piece on the bottom. You could put all the plastic parts together and all the iron parts together and all the brass parts together. Each of these is a kind of organization. Why don't you do this? Because none of them suits your *purpose*. You want the car to run. So you'll have to fit the parts together in a way that allows them to work in synchrony.

This is a simple example, but it illustrates a basic principle: *YOUR PURPOSE DETERMINES THE ORGANIZATION YOU CHOOSE TO IMPOSE ON THE DATA (THINGS) YOU'RE WORKING WITH.* If you were a modern artist working on a sculpture, you might very well want to take automobile parts and organize them by welding them all together. If your purpose was to just give up, dumping the parts in the back seat would be OK. You impose a functional purpose on the parts because that's what you want as a result—function.

If you think about this for a moment, you'll realize that many people wait until the data come in from research before they decide how to organize it. They say things such as "I have to see what I find out before I can put it together." This is an excuse for laziness or an indication that they haven't thought very much about what they're doing. Looking at the data doesn't reveal anything at all about organization. The organization is imposed on the data—according to the purpose.

A practical example of this occurs in all tax collection agencies. The data these agencies have concern taxes—laws and regulations and interpretations and procedures. These data can be, and are, organized two distinctly different ways in two distinctly different publications. In the guide to the tax code that is used by auditors, these data are organized in an encyclopedic manner—by the subject the law covers. Corporation law is covered in one section of this guide. Personal income tax law is covered in another. And so forth. It's done this way because the purpose of the guide is to make it easy for an auditor to look up the laws. Much of these data are also used in the *Instructions to the Taxpayer* which most agencies send out when it's time to pay taxes (file a return). The same data, though, are organized differently. In these instruction booklets (the good ones at least), it's organized *chronologically,* to correspond to the order in which the tax form is filled out.

Which organization is *right? Both.* The encyclopedic organization is right for the purpose of easy reference—but would not work at all for the purpose of telling you how to fill out the form. The chronological order is right for the purpose of filling out the form, but wouldn't work for those needing quick reference to the law. *Purpose generates the organization. The purpose is then imposed on the data. You can decide on organization as soon as you know your purpose; you don't have to wait until you have the data.* Computer programmers know this better than anyone. They always design the program before they start putting data into the computer. Coaches of baseball, football, basketball, soccer, etc., teams do the same, the structure of the team is set up in advance. People are then gathered to fill positions in the structure.

When you're looking at your reader questions and at your definition of key words, then, you need to follow a simple proceedure:

1. Think about your purpose.
2. Determine what organization is appropriate to your purpose.
3. Impose this order on the random elements you're looking at.

If you're thinking, "But there are thousands of purposes and thousands of ways to organize," you're technically right, but there are only a few basic purposes and thus only a few basic structures and organization patterns. If you learn the basic structures to impose on data, you can easily take care of the minor adjustments needed to make them appropriate to very specific structures. The basic purposes may be expressed as very general questions. Each kind of question indicates a different structure for the components of the answer.

Basic questions	Type of structure
How?	Chronological
What?	Definition
How _____ is it?	Comparison
How come?	Argument
What's wrong?	Problem (complex comparison)
Why?	Cause/effect
What is it made of?	Analysis (standard outline)
How does it work?	
or	
How does it fit together?	Systems analysis
What's the fastest	Critical path chart
way to _____?	

If you think about it, these questions cover almost all the kinds of questions you can ask. They can be made more complicated and more detailed, but a "How" question is still a "How" question, and the answer should still be answered chronologically. And "How good is it?" is not really a different question from "How might it be most efficaciously done?" Both require comparison.

Each of the types of structures named above is described and illustrated in the checklist at the end of this chapter. Use this checklist to remind yourself of how to set up each kind of structure.

Applying This Principle

The knowledge that for every purpose there is a corresponding unique structure has to be looked at in practical terms before it makes real sense. Here, then, are some ways in which the principle is applied during the brainstorming and research and writing processes:

1. *Organizing questions for the report:* Suppose you are working on a report that has as its goal the solution of a problem. You have a list of questions you might be asked by your readers:

   > What do we do about it?
   > Why did it happen in the first place?
   > How do we know that's the best solution?
   > What's the problem?
   > What do we want to achieve?
   > What are the alternatives?

   and about twenty more. You can't just put them into any order, even if you did think them up in this manner. But what's the best order? What's your purpose? Your purpose in the whole project is to answer the simple question "How do we solve the problem?" The answer to a "How" question is organized chronologically. So, the questions should be set forth in the order in which they must be answered to do the actual solving. They're in the chronological order of the research—beginning with questions about the background and finishing with questions about implementation of the solution. If you look back at Chapter 5, at the list of reader questions for studies of a problem (page 74), you'll see that that's exactly how these questions are ordered.

2. *Organizing the components of a key word:* In every key word definition given so far, the elements have always been organized. In practice, that's not how they come out of your brain. So you have to take them and put a structure around them.

   Suppose you were working on a report involving the subject *effectiveness*. You might come up with the following components:

   > *Effectiveness*
   >
   > Performance
   > Standard
   > Measurement
   > Difference

How would you organize these elements of your research and how would you organize your results about effectiveness? The answer to both questions is the same. Effectiveness implies comparison. You would set up your work to make this comparison between *standard* and *performance* clear. Thus, a chart something like Figure 7–1 might be helpful. Note that in this tabular form elements of the standard are set up to correspond exactly to elements of measured performance. Anything else would obscure the meaning.

3. *Organizing the answer to a reader's question:* As you are writing, you make dozens of organizing decisions. For each, all you need to know is what kind of question you're answering. You need to translate specific questions into the simple ones listed previously.

Suppose, for example, that you were answering the question, "Which of the alternatives should we choose?" The standard answer is "We should choose _____, because _____." This often leads to arguments because the readers may or may not agree with your initial recommendation, and may or may not wait until you've explained your reasons. The standard approach can lead to this problem because it doesn't take into account that the kind of question being answered isn't "Why?", which would allow you a cause/effect answer, but "How much better is _____, than _____?", which leads to a comparison structure. Such a comparison structure allows you to put your data first, and then draw the conclusion from it. Thus, you might get something like Figure 7-2. The comparison of alternatives against the standard and against each other makes forcefully drawing the conclusion and fighting through an explanation of how you got there quite unnecessary. The comparison structure placed around the data reveals the reasons for the deci-

FIGURE 7-1/PERFORMANCE EVALUATION TABLE

Performance standard	Measured performance	Difference
10 per hour	14 per hour	+4
17 a day	5 per day	-12
65 wpm	45 wpm	-20 wpm

**FIGURE 7-2/COMPARISON OF ALTERNATIVES AS THE MEANS OF
EXPLAINING WHY ONE IS BETTER**

Standard	Alternative 1	Alternative 2	Alternative 3
200 units per hour	265 units per hour	180 units per hour	245 units per hour
$10 per unit	$26 per unit	$9 per unit	$9 per unit

sion quite nicely without a lot of prose. There is an advantage
to using organization to make your point rather than trying to
make it directly. If you organize clearly, the data will make
your point for you. The reader will look at it and just draw
the conclusion from it. You won't have to push the point at
all.

   To apply this principle of one-purpose/one-structure, you must
analyze what you're doing very carefully. Then, once you know
what your purpose is, scan the checklist at the end of this chapter
and use the appropriate structure to organize your data or discussion.

FOCUSING AND ORGANIZING: A BRIEF EXAMPLE

By both focusing and organizing the materials you've developed
during brainstorming, you produce a complete outline of the final
paper—and you establish a strategy for the presentation. A simple
cover letter for your resume, the "job letter," which we've already
looked at in part in Chapter 6, will provide a good example of this
process and its results.

   Here's a complete analysis and organizing process in outline
form—from the initial assignment to the final written product.

Step 1: Analyze the assignment

The purpose of a job letter is to get you an interview. It can also be
used to give its readers something concrete to discuss with you
when you are being interviewed. Politically, it must be a tactful
letter and cannot cover anything personal. Since it's your letter, you

have the right to cover anything you want in the research process, but you would do well to stick to professional matters. The report is a part of your overall *policy* in that it reflects your interests and represents an effort to improve your overall situation. It has high priority. You have few resources available to help you do this research and you probably won't have much time to spend on study. The basic stumbling blocks you have to face are (1) not being able to get satisfactory information about the job and (2) having to get your letter past secretaries and personnel officers so that the person doing the actual hiring will see it.

Key words in assignment			*Readers*
Job	Letter	You	Person hiring
			Office secretaries
			Personnel people
			Review committee

Step 2: Analyze the readers' interests

The person hiring has the following basic questions:
1. Who are you? Do I know you? Should I know you?
2. What do you want?
3. What can you do for me?
4. If you're so good, why do you want this job?
5. OK, I've read the letter, what do you want me to do now? What's the next step we should take?

The personnel people have the following questions:
1. Should we send this one on to the person doing the hiring?
2. Are we safe if we do so?

Office Secretaries have these questions:
1. Would the boss want me to bother him/her with this?
2. Is this someone I want to work with?

The review committee has the same questions as the boss, plus:
1. Would we want to work with or for this person?

Given these questions, there are two general strategies to think about. First, if the answer to the boss's first question is "Yes," then the personnel people have the answer to their questions, and so does the secretary. If you are already known to the boss, you can be reasonably sure that the personnel office *will* send your application to him/her. Second, to answer questions about whether those in the office would like to work with or for you, you have to answer the boss's third question, "What can you do for me?" in a professional but restrained and modest way. You have to sound good without sounding pretentious.

Since the person doing the hiring is the primary audience, you should focus on answering this person's questions—and set up your answers to them so that the other readers' questions are answered at the same time. The boss's (person who is hiring) questions are organized in the chronological order in which they would be asked if you, instead of your letter, were to suddenly walk into the boss's private office. Your purpose in writing a letter is to *introduce* yourself (your resume). Introducing is a process that takes place chronologically.

Step 3: Analyze the subject

The three key words in the assignment have the following components (see Chapter 6, pages 92-94):

Job

1. Objectives: short-term and long-term
2. Tasks: inputs, outputs, processes, schedules
3. Rewards: money, benefits, personal and social rewards
4. Resources: money, people, facilities, materials, systems
5. A context: a physical environment; a social, religious, political, traditional (customs), and psychological context
6. A history: a series of chronological changes

Letter
1. Paper
2. Type
3. Ink
4. A form
5. An envelope
6. A return address
7. A stamp

You = A person (and all people have):

1. Objectives: short-term and long-term
2. Abilities: to handle input, output, processes, schedules
3. Needs: for money, benefits, personal and social rewards
4. Needs: for resources to work with (all the above)
5. Needs or desires: for the appropriate context for living and working
6. Needs: for stability or change, for growth or maintenance of status

The elements of the word *job* are organized in order of importance to many of those who fall into the category "person doing the hiring." Elements of *letter* are organized in the order in which they are dealt with during the writing process. Elements of *you* are set up to match the order of elements of *job*—totally arbitrarily.

Step 4: Focus by writing title

The title for this letter is very simple, but important to consider. It is:

JOB LETTER

It does not contain the word *I* or the word *me* or any other reference to the person writing the letter. Thus, the focus of the letter is on the word (subject) *job*. It is a letter about a job.

If you think, for a moment, about what the ordinary job letter sounds like, you'll see how important this focus on the job really is. Most such letters sound terribly egotistical. The writer says "I did this" and "I am that" and "I think this" and so forth. The letter becomes an "I" letter, in which the writer spends half the allotted space bragging and explaining why the job interests the writer. The title, though, indicates that the focus ought to be on the job; it suggests a strategy for the letter: Show the readers that you're right for the job by showing them that you know something about the job. The difference in these two approaches is obvious from the following illustrations:

Talk about yourself	I think that this is an interesting job for someone with my qualifications, and I am looking forward to the challenge it offers.
Talk about the job:	This job is particularly challenging to a biochemist because it involves practical applications of sensitive techniques that have only recently been standardized.

You will have to talk about yourself at some point in this letter, but the majority of what you say should be focused, by the title, on the job.

Step 5: Organize

The reader questions have already been organized, something you can do as soon as you work them out. The elements of the definitions have been organized too. The overall organization of the answer to the questions has not yet been worked out, though the title has suggested a focus for the answers.

The question that remains to be answered is: What structure should be imposed on the information you're going to present in each paragraph of the letter? The answer is: a comparison structure. The purpose of a job letter is to establish your fitness for a job; you're trying to compare your qualifications with the requirements of the job. Thus, your research questions will involve your seeing how you and the job are and are not consistent. You might set up your analysis thus:

Job element	Personal element
Short-term objectives	Are your short-term objectives consistent with your employer's?
Long-term objectives	Are your long-term objectives consistent with your employer's?
Tasks	Do you have the abilities to do the required tasks? Handle the schedule?
Rewards	Are the rewards adequate to meet your needs?

By doing this sort of analysis, and continuing it until all the elements have been thoroughly studied, you will find out whether you really want the job.

You could and should organize the answers to readers' questions 3 and 4 in the same way:

3. What can you do for me?	Discuss the specific elements of the job, explain what you know about them and what you have done that will indicate your ability to do the job. Compare yourself to the job, but mention the job first in each portion of your answer.
4. If you're so good, why do you want this job?	Discuss the elements of the job and then why the job interests you.

The specific elements of the job that you choose to discuss in answering these questions depend on the nature of the job and your qualifications. All things considered, though, a letter looks something like this:

Letter   *Comment*

Mr. James Jones, President
Electronic Wine Company
1212 Napa Road
Sunnyvale, California 95000

Dear Mr. Jones:

Thank you for taking the time to explain your company's operations last Friday (August 22). The automated ion transfer process we discussed was particularly interesting, and I would like to formally apply for the position of *ion transfer chemist* that we spoke of.

> Write to the person doing the hiring. Send copies to the personnel department.
>
> Here you introduce yourself as the person who called to talk about the job—and you let personnel know that the boss is expecting the letter. Many placement people suggest such a call to break the ice, and also to help you get information about the job.

This position is particularly interesting because ion transfer in wine requires great accuracy and has been attempted so far only on a very small scale. At _____ winery, we developed a small-scale ion transfer process for rectifying acid balance in premium wines. Our process was similar to the one you're contemplating using, but we did not attempt it on a large scale because of capital limitations.

> Here, one element of the job is developed. First the job element is described . . . then your experience is discussed. Note how low key this makes the letter.

Large-scale applications of such delicate processes are a special challenge to a chemist, one I have been working on since 1972 with John Jones at University of _____. Your company's size makes extension of this work possible, and I am looking forward to applying what we've found out recently to a production line process.

> Note that in explaining why you want the job, you focus once more on the job elements and then talk about yourself.

Your secretary indicated that you will soon begin interviewing. May I call him for an appointment?
Sincerely,

> You need not demand an interview, the request is enough. You will call.

Though this is a very short example letter, notice how it does answer the readers' questions—by implication it even may convince your prospective colleagues that you'll be OK to work with. It includes two central paragraphs in which the subject is discussed, the subject having been derived from the key word list. It has a clear focus on the job, which was indicated as important in the title. The comparison structure, job element/your experience, is carried out through the two center paragraphs, with the emphasis on the job. The overall effect of a letter like this is to make the person reading it reasonably sure that you know what you're about and that you are worth talking to.

NOTES TO MANAGEMENT AND STAFF

To Management

If you want to control the focus of the research and the report, try writing the title—very carefully—for staff. Give it to them and explain why this title is what you expect them to work toward. Don't give any leeway, or else the title will change as the staff impose their focus on the project. This sort of control isn't always necessary; it's just one way you can give staff a clear picture of what you want.

To Staff

In looking at *purpose* in order to determine what kind of structure to give to data, you should consider both your purpose in writing the report and the readers' purposes in reading. Taking the readers' point of view will often lead you to organize differently. The job letter is a good example. The comparison structure serves the reader; it helps the reader compare you to the job. It isn't going to suit *your* purpose unless you are really qualified for the job. This is why it's necessary for you to get information about the job so that you can decide whether or not you match up to it. In any report, decide very carefully whether to organize to suit the readers' purpose or to suit your own.

CHAPTER SUMMARY

By defining the focus of the paper through building a title from the key words in the assignment and by organizing the readers' questions and the elements of the key words, you establish the basis for a final outline. The title gives you a concrete indicator of what element of the assignment is most important to you, and thus leads you to use the components of that element's sum-of-parts definition as the major subheadings for the results portion of your paper. By assembling the organized readers' question list and the organized components from your sum-of-parts definitions, you develop a complete outline of the report. Later, by setting up the organization of your answer to your questions according to your purpose, you further organize. Diagrammed, the process is as shown in Figure 7-3.

FIGURE 7-3/ASSEMBLY PROCESS

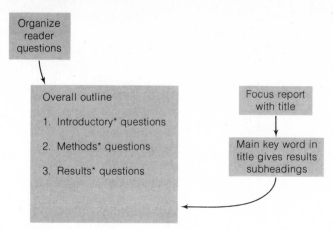

*These are not necessarily the kinds of headings you'll have in any given report.

A CHECKLIST OF ORGANIZING STRUCTURES: COMMON STRUCTURES

When you have to deal with any question concerning organization, use this checklist to help you think about how you should give structure to the data you're working with. Scan the purposes listed on the left-hand side of the page. When you find one that sounds right, look to see what the corresponding structure is, and how it may be used to structure data.

Since there are many *specific* ways of organizing, you'll always have to do some thinking about how to make minor adjustments to each of these basic approaches.

Purpose	**Basic structure**
1. To answer the question, "How?" To explain a process. To tell the story of something; to explain its history. If you're writing a manual, a set of instructions.	All elements or pieces of data go in chronological order. The graphic for this is the Flowchart.
2. To answer the question, "What?" To define something. To describe its parts.	$X = a + b + c + d + e$, where X is being defined, and $a, b, c, \ldots$ are the components of X. The components should normally be in some order of priority. If the thing being defined is a *process*, the components should be listed in chronological order.

3. To answer the question, "How _____, is it?" To evaluate. To show that differences exist. To deal with any value system.

Make a comparison. Set the elements of one kind of data opposite corresponding elements of the other kind of data.

4. To answer the question, "How come!?" To argue. To explain how you arrived at a conclusion. To present a legal case. To explain regulations.

Argument is a complex logic form that lawyers have refined over a long period of time. Data are set forth in four basic categories: issue, regulation, application, conclusion (the IRAC pattern). The issue statement involves defining the situation and listing the key elements of it. The regulation section also involves defining, this time a list of the key elements of the law, in the order in which they correspond to the issue elements. The application section involves putting these two portions together, explaining how each issue/situation element is dealt with in the law. The conclusion is a simple series of cause/effect statements: "Because _____ did _____, and the law says _____ about it, _____ is guilty." Obviously, the key to this pattern lies in the first step—issue definition.

5. To answer the question, "What's wrong?" To explain problems. To discuss poor performance.

The explanation of problems requires three steps. Should be ⟶ Is ⟶ Deficiency First, you have to present data about some standard of peformance. Events in and of themselves are not problems; the event must violate some standard and be perceived as doing so before it is called a problem. Then you present the data about the situation, listing it in the same order as you listed the elements of the standard. The deficiencies = the problems. The analysis and the presentation of problems should both be handled in this manner in order to avoid randomness. Presenting problems is thus a very complex form of comparison, in some ways like the IRAC pattern for argument. This basic comparison form recurs so frequently in our thinking that it may account for most of the research done in government or business.

6. To answer the question, "Why?" To explain what has happened or will happen. To discuss issues of *consequence*. To provide the basis for recommendations.

Explaining "Why" is often thought of as a simple thing to do. It isn't; it requires presentation of data concerning causes and this is one of the most difficult research and analysis tasks. The elements of an explanation of "Why" are:

    a. A list of all possible causes
    b. Data about how causes were elim-
        inated from consideration
    c. A statement about the cause that is
        finally determined to be *the* cause
        (or causes), including evidence to
        link this cause (causes) directly to the
        effect being studied

Without these elements, the cause statement
will not be valid and will lead the reader
to say things like: "Yeah, but what about
_____?"

7. To answer the question, "What is it made
   of?" To analyze. To describe a complex
   object.

I.

  A.

  B.

    1.

    2.

      a.

      b.   etc.

The standard outline form used by all high
school students is the form for analytical
statements. The analysis process involves
continual breakdown of things into some
form of component parts, and this form
permits the separation of main parts from
subparts, from subparts, etc.

8. To answer the question, "How does it
   work?" or "How does it fit together?"
   To describe systems. To describe anything that operates, has inputs, outputs,
   and processes.

Basic form: *INPUT* ⟶ *OUTPUT*

The arrow represents the connection, the process, between the input and
the output. In describing the elements of
the connecting process, you need to cover:

    a. Time required for the process
    b. Space required for the process
    c. Direction of the effort
    d. Method for getting the process done
    e. Energy required to get the process
        done
    f. Materials required to get the process
       done (people too)

There are a few systems where there is only
one input or output, much less only one
simple process. You're far more likely to
have to deal with structures that look like
this:

    Input *A* ⟶ Output *A*

    Input *B* ⟶ Output *B*

    Input *C* ⟶ Output *C*

Input $D \longrightarrow$ Output D

Input $E \longrightarrow$ Output E

Here, the connections are fairly complex. When you're working on such *systems*, it is thus essential to work with a *diagram* such as the one above. A good systems analysis book will give you a number of examples of these, plus the mathematical means for expressing all the relationships. (Though primarily intended for engineers, the best systems analysis book I've found is *Systems Dynamics: A Unified Approach* by D. Karnopp and R. Rosenberg, published by John Wiley & Sons, New York, in 1975. The first four chapters summarize basic systems analysis procedures clearly and completely.) When you get around to writing about such a system, it's essential to give the reader a chart of the whole business, so that the reader can see it in a nutshell before starting to read the prose.

9. To answer the question, "What's the fastest way to get to _____?" How should we schedule this work? How should we all set up this project so we don't get in each other's way.

Any trip or project involves people in a complex process involving more than one *time line* or *flowchart*. The *critical path chart* breaks the project down into three sets of elements:

    a. Actors
    b. Actions
    c. Time

The three are linked by various time lines, as indicated in Figure 7–4.

FIGURE 7-4/A SAMPLE CRITICAL PATH CHART

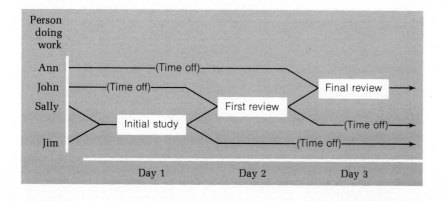

Rules for Using Structures

This simple checklist probably covers about 90 percent of the organizing structures you'll use. The other 10 percent are simply too idiosyncratic and too numerous to cover. Regardless of the structure you choose to impose on your data, there are some general rules that will help you avoid problems.

1. Data designed to suit one purpose should not be mixed in with data designed to suit another purpose. In prose as well as in tables, charts, and graphs, have one purpose for each unit of expression. Don't mix data about cause in the same sentence with data about effect, for example.

2. Even when you have subsections in a unit designed to suit a single, overall purpose (such as the four subsections involved in an argument), separate these from one another.

3. For any structure where the elements cannot be set forth in some *clear sequence*, use a chart, graph, or table form to present the data. Don't use prose. Prose is a sequential medium, one words goes down on the page at a time, and they're read in sequence. Because of this, it's very difficult to deal with something like a system analysis in English prose. How can you describe something that looks like Figure 7–5? The answer is, you can't. You have to use the visual form to set out the structure so that the reader can see it; then you can use prose to highlight what you've shown in the visual. A picture is worth a thousand words—when the data do not go together in some sequence. More will be said about this in the chapters on writing and data presentation.

4. Use the same structure over and over again—whenever you're dealing with the same purpose. Repetition isn't as boring as you might think—and it can lead to clarity.

FIGURE 7-5/A NONSEQUENTIAL SYSTEM DIAGRAM

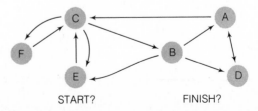

SECTION TWO SUMMARY AND THE ANSWERS TO SOME QUESTIONS YOU MAY STILL HAVE

Summary

The brainstorming for the project is over when you've done all five steps: analyzed the assignment, analyzed the reader, analyzed the subject, established a focus, and organized. The basic approach to each is:

—Analyze the assignment	*Identify key words* *Identify readers* *Answer key questions*
—Analyze the reader	*Determine what questions each group of readers wants answered in the report*
—Analyze the subject	*Develop sum-of-parts definitions of all key words you'll have to deal with*
—Establish a focus	*Using key words from the assignment, develop a title*
—Organize	*Organize reader questions* *Organize components of sum-of-parts definitions* *Assemble parts into an outline* *Organize answers to questions*

The result of the whole brainstorming process is a complete outline of the report that you will eventually turn in. It will guide you through the entire research process by keeping your attention fixed on your destination. With it, you'll be asked to get control over your research efforts.

Some questions I always get asked at this stage

1. It sounds so difficult, do you really have to do all of this before you do research?

Yes. Do you really think that it would take 5–7 years to train a research biologist or physicist or psychologist or political scientist if research weren't one of the most difficult things in the world? These very bright people often spend years mastering the five brainstorming steps and learning the techniques for gathering data. Most of these people, though, learn this process by trail and error. You can learn it in about 3 months if you practice it a bit.

2. It sounds like it takes weeks to do this brainstorming. How can you justify spending this much time?

   It takes about a third of a book to describe the brainstorming process because the steps are mental steps. There are just a lot of little things you have to do in your head to get a clear picture of your assignment. But it doesn't take very long to do these things, once you get the hang of it. For a short report, a short research assignment amounting to several days' work, this process can take you about an hour. For a really major project, one which you'll be expected to spend months working on, the process can take up to several days. Remember, you're going to check this stuff out with the boss at various points, so expect to lose some time here. I've seen the whole process take as little as 2 hours—and the outline covered a report that took 8 months to research. It looks like it takes a long time, but it doesn't, once you get some practice.

3. When do you know you've got it right? How does it feel when you're really finished?

   Knowing when you've got all the readers' questions anticipated, or when you've got a key word broken down into all its components is partly a function of experience and partly a function·of exhaustion. This brainstorming process will tire you out, and sometimes it's a good idea just to end it arbitrarily. No report is ever perfect, and going through all five steps in this brainstorming process will get you so much farther along in the thinking process than most people get at this stage that you may even find yourself covering the subject too thoroughly. So, don't worry about the process being "objectively complete." When you feel that you have satisfactory direction, that you know where you're going, stop. If you have some doubts, let the boss review what you've done; get some new energy and input from the boss or from one of your coworkers. If you are really dedicated, nothing you do will ever be completely satisfactory. Then, stop this brainstorming process when you feel you have enough to go on for the rest of the research effort. Later, when you get the final report

back, take some time to see where you succeeded and where
you failed. Learn for next time by comparing what you
thought you should do (on the basis of brainstorming) with
what the readers really wanted.

4. Do you have to do all this in order?

Of course. Brainstorming is a process, so its structure is
chronological. Even though there is some feedback from one
step to the next, even though you may learn a bit about the
readers' questions from the organizing process, try to finish
each step before going on.

5. Does it really work?

Try it. It works for anyone willing to put the effort into it. It
does not work for people looking for shortcuts. There is no
such thing as easy research.

6. What if there just isn't time?

If there isn't time to think, there surely isn't time to do any
research. Take the time, even if it means doing some work
after hours. It will pay off, professionally and personally.

SECTION THREE

PLANNING RESEARCH AND COLLECTING DATA

Research is the process by which you answer the questions you've decided the reader wants answered—about the subject you've defined. Research can take dozens of forms: interviews, tests, observations, searches of records, studies of others' research. It's a reasonably difficult process; it requires *planning*.

Planning means organized thinking, goal setting, problem analysis of alternative methods of research, and careful control over the whole research process. In even the simplest research situations, you will collect enough data to "swamp" your brain. Unless you plan for it, you'll find you have trouble remembering all the data—much less interpreting it.

The research planning process takes four basic steps:

1. Figuring out what data you need
2. Finding data sources
3. Planning and conducting data collection
4. Planning data interpretation

In the four chapters that follow, these steps are discussed and you'll get an *overview* of what good government research requires. Research requires you to think about a number of things at once; it's difficult ever to feel comfortable and secure about what you're doing, because so much can go wrong. The discussions in the chapters that follow are brief, but designed to give you an idea of what you need to think about as you prepare to collect data. A complete view of research processes will involve considerable further study. (See the brief bibliography at the end of this book.)

FIGURING OUT WHAT DATA YOU NEED

8

Formal research sometimes frightens people because it sounds so terribly like chemistry or physics. It isn't anything to be really hesitant about; nearly every adult has conducted at least one or two extensive research projects. If, for example, you have bought a car, and taken the whole project seriously rather than impulsively, you've done some pretty fancy research. You probably consulted several reliable experts (mechanics), you probably did some extensive secondary research (*Road & Track, Consumers Reports, Car and Driver*), you probably did some careful collection of primary data about each car (road testing), and you probably conducted a survey to gather opinions about the cars you were considering (asking friends, car salespeople, etc.). The only difference between this research and the kind you do for government is the subject—and the fact that you're not risking your life on the results of the research you do on the job.

You're probably reasonably familiar with the problems you often encounter while conducting research. You've encountered the problem of unreliable data (the stuff in the warranty), of bias among those whom you've asked for an opinion (no Porsche driver would admit to liking anything but a Porsche—regardless of the truth), and of having lots of data that just don't apply to *your* situation (some magazines don't do road tests on family cars, but you can always get data about any car over $30,000).

You're probably also familiar with many of the general approaches taken to getting around these problems. You may know, for instance, that you can't ask a seven-year-old, "Did you do it or not?!" and expect to get a reliable answer. But if you're sneaky, and you ask "What did Mr. Smith say after you broke the window?", you'll often get an answer to your real question. Similarly, you've probably learned who to trust and who not to trust.

In short, if you're a normal adult, formal research should not be a very new business. The difference between it and what you do everyday is simple: It's formal. It requires a bit higher degree of reliability; it takes more time and money; and it isn't research you are doing for yourself, so someone else has to suffer if you make a mistake. The people who purchased Edsels didn't hurt anyone but themselves; the person who did the marketing survey that led to their design and production must forever bear the stigma of having cost millions of people millions of dollars. So, formal research is just like regular, personal information gathering, only more so. It requires the same imagination in problem solving, but it must be guided imagination.

The first step in this formal research process is to decide what data are needed. Everyday research often fails to make this a formal step. We often collect whatever data happen to be available. For example, we don't demand that consumer magazine staff collect the data *we* want about a food processor; we take the data they give us even if some is not really useful and some isn't appropriate to our particular needs. In research *you* control, *you* have to decide what data you want.

The Problem

The problem with selecting any particular kind of data to collect is that there's almost always something wrong with *anything* you decide on. This problem is complicated by the difficulty in determining what *units* to measure things in, even when you've figured out what you want.

The Problem of Deciding What to Measure

The initial problem is how to decide what to measure, what kind of data to collect. The examples below will make this clear.

Example 1: Educators have long sought to measure academic achievement and potential for real-world success with standardized tests. They've spent tens of millions of dollars on research to design such tests only to find that the results get less reliable as they find out more. Reading tests, for example, do not always test reading ability. They test for certain cultural background; the child without a television or a keen interest in sports will have trouble with a passage about a football game. The words will simply be mystifying. Similarly, a child from the inner city will not likely know terms in a story about farming. The list of this sort of problem is almost endless. In addition, test-taking ability may be a greater factor than reading ability in scoring high on these tests. Many parents have noticed that their children read quite well but don't do well on tests. So, what do you measure if you're trying to find out something about children's ability to read?

Example 2: Recently, police departments have undertaken extensive studies of the effectiveness of preventive programs—burglary prevention, delinquency prevention, etc. They take a set of carefully planned actions and then try to measure the effect of these actions on crime rate. They encounter numerous problems: (1) As people become aware of the prevention program, they report a higher proportion of crimes, so it looks like crime is rising when it may really be falling. (2) Crimes such as burglary can be reported under other categories—if the reporting officers want to—leading to questions about whether crime rate goes down because the officers want it to. (3) The *chance* arrest of a major burglar may reduce crime rate significantly, but not be an indicator that the special program has done anything at all. What, then, can the police researcher measure to reveal the effect of the program on crime?

These are, of course, classic research problems, but even simple research within an office can be this difficult. For example, the simple task of hiring someone for a responsible position can be a researcher's nightmare. Do you measure past performance as an indicator of future performance? Do you give a test to measure skills? Do you look at how the person acts during the interview? How do you distinguish between easy-going glibness and real understanding? First, what do you decide to measure? Then, how?

The problem of deciding what to measure is really four *problems: Reliability, Objectivity, Applicability, Measurability.* In order for research to be successful, each of these problems must be solved.

The Problem of *reliability:* The person who reads the results must be confident that the data presented are reliable, that is, that if the experiment were conducted again, the same results would be recorded (within an acceptable range of error). Suppose, for example, that an office questionnaire shows staff to be quite disgruntled with a particular policy. Before taking action, the boss needs to know that the questionnaire results reflect real feelings—not just staff impatience with a questionnaire delivered on a Friday afternoon just before quitting or on Monday at 8 A.M. Data in this example might also be unreliable because: (1) someone everyone really liked had just died and everyone felt bad, (2) payroll office had just given everyone a $100 a week raise in error and everyone was so happy *no* policy could be bad, or (3) the governor had just announced that a tax cut would force layoffs on a massive scale. Any one of these circumstantial events could influence the kind of answers given on any given day. The results would be unreliable unless these sorts of things were accounted for.

The problem of *objectivity:* The person who reads the results must be sure that, however reliable they may be, they represent an answer to the real question being asked. If the question is, "Can Johnny read?", the answer must be "Yes," or "No." It shouldn't be "Yes, he can take reading tests on material familiar to white, Anglosaxon, Protestants from farm areas. The problem of objectivity, then, is a problem involving making sure the questions being asked aren't biased and the methods used to collect data aren't biased.

The problem of *applicability:* The data have to apply directly to what the person reading the report is looking for. To answer a question about *office* morale, for example, you don't collect data about the divorce rate of office employees—unless you can show that it applies, that employees are getting divorced because they hate their jobs. In short, you must establish a link between the data you collect and the question you're answering. This link must be absolutely secure.

The problem of *measurability:* The data you collect must be data you can give some numerical value to, so you can measure it in some way. You have to be able to make a clear distinction between one bit of data and another. Opinion surveys are one example of research methods that suffer from measurability problems. If you find that one person says, "The President's doing a rotten job" and another says, "The President's doing a good job," you might assume that this is an indication of some clear difference. But you might be wrong. One person may be an optimist, and declaring the President to be "good" might be a pretty weak statement; the other could be a pessimist, and declaring the President to be "rotten" may be high praise indeed. You can't tell because you haven't established any numerical scale for these responses. Doing so with these two types of people would be almost impossible, anyway.

THE GENERAL SOLUTION

While there are no generalizable solutions to any particular research problem, there are two strategies, or approaches, that help most researchers *work out specific solutions* to these problems. The first involves making a distinction between direct measurement and indirect measurement; the second involves forcing yourself to think in measurable terms by designing what are often called *data shells*.

Direct and Indirect Measurement

Sometimes, the collection of data is difficult because you try to measure things directly, you try to get information directly from the source. While this is admirable in theory, it's often troublesome in practice. It's hard for example, to collect data about horses *from* horses. It's hard to collect data about people *from* people. Direct evidence about how people feel or think is almost impossible to get in any reliable manner. The trouble is that government research is *usually* about people. For example, an Air Force colonel I knew once tried to collect information about the ability of an air base to handle traffic. He asked people on the base if they could handle their present workload, and if they could manage to take a few more planes. Their response? "Yes sir!" The result: they fell behind when he sent in the planes. Direct questioning just doesn't get reliable information most of the time.

Physicians long ago worked out a solution to this problem. They always have difficulty getting direct evidence regarding the existence or progress of a disease inside a patient's body. After all, the direct evidence might require examination of the inside, and few people like to be opened up just for diagnosis. So the physician has learned to collect *indirect* evidence, to look at symptoms and to draw conclusions from these. For example, a patient may come into the office complaining of extreme headaches, high fever, difficulty breathing, cramps—all of which came on suddenly. The physician may *suspect* meningitis. More information about symptoms may be gathered, but it's really too much to ask the patient to submit to any kind of painful tests until the physician is already almost *certain* that the symptoms are really *indicating* meningitis. In many cases, a treatment will begin before the actual disease organism causing the disease has been found.

In dealing with research into people, looking at symptoms is all-important. If, for example, you wanted to know whether a school reading improvement program was having any real effect, you might go looking for information about symptoms of *effect*. You might look at:

1. Book orders at the local bookstore: Are the students in the program actually buying more books? If they *are* you've got a good indicator, or symptom, of success.
2. Records from the local library: Are the students taking out more library books; are there more students with library cards?
3. Sales of *good* children's magazines: Do local retailers say they've noticed any increase in such sales?

None of these is a direct measure of any change in reading skill among students, but all are very concrete *indicators* of increased reading and thus of increased interest and skill. No, you can't be absolutely sure that these indicators are correct, that you've really got the increase in skill. Yes, they're more reliable measures than you'd get if you *asked* the children or their parents about their ability. And they're more reliable than the test scores on standard tests—which are biased.

The assumption behind indirect measurement—measurement of symptoms—is that it is better to measure something concrete than to attempt to measure something subjective. Book sales are concrete. The evidence for them is absolute—sales slips, order forms. The *direct* evidence for increase in reading skills (opinions from teachers who *want* the program to succeed, opinions from students, test scores) is either not concrete enough or not reliable enough. And, like the physician, you cannot actually go into the students' brains to collect data.

In planning a research effort, in thinking about the data you might want to collect about your subject, here are some good general rules for keeping focused on indirect (concrete) evidence:

1. *Measure actions, behavior, and results of behavior rather than opinions.* You want to find out something about office morale—measure turnover rate, sick leave, number of complaints received by grievance committees, etc. Don't ask people if they feel good about the job; they may well lie to you to protect themselves, or they may lie to make things seem worse than they really are.

2. *Observe; don't confront.* People will change their behavior if they think they're being watched. If you're worried about possible fraud in an office, make observations without letting anyone know what you're doing. Otherwise, you'll get good behavior for the time you're there. That's why auditors have learned to ignore what people say and go straight to the concrete indicators of behavior—the records.

Although it will take some imagination to work out a research plan that focuses on indicators or symptoms, it's possible to do so in almost every situation. Here are some of the more innovative solutions to research problems I've seen in the past few years:

1. To measure the effectiveness of a special burglary prevention program in a residential neighborhood, the police in a California county collected data about the number of deadbolt locks sold and installed from the time the program began to its end. A large increase in sales indicated they had made the message of the program clear—prevention begins with the resident. They also checked the number of community "block groups" formed to provide neighborhood "watches," and they discussed the effects of the program with burglars who had been caught in other areas in the county.

2. To determine whether senior citizens felt they were being forced into making a "donation" at a federally funded lunch program, officials moved the donation box to an obscure area of the dining room—where no one could see how much a person was placing in the box. Donations did not decline, indicating that the people who were giving money were doing so because they wanted to, not because of the pressure of the rest of the program members looking on.

3. To measure the effectiveness of an agency training program, several groups of new employees were put on the job *without* going through it. Their performance was compared with that of groups that had been subjected to the training. There was no difference, indicating that the questionnaire previously used to evaluate the effectiveness and usefulness of the training had been an almost useless measure. The training also

appeared to be less than useful, though further study was indicated before this conclusion could be made conclusively.

4. A police officer got a good indicator of how much business revenue the city would lose if police cracked down on prostitutes in a booming "nite club" area by simply stationing a car outside each of several bars at random intervals. The difference between bar sales when the car wasn't there and bar sales when prostitutes avoided the bar because of the police presence was significant, indicating that sales tax revenues might go down if a crackdown was initiated. (The report wasn't made *public*, of course.)

Thinking in Measurable Terms by Designing Data Shells

You can help yourself plan research by turning vague thoughts about what data you want into concrete pictures of what the data will look like when presented. This involves designing graphs, tables, charts, and diagrams that you'll be able to use in the final report. These graphics, drawn out but without any numbers filled in, will help you think; they'll organize your thoughts about the data and keep you focused on one question in the report at a time.

What scientists call *data shells* are really very common items, used everyday by companies and government to help people think in numerical terms and to help them make sense out of all the data they've got in their heads. Perhaps the most well-known example is the Internal Revenue Service Form 1040—the income tax return. This form is really a very complex table used to display data about a taxpayer's income, deductions, tax liability, and withholding tax. The form is not beautifully designed, but imagine for a moment where you'd be on April 15 without it. Suppose all you got from the IRS was a request for a return—no form, just a request that you read the instructions and figure out your tax. Without the data shell, the empty table, you'd be lost.

The same lost feeling often creeps over people when they look at an outline of a paper and try to decide what data to collect. There are so many problems to be overcome in research that it often seems mere chance that one method of getting information is chosen over another. Designing a graph or a table sometimes helps you get going in the right direction.

Suppose, for example, that you were looking for a job and that you had four good offers. Your question is, "Which do I choose?" This is a difficult research question. If you think about it for a moment, you will probably find yourself weighing one job against another in a rather random fashion: "Well, if I take job A, I get a really good salary, but who wants to go to South Yemen with a wife and four

FIGURE 8-1/JOB COMPARISON: BASIC FORM

Criteria for evaluation	Job A	Job B	Job C	Job D

girls? If I take job B, I get to go to Atlanta, but the company doesn't have a good benefit package." And so forth. What you need is some *form* to your deliberations, some form that gives everything meaning, that tells you what all the data you have means. Since you know that the question you're answering requires comparison, you could get some order to your thinking by setting up a table such as the one shown in Figure 8–1. Notice how the form of the table organizes the thinking you'll do.

There is yet something missing in this simple table—the criteria for evaluating each job. You can't set up such a table without the criteria. What they are depends on your own value system, but Figure 8–2 shows an example of what you might come up with.

FIGURE 8-2/JOB COMPARISON: BASIC FORM WITH CRITERIA FOR EVALUATION

Criteria for evaluation	Job A	Job B	Job C	Job D
Salary (minimum $20,000)				
Benefits	✕	✕	✕	✕
a. Retirement				
b. Health				
c. Dental				
d. Vacation				
e. Travel				
Overtime				
Climate				
Status				
Have to commute?				
Job for spouse?				
Good schools?				

You now know what kinds of data you're going to collect about the jobs; each of the criteria sets up a category of data. You've broken the single question, "Which do I choose?" into a series of very specific comparisons. Your next question is, "How do I assign a *number,* a numerical kind of value, to each of the criteria?" Doing this, without having the data about each job in your head, will help you set your priorities. Some of the criteria will be easy to set forth in numerical terms—salary, fringe benefits—but you'll have to do some thinking to give numerical value to weather, social status, and the like. Maybe you'll end up with something simple like a scale of values "great weather, fine weather, good weather, mediocre weather, poor weather, rotten weather," but working from the table form will almost *force* you into some kind of numerical value system.

This is the reason to design tables *before* you go out to collect data—while you're designing them, you are almost forced to think about how you are going to take *data,* about how you are going to measure things. There is no research that I know of that explains why this happens, but it's probably because people are used to seeing tables and charts and graphs associated with numerical values. You see a table form and you immediately began to think about numbers.

Designing data shells begins with knowing the question you want to answer. Start, for example, with a simple question, "Why has public schooling increased in cost while the number of students has declined?" The two elements of this question are (1) students and (2) costs. They are being dealt with in terms of a trend (decreased, increased). The graphic form for this sort of relationship is the line graph shown in Figure 8–3. This is how you would express the relationship graphically, *regardless* of the data you collected. The next step is to put some units on each axis, to mark off some scale. Dollars on one axis will do, and numbers of students will do for the other, as shown in Figure 8–4.

FIGURE 8-3/FROM QUESTION TO GRAPH

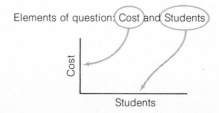

FIGURE 8-4/MARKING A SCALE

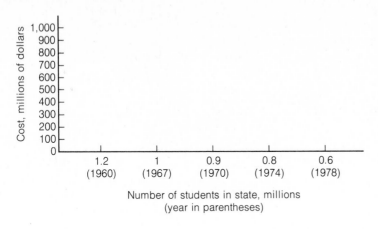

The next question is which costs to measure. There are many kinds of costs in the overall school budget that you might look at: administrative costs, special program costs, transportation costs, counselling costs, costs of basic skills programs, athletic program costs, etc. You could easily look at each of these separately, as shown in Figure 8–5. Where does this get you? To a concrete series of indicators of the causes of the increase in costs. By determining which costs have gone up, in relation to enrollment, you can identify the cause, or at least you can get some good *indicators*. For example, if you found that basic skills programs costs stayed stable in relationship to number of students, as indicated in Figure 8–6, you might argue that the cause for the increase is the increasingly broad education given at the school. Other similar arguments could be made, depending on what data you collect.

It is important to note that *the act of making the graph or table or chart actually stimulates your thinking,* actually helps you think about what data you can use to answer the basic question you've taken from your outline.

NOTES TO MANAGEMENT AND STAFF

To Management

Research takes immense amounts of staff time and thus costs you a lot of money. Attempts to collect direct data are particularly

To Staff

The process of designing data shells has some real advantages in terms of your total research and analysis effort. First, you can

FIGURE 8-5/TURNING A BASIC GRAPH INTO A NUMBER OF SPECIFIC GRAPHS

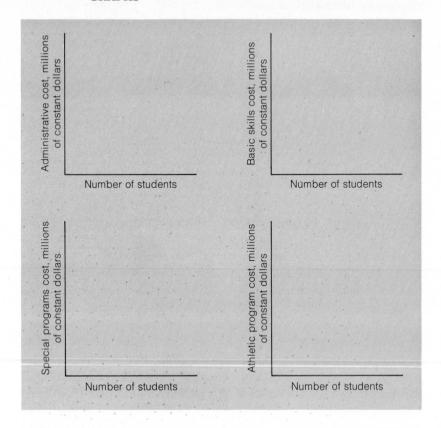

FIGURE 8-6/A DATA SHELL WITH HYPOTHETICAL RESULTS ADDED

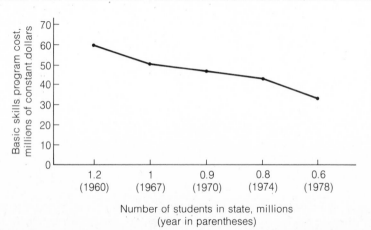

To Management *(continued)*

expensive, because they usually involve staff in making out questionnaires, interview questions, etc. *If* the question can be answered with reasonable accuracy through indirect means, the cost is likely to be considerably lower, because it will involve only the researchers. The subjects of the study are not a part of the study process, they're just observed. Even better, indirect measures are often made with already existing data. To study staff morale, for example, you need only the available records on sick leave, turnover, etc. In many cases, indirect measures will be handled in this way, reducing the cost of the research considerably. If you want a more complete view of the sorts of things you can learn from indirect sources such as common office records, invite your department's internal audit staff to go over these records with you.

To Staff *(continued)*

almost always get information about a subject if you tell the people who have the data *exactly what you want,* and one of the best ways of doing this is to give them a form to fill out. In short, you can often use the data shell form as a means of collecting data, as well as a way to help you think about what data you want to collect. Second, you'll often be asked to do some simple statistical analysis on your results to ensure their significance. Statistics often tend to get in the way of your thinking process. You can get some concrete advice from your agency statisticians or computer programmers (both can help) *if* you can show them in a very concrete manner exactly what data you expect to collect and how you plan to use it. I've found that the data shell is the best way to do this. In fact, if you take copies of your preliminary data shells to the person who will be in charge of the statistical analysis, this person can often help you further design your research, can tell you what you can and cannot do with your data. But you must go to these people with something very concrete; otherwise, they won't know what you want, and you'll likely come away more confused than when you contacted them. Finally, having a data shell for information you're going to collect gives you a place to put the data as it is collected; you've organized your note taking.

CHAPTER SUMMARY

Knowing what questions you have to answer, you next must decide what data you need to answer the questions. The data must be reliable, objective, applicable, and numerical. To help yourself get this sort of data, focus on collecting indirect evidence rather than spending all your time and energy on trying to collect direct evidence. (Don't ignore direct evidence, but make sure you confirm any you do collect by comparing it to your other indicators.) Before you actually begin to go out to collect data, help yourself think about how you're going to measure things by designing all the tables, graphs, charts, diagrams, etc., you'll eventually use in presenting your data. This will focus your thoughts quite quickly on the questions of measurement.

On the pages that follow is a checklist of graphic forms that you may find useful in thinking about how to present and analyze your data.

A CHECKLIST OF COMMON GRAPHIC FORMS

It's often quite useful to look at your options before you actually begin to design graphics. Seeing the forms can help you see what you're really trying to do. To use this checklist, isolate the question you're trying to answer, and then scan the list to see if there are forms you can use to help you answer the question. There may be more than one form you can consider, so go through the whole list before you make your decision.

You may find that you'll use several graphs or tables to cover the same question. You may find that you'll have to adapt these basic forms to suit your particular purpose.

1. *The basic comparative table:* The table consists of a checkerboard arrangement of empty boxes, into which you put numbers. It is used, primarily for comparisons, to show *exact values*. It looks like Figure 8–7.

2. *The bar graph:* This form is used to make comparisons of the same sort as are made in tables, except here the numerical values are not as important as the visualization of the differences. There are two basic types of bar graphs, both of which are shown in Figure 8–8.

FIGURE 8-7/COMPARATIVE TABLE

		1	2	3	4	5	6	7	8	9
					Things to be compared					
Comparison criteria	1									
	2									
	3									
	4									
	5									
	6									
	7 Sum									

FIGURE 8-8/BAR GRAPHS

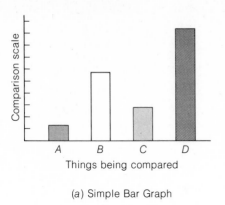

(a) Simple Bar Graph

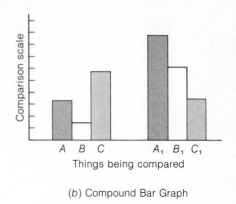

(b) Compound Bar Graph

3. *Line graphs:* Line graphs are useful for showing relationships of things that occur over time and relationships between things that change in relation to one another. Values are shown by a rising or falling line, and the emphasis is on this rise and fall more than it is on the actual values being dealt with. There are three basic types of line graphs; all these are shown in Figure 8–9. Note that the multiline form allows you to look at how several things change in relation to one another as time also changes. In the cumulative effect form, you can show the effects of three or four things on a total function—as the whole business changes with time. At any spot on the time line, you can calculate the percentage of the whole attributable to any of its components.

4. *Decision tables:* This is a special kind of table designed to show how a conclusion was reached—graphically rather than in prose form. It involves comparing various alternatives against criteria set up in declining order of importance. As you move down the list of criteria, only the alternatives that have met previous criteria are given data, only these are still compared. Figure 8–10 shows an example. Note that in using this form you show the reader the progress of your thought without having to write about it. As you cross out the boxes below the point at which you eliminated an alternative, you focus attention on those remaining.

5. *Periodicity charts:* This special form of chart is designed to show how a number of things change in relation to each other and to some

FIGURE 8-9/LINE GRAPHS

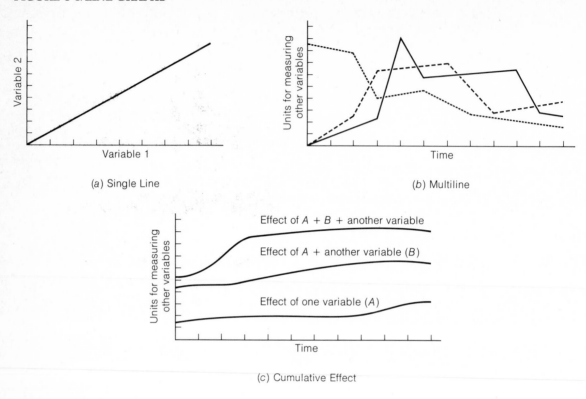

(a) Single Line

(b) Multiline

(c) Cumulative Effect

total quantity as time changes. Note in Figure 8–11 that you get a very complex chart, one that reveals many relationships in a single form.

FIGURE 8-10/DECISION TABLE

		\multicolumn{10}{c}{Things to be compared}
		1	2	3	4	5	6	7	8	9	10
Criteria, in order of priority	1	10	10	6	5	10	10	3	10	6	10
	2	10	9			10	6		10		10
	3	10				10			10		3
	4	9				10			10		
	5					10			10		
	6					10					

**FIGURE 8-11/PERIODICITY CHART: AMOUNT OF SHADED AREA
EXPRESSES PERCENTAGE OF WHOLE AT
ANY SPECIFIED TIME**

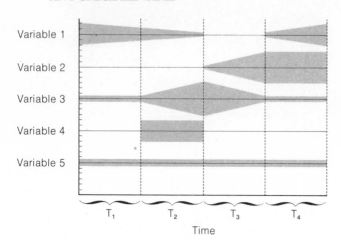

6. *Maps:* Maps show spatial relationships. They're useful any time the question you're answering has anything to do with place and time relationships. Maps can be realistic or schematic. They can be colored, cross-hatched, contour-lined, numbered, and overlaid one on the other. There are so many kinds, that examples here would hardly begin to cover them. Skim through a history book to see the dozens of ways maps can be used to present data about changes involving time and place.

7. *Flowcharts:* Flowcharts show the relationships among elements of a process and are primarily designed to show decision-making processes. The normal form looks something like Figure 8–12.

8. *Trees, or similarity charts:* These charts are designed to show two things at once, similarity among items and the flow of some trait

FIGURE 8-12/FLOWCHART

FIGURE 8-13/TREE, OR SIMILARITY CHART

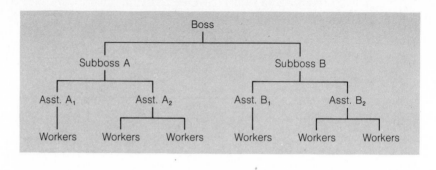

from one item to the next. The most common form is the organization chart, as shown in Figure 8–13. Note that you read level of similarity horizontally and flow of authority vertically.

The same kind of similarity/flow relationships can be used for any number of other subjects, for example to trace the history of people after high-school graduation (Figure 8–14), where diverging lines indicate the slow separation and regrouping of members of the original, similar group.

FIGURE 8-14/WHAT HAPPENED TO THE CLASS OF 1957

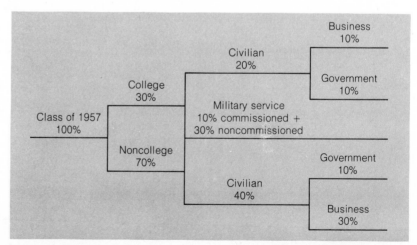

Note in this figure that you can trace the route taken by various portions of the class of 1957—backwards from the points of dissimilarity to points of similarity.

FIGURE 8-15/SYSTEMS DIAGRAM

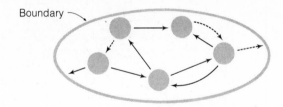

9. *Systems diagrams:* Systems diagrams are a special form of map. They're used to show how several things interact within some form of boundary. They're useful in environmental studies; in studies of communication, cooperation; or in any endeavor that requires people or things to interact with one another. Their elements are (see Figure 8–15) circles, which represent the elements of the system; solid arrows, which represent direct interactions; and dotted arrows, which represent indirect interactions.

9

FINDING DATA SOURCES

While using the data shell technique to help yourself think about what data you might like to collect, you will quickly reach the point of wondering "Where on earth can I find that out!?" Answering this question takes you from the realm of the theoretical into the realm of the practical. It's the beginning of the actual field work—the actual data collection process.

The question about where to get a particular bit of information should not be asked, of course, until you've finished deciding what information you really want. You make a full effort to figure out what data you need. You jot down all your data needs, regardless of what you think about the availability of the data. *Then*, you go looking for it. Separating these two processes is important because if you do them both at the same time, the tendency is to reject suggestions that you need certain data simply because you can't immediately see where you might get it. I've heard many, many government researchers—experienced as well as novice—say things like "Well, I admit it would be nice to have that information, but there's just no way we could collect it in time." They've usually rejected the idea of looking for data before they've ever thought about where to get it.

The trouble with this attitude is that it severely limits you in your research effort and it's completely illogical. If you decide that you want a particular bit of information, it's almost certain that you can get it reasonably quickly and at reasonable cost in time, energy, and money. You sometimes have to be a bit innovative in your thinking to find convenient data source. *If you're willing to do a little imaginative thinking, the data can be found.* In fact, your problem is likely to be that there is *too much available data,* and you'll have to spend half your time eliminating data from your project files.

The reason you should not reject any data need off-handedly is that there is simply an immense amount of data available on almost any subject you could possibly be interested in. There are literally millions of file cabinets just stuffed with information on every aspect of American society—from who eats peanut butter and jelly sandwiches to what the rate of inflation is in even the smallest community. The government spends billions of dollars every year to gather and store this information. Businesses spend billions more analyzing the people who buy products. And almost all this information is yours for the asking—if you can simply find the particular bits of information you want. And, if you're studying a limited subject, such as something that concerns only your own county, state, or agency, you'll still find plenty of information. The records you keep on your own program will probably contain more than enough information if you've thought about what you're doing and what you really need.

There are two kinds of data available to you: secondary data and primary, or *raw,* data. The secondary data are in the form of already prepared reports, statistical publications, reviews of operations, and government reports. The primary information takes just about every form possible, from census data to contract information. It's a bit harder to find the primary data, so initially we'll concentrate on finding the secondary information—the stuff that has already been collected and analyzed.

PROBLEMS

There are two problems to overcome before you can get at either secondary or primary data. The first is figuring out who has the data. The second is gaining access to it.

SOLUTIONS

The problems are obvious and don't require much discussion. The solutions are also pretty obvious, but they deserve some special attention. Before you can begin to identify data sources, you need to establish a positive frame of mind. Begin your research with the attitude that if the information you need is important to you, it's probably also important to other people. There are probably dozens of organized groups within the United States who have sponsored or conducted research into such seemingly obscure topics as:

1. How to set up a lobby so that the public feels comfortable
2. Predicting workload in an office over holidays
3. The number of business licenses issued to *any* identifiable subgroup of the general population
4. How many people can walk over a patch of grass (any variety) before it begins to erode

Sitting in your office, you may think you have a unique problem that no one has ever even thought of before. Most of the people I've done research consulting with over the last few years have felt this very strongly. They've *all* been wrong. We have never failed in a search for information on any subject. If it's important enough for you to study it *now*, then it's been just as important to someone else in the past. This does not hold true for sciences, but it does for studies of people.

Once you decide to admit that your study is probably not fundamentally unique, you can begin to look for the data that is already available. The basic strategy for this search is to find *one source* and then use that source to help you locate others. You "pyramid" into the system, as illustrated in Figure 9–1. To identify your entry point into the data system, you need to think carefully about other people who might share your interest in the subject. You need to make a list of all types of people who might have data you need.

The same advice goes for efforts to get at primary, or raw, data. There are vast resources, but to find them you have to think carefully about who would have the data and what form it might be in. Once you've done this, you have to solve the next problem, of getting access to the data. As people are naturally hesitant to give information to the government, for fear that it will be used against them (probably to increase their tax bill), you need to overcome considerable resistance before you can gain access to data. *Demanding it won't work in most cases.* Besides, if you demand data, you will probably have to go to court to get it and this takes more time than most administrative researchers have. No, you'll just have to ask for

FIGURE 9-1/THE RESEARCH PYRAMID

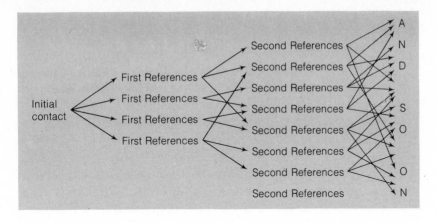

it. And ask politely. In your request, make sure you *cover* the following:

1. Who you are and who you work for
2. The fact that you are not out to get anyone
3. The exact nature of the information you want
4. Why you want it
5. What general good will be done with the data
6. The exact form the data should be in
7. That everything will be kept strictly confidential
8. That you'll name no names, that you're interested only in *general* trends or characteristics

If you cannot give these last assurances, expect some resistance. Once you've done this, most people are quite willing to open up their office files. If they don't, you may also have to assure them:

1. That you will destroy the raw data once you have finished analyzing it (and if you promise this, do it)
2. That the work you're going to do will directly benefit those who are supplying the data
3. That you'll give them some good public relations when you finish the report

EXAMPLES

This is very simple advice to give, but very difficult advice to follow. Here are three examples of how government researchers have located usable data about subjects you would expect to be difficult to study.

1. *The impact of a city transit workers' strike on city revenues.* In this study, the researchers decided that they could not predict impact unless they knew what the transit strike was doing to each of the *sources* of the city's income—taxpayers. However, they also knew that the business people involved would be hesitant to advertise *their* losses. They were also faced with the problem of the *timing* of the data collection. For sure, they could get data from the city's businesses when regular, quarterly reports were compiled, but they couldn't expect to get the information on a day-to-day basis. They needed to know immediately whether business was being hurt by the strike. To determine this, they decided that the indicator that was easiest to measure was the number of people still going into the downtown areas. If the number was dropping rapidly, they could quickly report that business was likely to be hurt by the strike. If the number stayed high, they could assume that the strike was going to have a lesser impact. They could report these preliminary findings to the negotiators immediately.

   Where, though, would they find information about the number of people still going into the downtown area? They could, of course, take a survey of 10,000 people selected at random, but this would cost more than settling the strike, so they rejected this conventional idea. The question was, then, *who* might have information about the number of people coming into the downtown area? Here are a few of the people they tentatively identified.:

   a. Taxi companies: They would notice any increase in business very quickly, because they'd have to put more cabs on the street to handle it. An increase in their customers would indicate that at least some of those not coming into town on buses were still coming into town.

   b. Parking lot operators: A sudden upswing of business here would also be immediately noticeable, and noting the *time* of customers' arrival and departure would tentatively identify shoppers (separating them from business commuters). The time is, of course, marked on each parking lot stub.

   c. City parking meter collections: Greater revenue here would indicate that more people were driving into the city.

d. Highway patrol: Police agencies might record whether there was a massive increase in traffic, and respond to it by putting more people on the roads.

All these sources were sources for indicators only, and they were certainly no substitute for the data that was later collected to confirm the findings of the initial research—that is, the actual revenue figures. But the research team was able to say, in a day or so, that the number of people coming into the city had declined very significantly. There had been no upswing of activity in the above forms of alternative transportation. The city had no choice but to settle the strike or lose revenue as a result. People were just not shopping in the downtown areas.

2. *A middle-management to upper-management communications problem.* In this study, a top administrator felt that she was not getting accurate information about line operations from middle managers who were responsible for these operations. She felt there were problems that were being sugar-coated before she was informed of them. She wanted to find out what the real problems were and where the information about them was being held up or altered.

Her problem, of course, was that she did not want to create problems where none existed. She did not want to hold interviews with line staff and ask questions about the middle managers. She didn't want a questionnaire circulated, because this would suggest mistrust. She would create a poor supervisory atmosphere in doing this sort of research. She simply had to conduct research without letting everyone know about it. Where could she find information about a subject that those in middle management would want to suppress? She found it in the office file cabinets.

She solved her problem thus:

a. She reasoned that people *keep* copies of memos, suggestions, and complaints that *they* send up the chain of command. These copies would be in the files of the immediate supervisors of line staff. The secretary in charge of these files would know exactly where they were.

b. She already had copies of memos and reports sent to *her* by the supervisors and by their supervisors.

c. All she had to do was to compare the information from these two sources to determine what sorts of information was being screened from her. She could do this without causing any trouble for those supervisors who *were* transmitting information about problems accurately. She simply requested one of her staff to go into each supervisor's office file to gather copies of the original problem memos. The supervisors might object, but at least there would be no public reaction; the whole affair could be kept within the managerial boundaries of the agency.

The normal procedure in such a "management audit" is to try to collect information directly from the sources involved. Staff and management get into a long and complex interview and questionnaire process, which often causes more trouble than it's worth. By finding an already existing data source, this manager was able to avoid the chaos of such direct confrontation research. She was able to solve the communication problem without creating more problems.

3. *The impact of a new tax on business revenues on the business community of a small city.* The city council in this case wanted to increase revenues by increasing business fees and by instituting a tax on hotel accommodations. Legalities aside, the city administrator needed to know what the business community would do if this was done. The proposal was made, and the city's business people did everything short of threatening murder to convince the city officials that this would ruin their businesses.

Management analysts for the city were asked to determine how much of this outcry was genuine and how much was merely for show. Would the businesses really move out of town? Would the increases really give the shopping centers in neighboring communities a pricing advantage over the city's merchants? These were the questions; the problem was to find information sources that could be relied on. Asking the business people in the city wouldn't do, nor would a survey of customers—who would have a vested interest in anything that would keep prices down. The sources finally selected were:

a. *The chamber of commerce's own advertising brochure.* Advertising to attract businesses to the community in the first place would give the researchers a good indication of the relative importance of tax rates in the decision to locate a business. If the advertising stressed this issue, it was probably something to take seriously. If not, then the businesses would likely stay because of the other benefits of the area. The researchers found that the tax situation received very little emphasis in these advertisments; they stressed a healthy economy, stable clientele, and good potential for growth. These, then, were the things that would act to draw and keep businesses in the city. Taxes were not a major issue.

b. *The current response of the city's residents to price differentials between city merchants' goods and those of merchants in outlying shopping areas.* The question here was simple: When outlying shopping centers had large sales, did city customers abandon city merchants and do their shopping elsewhere?" Data about this could be collected without ever asking a single shopper. It was done thus:

   (1) Researchers identified, from old newspaper files, those periods when outlying shopping areas had major sales that brought their prices to a significantly lower point than those of in-city merchants.

   (2) City sales tax revenues for these periods were compared to revenues for periods when the price differentials were smaller.

   (3) Revenues from the bus line that carried intracity passengers were also compared for these two kinds of periods.

   The researchers found that revenues during periods when the outlying shopping center merchants had a significant price edge over in-city merchants did show a decline, but only a very small one.

   On the basis of these findings, the researchers felt that most of the complaints from merchants were not serious. They recommended that the city increase the taxes. To make business happy, they earmarked *some* of the increased revenues for a regular "Shop in in _____" advertising campaign; research and politics were admirably blended.

These examples don't even begin to indicate the millions of innovative approaches to research that can be taken—if the researcher spends some time thinking about what data are really necessary to answer a question and then spends equal time thinking about all the possible sources of the data

NOTES TO MANAGEMENT AND STAFF

To Management

It often takes some time for staff to locate sources of existing data—either primary or secondary. It takes telephone calls and trips to libraries and other data depositories. The

To Staff

There is an almost irresistible urge in any research situation to do something *new*, to find out something that no one has ever found out before. There is a similar urge to

To Management (continued)

time spent often *looks* wasteful because it may take ten attempts to find one reliable source of existing data about the subject at hand. But, even though this process takes a lot of time, remember that it takes much less time than any effort to *generate new data*. For example, it may take 4 hours of thinking and talking for staff to find a good source of data about welfare recipients in a county; in the same time, these four people could easily design and have typed a complete questionnaire to send to every welfare recipient. The collecting process then makes the difference. Working with existing data, it is often possible to collect an immense amount of information in a few days; a questionnaire seldom takes less than a month. *The time spent in finding existing data sources is recouped in the process of collecting the actual data. Overall efficiency is the result.*

Since most staff I've worked with have been hesitant to spend the time to identify sources of already existing data, I feel very strongly that management must actually encourage staff to take this step. This can be done in a number of ways:

1. *Post lists of data sources.* It's not a bad idea to have a large poster with the names and telephone numbers of data sources for subjects commonly dealt with in the office. Such a list will probably be useful in everyday work as well as research efforts.
2. *Require an evaluation of alternative data sources.* A good review step is to ask staff to supply you with a list of data sources considered, with brief comments about why some were finally selected and some rejected. You could do this by using the Data Source Evaluation Form at the end of this chapter.
3. *Include time and money for a data source search in the project budget.* You can let staff know that you feel the search for existing data sources is valuable by putting a dollar value on it. You can specify, for instance, that long-distance clls to inquire about data sources are OK, or that staff may take

To Staff (continued)

think about the project you're working on as *unique*. Resist both urges; they're silly.

First, if it's worth studying, it's already been studied. And, it's been studied more extensively than you are likely to be able to do with the limitations of time and money that are placed on most government research projects. Your job is not to create new knowledge (though that's nice if you can manage do it on the side) but to find and use information to make decisions, to design programs, to improve operations. Only in very special circumstances will you have to generate information on your own.

Second, every project is unique, but only in some very minor way. The basics of almost every program evaluation, for example, are the same—you measure the same things in roughly the same way. Even the program you work in is unlikely to be unique except in some very minor ways. Government agencies *all* deal with the collection and allocation of community resources; the problems one county faces in doing this are going to be very similar to the problems another county faces.

So, spend some time in the office trying to locate sources of existing data about your subject. Use the telephone. Talk to other people in the agency about the subject and to people from outside the agency. Explore all avenues you can think of before you decide that you have to go out and generate your own data. This way, you'll usually get the data you need with little effort; if you really do need to collect new data, you'll also be able to justify your actions.

To Management (continued)

> office time to go to the library. If you
> indicate that you think the effort is
> worth it, staff will put out the effort.

SUMMARY

*There is little need for a researcher to collect new data in order to
answer most questions, because there is an immense amount of data
routinely collected, stored, and reported by government, business,
universities, and private research groups. To get the data, you have
to identify exactly what data you want. Then you must spend some
time thinking about where to locate it. Doing this by "pyramiding"
into the data system is one way of saving yourself the time and
trouble of generating new data. In looking for existing data, make
sure you are very careful to assure your sources that they will not be
hurt by giving you the information and that there is a real need for it.*

A CHECKLIST OF DATA SOURCES

When you're looking for information, you can usually get it from one
or another of the sources listed below. These sources collect and
store vast amounts of data about people, programs, and conditions in
the United States and abroad. To gain access to the data, you'll
usually have to be quite careful about how you explain the need for it
and about what form you request it in.

Internal (In-House) Sources

Management information systems

Personnel files   Daily, weekly, monthly, quarterly, semiannual,
and annual reports

Budgets

Expense records

Travel records

Time sheets

Correspondence files

Retirement, insurance, and Social Security records

Minutes of meetings

External Sources

Reports by other local, state, and federal agencies

Reports from industry, trade journals and corporate yearly statements

Reports and files of community service organizations, such as the chamber of commerce, charity organizations, unions, fraternal organizations, foundations, and political parties

Newspaper and magazine files

University and college faculty studies

Libraries

Public records of marriage, health, parentage, age, welfare, place of business, property ownership and use, and taxation

Census bureau data

Sales and inventory data

As you think about the data you need, you may find it useful to skim this checklist. It may remind you of a kind of data you could use, as well as possible sources of the data.

Data Source Evaluation Form

As you think of various data sources, you may find it useful to evaluate them in a systematic fashion. The form on page 159 may help you do this.

DATA SOURCE EVALUATION FORM

Criteria for evaluation	Alternative data sources			
	1	2	3	4
Reliability				
Objectivity				
Vested interest?				
Political bias?				
Measurability				
Applicability				
Is situation being studied similar to situation previously studied?	NOTES ON APPLICABILITY			
Cost				
Form of data				
Amount of data				
Ease of access				

10

PLANNING AND CONDUCTING DATA COLLECTION

Once you have taken care to think about the data you need and to identify sources for this information, you find yourself about to start the leg-work of research. You may even have done a little of it by this time, but the majority of the data collection effort is yet to come.

Collecting data from secondary sources is really quite easy; you write for the report or article or other piece of existing data, you read it, and you take what you need from it. Collecting primary data—data in the form of bits and pieces stored in files or in people's heads—is more difficult. Avoid it if you can. If you can get all the data you need in other people's reports, do so. If you can't, if you have to go out and get raw data, which you must then synthesize and make sense of, you'll need to do some careful planning.

THE PROBLEM

*The basic problem you face is that the way you collect data—even
existing data in files—can influence the kind of data you get.* Everything you do can have an influence. You may even generate the
answer you want, rather than the truthful answer, by choosing the
wrong method. Every aspect of your method can have an influence
on the validity of your results—the timing of your collection, the
way you encounter people involved, the explanation you give for
why you want the data, your appearance, your voice—everything
about you and the way you go about collecting data.

The classic example of this problem took place in 1948 during
the Truman–Dewey campaign for the Presidency. Opinion polls
were a relatively new "science" at that time, but they were highly
regarded as indicators of what the public would do in the election.
They showed Dewey with a comfortable lead all through the campaign. People were so certain that Dewey would win the election
that newspapers printed the headline "DEWEY WINS" even before
the results were in on election night. There is a classic political
photograph of Truman holding up one of these newspapers; he won,
in spite of the polls.

What went wrong with those polls can still go wrong today, even
with computer projections, millions of dollars of research effort, and
decades of refining survey methods. In the 1978 midterm elections,
Minnesota political pollsters miscalled the senatorial races badly. In
California, several "too-close-to-call" races ended up being landslides.

The problem is, of course, that research methods for studying
people are just plain unreliable. There are too many things that can
go wrong, too many variables to take into account, for them to be
successful all the time. In the Truman–Dewey election, the pollsters
made a number of gross errors in their survey technique. The errors
were easy to recognize after the fact, but they were very difficult to
anticipate.

1. The pollsters used telephone surveys at a time when the telephone was not in general use. Poor families did not have
   telephones, and since poor families tend to vote Democratic,
   the survey missed a lot of potential voters who were strongly
   on Truman's side.
2. They forgot that people sometimes *lie*. There is often a
   "right" answer to a question about something as important as
   an election. The socially correct answer in this case was to

say you were going to vote for Dewey, the safe, respectable person. But there isn't any lying in the voting booth; there the real preference of the voter comes out. (This same phenomenon can be seen in more recent elections. There are very few liberals in California who will admit to voting for Ronald Reagan during the 1960s, but he won by landslides each time he ran for governor—at least a few liberal Democrats must have voted for him!)

3. They forgot that people change their minds. When a candidate looks like a sure loser, a lot of people switch their votes in sympathy for the underdog. If the candidates are both reasonable people and there are no issues on which they are violently set against the general public opinion, people will often switch votes at the last minute—to preserve the two-party system, to make one candidate feel better about losing, or some such reason. They often succeed in turning the election results upside down.

While it is doubtful that you will ever conduct a political poll, the same kinds of problems will face you every time you try to collect information about political questions—about people and programs. You'll have to be very careful to avoid problems such as the following:

1. *Timing problems.* It's extremely important to time your collection carefully. If, for example, you plan to look at complaints being sent to a consumer affairs agency by consumers from a given area, make sure you collect the data before you announce that you're doing so. Otherwise, special-interest groups will flood the agency with complaints, knowing that now is their chance to be heard. You thus get a biased view. The same kind of strategy is important in any internal study. If you talk to an office manager and reveal that you're going to solicit suggestions from his/her staff, you can count on that manager trying to influence the nature of these suggestions. In short, you have to time your efforts so that no one with a vested interest can see what's happening until the data are already in.

2. *Your personal appearance.* If you happen to get involved in research that requires you to meet people who will supply you with data, make sure that you look like you belong in their company. Dress to suit your audience. If you're going to visit a school, dress casually. If you're going to collect data about operations of a legal agency, wear the "legal" three-piece suit. Try not to stand out, because the minute you stand

out, you're a threat, and you'll get really hesitant responses from those you're working with.

3. *Your own bias.* Every word you use reveals how you think to those you're collecting data from. Without even knowing it, you can set up the answer you're really looking for, you can make the person give you the answer you want to hear. Even very experienced surveyors have this problem.

4. *Giving the people you're dealing with too much or too little information.* You need to tell people what you're doing, or else they will be hesitant to give you information. But if you tell them too much, you can make them even more hesitant. Or, you may allow them to understand the subject too well so that they can exercise self-interest in answering the question or showing you data.

The second kind of problem in deciding how to go out to collect data is that there are no right answers; there are only intelligent choices. Every data collection method has advantages and disadvantages. Every strategy for collecting data is good for some things and not so good for others. There are long-standing feuds, for example, between advocates of *interactive research* and advocates of *passive research*; between advocates of using *existing data* and advocates of *generating new data*. The feuds are worth looking at briefly.

Interactive versus Passive Methods

Interactive methods of collecting data involve direct contact between the data collector and the people being studied (in interviews or group discussions). The researcher who practices this method believes that you can adjust to situations, can force people to answer you, can get more substantive answers by having the interviewees react to you. They employ techniques such as asking leading questions, arguing to see how strongly the person holds an opinion, and questioning everything the person may say. In doing so, they say they get to the bottom of things, they go below the surface responses. Advocates of passive methods say they create the data they want.

Passive methods involve little or no contact between researcher and the people being studied. The researcher takes very limited data, but makes sure that there is no way the reliability or objectivity of the data can be questioned. The collection method involves gathering existing data about a situation or making observations without those being studied knowing about it. Thus, there is no way they can respond to the researcher and bias the results. For example, someone who believes in passive methods would not *ask* you about your preferences for certain foods; instead, the researcher would try to figure out a way of detecting these preferences without your knowing about it. This might involve standing behind you at the lunch counter, or asking a supermarket checker to remember what you bought when you went to the store. The passive research advocate might even go so far as to analyze your garbage. The idea is to avoid letting you know that you're being studied, so you can't possibly take any action to make the results come out the way you might want them to. The advocates of passive research say the method ensures reliable data. Advocates of interactive research say it's shallow.

Deciding who is right in any given situation is hardly easy. It's probably a good idea to use passive methods first, to collect as much data as you can without anyone knowing what you're doing early in the research. Answer as many questions as you can with these data. If you need more data, and interactive methods are the only ones you can think of to get the data you need, then introduce some of these methods—send out a questionnaire or hold an interview.

Using Existing Data or Generating New Data

Existing data has the advantage of being objective. There is no way that the bias of the researcher can influence data compiled before the research effort begins. Thus, many researchers tend to want to use this kind of data as the basis for conclusions about the subject. There may be less of it in some cases, it may sometimes be a bit old, but you can always count on it. In most cases, such data have been collected as a matter of routine, simply to maintain a record of activities. There is usually no significant bias to such data. And when there is a bias, it is unlikely to be *your* bias. The information won't be tailor-made to help you make *your* point. It will, from your point of view, be objective. You cannot influence the data in collecting it.

Those who advocate generating new data through experiments, questionnaires, interviews, etc., suggest that the problems of methods can be solved, that it is possible to adequately control the research process so that an interviewer does not significantly affect the responses of the interviewee. They recognize the problems that made the Truman–Dewey polls so ineffective, and they say that a carefully designed survey or interview can overcome these problems.

It's probably best to hold to the middle ground in this feud too. Existing data is certainly attractive if you can get enough of it to answer all your questions. In a great many cases, you can. But there will always be some cases where you'll have to generate new information, where you'll have to design an experiment or prepare for an interview. In finding the best applicant for a job, for example, no one has yet devised anything as good as the interview—a confrontation situation. The data about individuals that you can get from existing sources is just too biased.

SOLUTION

Research is an extremely complicated business. Each project will require imagination. But there are some good general rules to follow that may help you gain control over whatever method you choose for collecting the data you need.

Plan Everything

No matter what method you decide on, you have to know exactly what you're going to do at each step. Before you go to a set of files to collect data, know exactly what you want and exactly what you're going to use it for. Know who you are likely to meet in the office and exactly what you will tell them if you're asked what you're doing. If you're getting data from some other agency, know exactly who has official control of the data and what their responses might be to your request. Have an answer for every question you might get asked about the reasons for your research.

Try Not to Let the People You're Studying Know What You Want—Or that You Want Anything, if Possible. It will be extremely difficult to keep research goals a secret, just as it will be difficult to keep your personal bias a secret. The best method is to keep people from knowing that you're conducting a research project in the first place. If, for example, you want some statistics on turnover in an agency unit, don't go to the unit supervisor and announce that you're going to be looking at this. Go to personnel and look through the central files. No one being studied need know.

If you can't keep your research a secret, at least try to keep its goals from being known. Invent some perfectly honest but very general goal to explain why you're interested in the subject. For example, don't say "We're investigating the performance of three field officers because we've received numerous complaints about rude counselors and extensive delays in processsing requests for funds." Instead, say "We're here to do a study of the procedure for processing requests for funds. We would like to see how you do it in this office so that we can compare your procedure with that in other offices."

Avoid Loaded Words in any Part of Your Research. You can often expose your bias in the most innocent ways, simply by using the wrong word. For example, a researcher recently asked this question in a survey of voters in a congressional district:

"How do you feel we should deal with the problem of abortion?

a. Forbid it entirely.
b. Allow it only under special circumstances.
c. Allow it as long as a physician recommends it.
d. Allow it as a matter of personal freedom."

The question is full of loaded terms and betrays the bias of the person asking it. First, why should we have to "deal with" anything? This phrase is only used when we're faced with a serious situation and we view it as negative. Second, who says abortion is a "problem"? It's a biological phenomenon. In one sense, it's a medical technique. The writer here has made it into something *wrong* and then asked for an "objective" answer. The researcher has allowed us the option of choosing *d* only if we happen to be brave enough to say that the problem—the thing that is *wrong*—may not be wrong. The researcher spent time making sure the whole range of answers was available to the respondents but neglected to pay any attention to the bias in the question.

This kind of biasing is so easy to find in almost every questionnaire that questionnaires have become highly suspect as research tools, but it is just as easy to bias other forms of research by choosing the wrong word here and there.

Double-Check Your Results. It's very easy to get results that "prove" what you want to prove. It's easy to see what you want to see in a set of results. To avoid this, it's a good idea to plan some form of *check* into your research. For example, a survey of employees to find out if they feel they are doing useful work ought to be taken at several intervals. At the first interval, you probably won't get very thoughtful results; the answers to these questions will be rather shallow. Asking the same question at a later date will give you answers that are the result of some more intensive thinking. The first set of questions just starts the employees thinking about the subject.

Identify and Control for Variables. In any situation, there are a number of factors that can affect results and make them less than representative of the "truth." For example, many personnel officers will admit that the best time to go for an interview is midmorning. The interviewers are in a better mood, and less tired, at this time than at any other time during the day. If you know this, and if you're an interviewer, you can take action to control for it. You can, for example, schedule fewer interviews in the afternoon—so that you have time for breaks and thus time to restore some of your energy.

In designing any research collection method, it's important to identify as many of the things that might influence the results as possible. In questionnaires and interviews, the two methods that involve some form of personal contact between the researcher and the subjects of the study, some of the variables to control for are:

Questionnaires: Length, number of options in answering, ordering of multiple-choice answers, loaded words in the question, possible misinterpretation of one question (ask several about the same thing!), use of jargon, and reader identification of the agency person who is conducting the survey

Interviews: Age, sex, height, weight, manners, voice, dress, attitude of the interviewers; time, place, circumstances of the interview

Obviously, these are just general categories. The specifics that need to be controlled for make a list several chapters long.

Always Collect Data in Concrete, Numerical Form. Whatever method you choose for collecting data, make sure that what you get can be expressed in some numerical form. Unless you're actually interested in *opinions* as results themselves, don't collect data in this form.

To get data in concrete form, of course, means that you have to have designed the overall report very carefully. The questions you produced during brainstorming have to be questions that *can* be answered with concrete data. They have to be specific questions. For example, the question "Should we lease _____ computer to improve payroll office efficiency?" is too broad. It needs to be broken down into more specific questions before data can be collected to answer it:

—"Which computer is fastest?"

—"Which has the largest capacity?"

—"Which will fit into the corner of room 236A?" And so on.

PROCEDURE FOR METHODS PLANNING AND DATA COLLECTION

The business of designing adequate methods is so complex at times that it's useful to do the methods planning in a very strict order.

1. Identify data sources.
2. Identify alternate sources in case something goes wrong.

3. Determine the form of data desired.
4. Set Priorities.
5. Determine who must be contacted to get data.
   a. Existing data—the person in charge of the files or reports
   b. New data—the people you want to get information about, the people you must get permission from
6. Analyze each source to determine what variables could influence the nature of the data available.
7. Identify alternative methods for collecting each kind of data.
8. Analyze each method to determine which will give you the most reliable, objective, applicable, measurable data.
9. Select methods.
10. Schedule data collection.
11. Collect data: Control for all variables identified in Step 6.

EXAMPLE

If this looks complicated to you, you've come to the right conclusion. Research isn't something you can just do. It takes far more thought than most people usually give it, as this example will show.

The Situation

In late June of 197__, an agency of the state of New York hired a new Assistant Program Director. By December of that same year, the agency director was hearing rumors that this person was doing an absolutely terrible job of supervising. The program he was in charge of was politically important and relatively sensitive. The agency could not afford a scandal. The director requested a study of this person's operations so that a decision could be made to replace or retain him.

This kind of study goes on all the time in government work, at all levels. If you stay in government, you'll eventually get involved in such an administrative study.

The basic question being asked was "Replace or retain?" This question involved a number of subquestions:

—"Is he doing a good job?"

—"Are the complaints—rumors—substantive?

—"Are the complaints *valid*?"

—"Will the problem solve itself?"

There were at least two dozen other questions to answer. We'll look at one *question* and how it was studied: "Are the complaints valid?"

To determine whether the complaints being heard in the hall-ways of the agency were really valid, it was determined that data would need to be collected about what the complaints were, who was making them, and the causes of the complaints.

Methods Problems

There were a number of problems that had to be overcome in this study. First, the study had to be kept confidential. It was not fair to start full-scale investigation. It also would be a bad idea to let anyone know what was going on because that might lead to chaos in the program and cause adverse public reaction. Second, the data col-lected would have to stand up in an administrative hearing. If the person was going to be replaced, he could be expected to demand a hearing. If not, complainers might eventually demand such a hear-ing. Third, the study could not in any way encourage or discourage complaints. It had to be strictly neutral.

The Sources of Data

There are a number of possible sources of data about this sort of situation. For this particular case, these included:

1. Minutes of meetings—serious disputes would be revealed here.
2. Program policy files—changes in policy that might have caused disputes might be found here.
3. Personnel files—if complaints were caused by shifts in per-sonnel policy within the program, the results of these shifts would be found in the new manager's personnel action rec-ommendations.
4. Program workload information—if complaints were about too much work, they could be confirmed from this source.
5. Past records of grievance committees—if the complainers in this case had a record of complaining about everything, the validity of the complaints would be suspect.

Looking at these sources would give you a reasonable indication of whether or not you had a serious problem on your hands. The remaining sources of data were:

6. The new manager himself—this person could describe the reasons for any actions.
7. The employees—these people could explain what they didn't like (or did like).

Form of the Data

1. From minutes of meetings you would want data about the number of disputes over such things as scheduling, policy changes, and personnel actions. You would want data about who the disputes were between and the number of disputes per person.

2. From program policy files you would want to find out what policies had been changed, and who had been involved in setting the original policies and what their reasoning had been then. This information could be compared to that from minutes of meetings.

3. From personnel files you would want to see whether those who had been advancing under the old manager had ceased to advance. You would tabulate the number of *changes in mobility* evident in the new manager's actions.

4. From program workload information you would want data in the form of overall workload, workload per employee, and workload per program unit—for a period before and after the new manager's starting date.

5. From past records of grievance committees, you would want numbers of grievances filed, by work unit and by person. You would want number of grievances filed by subject.

After you had collected these data, you could consider confirming any findings from the two parties being studied.

Priorities

Data about the nature of the complaints would be primary. You can go no further without this. Data about the people making the complaints would come next. Data about the causes would have to be last in priority, because it would do you no good without the first two.

Contact People

All the data in the first grouping of sources can be collected as a part of the normal management process. It can be requested and examined without causing undue alarm.

Variables that Influence the Nature of the Data

1. Data from minutes of meetings could be influenced by changes in personnel and by changes in political climate, also possibly by changes in the views held by some personnel.

2. Data from program policy files would be difficult to influence, though a person selecting policy files to study might not get a really representative sample if he or she had a bias about what policies were important to study.

3. Data from personnel files would be subject to considerable interpretation by those studying them. Those looking at the files must control for their own bias in this situation. They must figure out how to measure changes in mobility without injecting their opinions into the subject.

4. Program workload information would be unbiased except for some possible problems if workload measures or standards had changed.

5. Data from grievance committee records would be subject to a great deal of interpretation, and the writer of each record would surely introduce a bias into each account.

Alternative Methods for Collecting Data

All the existing data could be collected in two ways—by the researchers themselves or on request. Data gathered directly from the people involved could be gathered by questionnaire, by individual interview, or by group interview.

Methods Analysis

Existing data are best gathered by the researchers themselves; otherwise, those supplying the information would be able to communicate with those being studied, or they might impose their own bias on the data—deciding what was and what was not important.

Each of the *interactive* methods for gathering data directly from the people involved would have distinct advantages and disadvantages. The questionnaire might give people too much time to think about any complaints they might have—it might actually create a bad situation. But it would be the most neutral form of collection method. Private interviews would make it easier to find out the intensity of the feelings about the complaints but would also create distrust among staff, who wouldn't know who was saying what behind the closed doors. Group interviews have the advantage of getting things out in the open for all to see, *if* those involved are willing to talk freely in front of superiors and coworkers, and if the interviewer can keep the participants from feeding on each other's feelings.

Selection of Methods

First, collect all data from existing sources. Second, hold a group interview with complainers, some noncomplainers, and the manager in question.

Schedule

1. Collect all data about the nature of the complaints.
2. Collect all data about the people involved.
3. Collect all data about cause.
4. Hold a group interview to bring everything out into the open if necessary.

Controls for Variables

1. To control for changes in personnel when examining minutes of meetings, classify comments according to the philosophy behind them. Record disputes as between "those favoring an open-door policy and those favoring restricting public access to files" rather than according to names.
2. To control for changes in political climate, record the number of people taking each side of the issue. Note any sudden shifts in view and identify possible political shifts that may account for the sudden change in views of meeting participants.
3. To control for bias in selecting policy files to sample, have a list of important files prepared by someone who uses the files, by the secretary who handles them, by a supervisor, and by yourself. Where all agree, where the same subject is mentioned on all lists, this is what you would call "important."
4. To control for possible misinterpretation of *mobility* in looking at personnel files, have the personnel office supply you with a set of *their* criteria for looking at the subject.
5. To control for changes in workload measurement, translate all workload figures into units of time and units of relative difficulty. To do this, you'll have to set up a scale of "difficulty."
6. To control for writer bias in looking at grievance records, identify all writers and determine what their *record* is in terms of taking a positive or negative stance regarding grievances.

This is only a sketchy overview of the effort that might go into planning the research into existing data. The planning for the interactive research is more difficult:

1. To control the group interview situation, select a neutral site—not the manager's office, not the union meeting hall.
2. To control for *time*, select a midweek period, when everyone is neither grumpy about having to come to work on Monday nor anxiously awaiting the weekend.
3. To control for the possibility of several complainers taking over the meeting and turning it into a "roast," make sure every question you ask is answered by all participants in writing and that you tabulate results on a blackboard or similar device before you explore the answers verbally.
4. To make sure everyone is willing to talk, have the new manager call the meeting as if it were a meeting to discuss office operations. Do not mention any investigation.
5. To keep the meeting from getting out of hand, stick to a preplanned agenda.
6. To keep people from feeding on each other's feelings, make sure you ask them to write down how strongly they feel about a subject before any talking is done.
7. General controls: Dress casually. If several people are conducting the interview, don't all sit together at the head of a table (as if you were conducting an inquisition).

This example is intended to show the pattern of the thinking you need to do to plan methods—it isn't in any way a complete examination of the project. In fact, the research that went into this project took about 2–3 hours to design and about 2 weeks to conduct—hardly anything you can describe in a few pages.

As a sidelight, you may be interested to know that the manager was not replaced. He had made a major mistake in management, though. He had changed policy and workload without explaining his reasons for doing so. And in doing these things, he had moved several key people into positions he thought were important but they thought were unimportant. These people were the complainers. Having found this out during the *existing data* stage of the research, the researchers were able to solve the problem during the group interview, where they could discuss the changes in direction that were being made in the program and point out how the personnel changes reflected these shifts in policy. The interview, which could have been a real hate session, ended up being productive.

NOTES TO MANAGEMENT AND STAFF

To Management

The biggest danger in administrative research is that the research process itself can cause problems as easily as it can identify problems that need solving or find solutions. The mere suggestion that something is being investigated can often make people start to think of reasons why it *should* be investigated. Interactive methods, such as questionnaires, interviews, and some experiments, tend to generate this sort of response unless they are very carefully controlled. It's a good idea to review all such research plans very carefully to make sure you really want to deal with the problems they may cause. It's also a good idea to encourage use of existing sources when they can be used to give you a reasonably decent answer. These sources can't be influenced too much by the collection process, and they don't involve a lot of research time. Most importantly, they allow research to be conducted confidentially; you don't have fifteen people wandering through your office asking leading questions.

To Staff

A simple caution is all that you need to remember when you're designing methods: *YOUR JOB IS TO COLLECT RESULTS, NOT TO CREATE THEM.*

You're going to be held responsible for the decisions that are made on the basis of your research—at least you're going to be responsible for the objectivity, reliability, and applicability of your results.

CHAPTER SUMMARY

The methods you use to gather data can, and will, influence the nature and the quality of the data you collect. As you design your methods, you need to control for a number of potential problems including:

> 1. *Your own bias*
> 2. *How you interact with those you're studying*
> 3. *Time, place, and circumstances of the research*
> 4. *The language you use in dealing with people involved in the research*

You must be extremely careful in designing your research methods to make sure you are not creating results and that the method you select is the most likely to give you reliable, objective, applicable, and measurable results.

To help you evaluate methods, a brief set of guidelines to basic methods is given on the following pages. In looking over these guidelines, remember one simple rule: THE CLOSER YOUR RESULTS ARE TO WHAT YOU EXPECTED TO FIND OUT, THE MORE LIKELY YOU DID SOMETHING TO INFLUENCE THOSE RESULTS.

RESEARCH METHODS GUIDELINES: COMMONLY USED METHODS

1. Using existing data in already published form. Since this sort of data is easiest to collect and analyze, it's usually the first kind of data you should try to collect. However, using such data is not the answer to every research problem. It's best used in making general policy decisions; it's best avoided when the decisions to be made involve specific people, places, or events.

Advantages

a. It's available.
b. It's cheap.
c. It's convenient.
d. It can save time and money.
e. It can permit you to use information you could never afford to gather on your own.
f. You have no way of influencing the results, no way to inject your bias.

Disadvantages

a. It doesn't always apply to your specific project.
b. You didn't control the methods use to collect the data; you cannot tell how reliable it is.
c. It may not be perfectly applicable to your specific situation.
d. It may not be organized to suit your purposes.
e. *It may not be complete data for you purposes.*

2. Using existing raw data. In general, the data already sitting around in files is really quite useful. You can almost always identify a source of information you can use—if you can get permission to do so.

Advantages

a. It's available.
b. It's cheaper than generating new data.
c. It's convenient.
d. If you can gain access to it quickly, you can often answer a question very quickly.
e. In most cases the supply of data is massive; you could never duplicate it in any single research effort.

Disadvantages

a. You have to get permission to use it, and this is sometimes a political problem.
b. It's often stored with lots of data you don't want. It requires a search.
c. It's often incomplete.
d. You don't know how it was gathered.
e. Its availability can be politically influenced.

Advantages (continued)

f. You cannot influence those who put it into the file or into the computer. You can't introduce any bias except by selecting only portions of it.

Disadvantages (continued)

f. It may not be exactly what you want.

3. Observing operations or people. This seemingly innocent method is useful in many circumstances where you don't have any data you can use in files but you don't want people to know you're doing research. It is, essentially, a form of "stake out." You identify the operation you want to study and then you watch it— secretly.

Advantages

a. It's relatively cheap.
b. You don't have to ask any questions, so you don't have to worry about getting biased answers.
c. You *may* discover things you never anticipated.

Disadvantages

a. It's sneaky, and people will resent it if they catch you.
b. Your very presence may cause a change in the operation or behavior you're trying to observe.
c. Your observations will very likely be gathered in random order, making interpretation difficult.
d. It's illegal in some cases.
e. Your observations may never be complete; you may not see or hear what you want to.
f. You can't ever do it again. Once you're identified as a researcher, you are forever suspect.

Suggestions for observations

a. If you have to do it, "go underground." Get yourself a position among those you're studying. Work with them.
b. Make sure you know the business before you go into any observational situation. Know what you're looking for.
c. Don't stir things up. Listen and watch, don't talk.
d. Don't allow anyone to know that you're observing them.

Self-conscious people do not make good research subjects.

4. Experiments. The opportunity to conduct experiments occurs more frequently than many people imagine during government research. For example, if you really wanted to find out what would happen if you cut the budget, there's one sure way to find

out—cut it. Make it seem as if the cut is permanent and see what happens. You can conduct such experiments in many cases, but you'll have to take the often unpleasant consequences.

Advantages

a. You get absolutely reliable results.
b. You may discover things you could never anticipate.
c. You may solve the problem you're studying in the process of doing the study.

Disadvantages

a. You can destroy a sense of teamwork by experimenting.
b. People can be hurt—permanently.
c. You can be sued.
d. You can be fired.
e. You may destroy the agency's public image.
f. You may do damage to people and systems that you can never repair.
g. If you make one tiny mistake in designing your experiment, you can invalidate all your results—and still run all the risks.

Suggestions for Experiments

a. Don't—if there's any chance of hurting anyone. There are so many other ways of collecting data that experiments shouldn't be used if there's any chance of harming a person.
b. Don't—unless you have an absolutely perfect experimental design.
c. Make sure the experiment you design allows for all possible factors that could influence the result.
d. Choose the least dramatic form of the experiment, the one with the least potential for disruption.

5. Tests. Tests are like experiments in some ways. They involve the researcher in some form of manipulation of people and situations. This is usually accepted—as long as those involved know they're being tested.

Generally speaking, tests are used to confirm data already gathered from other sources by other methods. They're useful once you have narrowed the scope of your study to two or three alternatives.

Advantages

a. Properly designed tests are reliable.
b. Tests allow you to discriminate very precisely between two alternatives.

Disadvantages

a. Tests have to be designed to give "either/or" results.
b. People don't like being tested in many situations.

Advantages (continued)

c. Tests are usually cheaper than interviews or questionnaires.

Disadvantages (continued)

c. Some people like tests and do well under pressure; others do poorly on tests but do well in work.

d. Results can be tampered with under all but ideal conditions.

e. Tests very often reflect the bias of the tester in ways quite difficult to control.

Suggestions for tests

a. Make sure your test actually measures the thing you're trying to measure. Don't give a verbal test to measure a nonverbal skill. The opposite is also true.

b. Avoid tests for such vague things as "attitude" or "preference." They're too easy to bias in these cases.

c. Always design your test so that it gives you black and white results, so that you don't have to interpret too much. If you find you're going to have to do a lot of interpreting, try another method or another data source.

d. Test the test. Try it out on a small group that you *know* will do well, or that you know will have certain abilities. If they do poorly, you may have to redesign your test.

6. Single interviews. While there are a lot of problems involved in interviewing people, the interview is sometimes the only way to get certain information. There is no better way of collecting data about job applicants, for example; the other sources of data about the applicant are simply too biased.

Advantages

a. You can get information in this way that you could not expect to get in any other manner.

b. In the process of the interview, you may solve the problem you're studying.

c. You give those interviewed a sense of importance, a sense of participating in the workings of the office. They are likely to accept the results if they're thus consulted.

d. You can generate interest in the subject studied.

Disadvantages

a. The subject of the interview is usually biased.

b. In your interaction with the person you're interviewing, you may significantly influence the results.

c. Interviews are very hard to control.

d. Results vary according to the time, place, and circumstances of the interview.

e. Interviews are expensive.

f. Interviews often disrupt normal routine.

g. You may generate a problem during the interview by changing the subject's perspective of the situation you're studying.

Suggestions for interviews

a. Thoroughly plan your interview. Try to anticipate every possible response to your questions so that you aren't surprised by anything. If you're thrown off-balance, you may close communication channels.

b. Always use plain, simple language, but do not attempt to talk down to the person you're interviewing or to adapt your language to that of the interviewee. If you feel that your language will be a barrier to communication, hire someone familiar with the language patterns of the interviewee to do the interview for you.

c. Don't make comments about answers. Listen.

d. In general, don't argue (unless the purpose of your interview is to see how the person handles arguments).

e. Prepare your questions in advance.

f. If you're interviewing more than one person, make sure you ask the same questions in the same order in the same tone of voice.

g. If you have time to do so, repeat questions—in altered form—at random intervals during the interview. you will want to compare results.

h. Make sure that the interview is convenient to the interviewee. Otherwise, you'll get hurried answers.

i. Make sure that you confirm the data you get from an interview with the data you get from other sources. The interview can be manipulated by anyone with even reasonable thinking ability—watch for this.

j. Try not to reveal the reasons behind each question; if you do, you'll find that the answers can be designed to be *right* rather than truthful.

k. Never underestimate the sophistication of the interviewee. Never overestimate the value of the results you get.

7. Group interviews. The group interview is very much in vogue now, and will probably continue to be popular for some time. It is a useful management tool for establishing a consensus among those interviewed. It often also produces dramatically unexpected results; the group dynamic can often make people reveal their true feelings. It can also turn people into simpering "yes, boss" types. In short, it's both a very good and a very bad research technique. Much of its effectiveness depends on chance. It has all the advantages and disadvantages previously mentioned for single interviews, with these additional items:

Advantages

a. People who feel threatened in single interviews often come alive and open up their hearts and souls when protected by a group.
b. You can collect a tremendous amount of data in a short time.

Disadvantages

a. Because you're dealing with a group, the reliability of any one response to a question is likely to be highly suspect. Group interview results should be thought of in very general terms.
b. Things often come out during group interviews that can be harmful to the people involved. Statements made in the heat of the moment are exposed for all to see; you can do a lot of harm with a group interview.

Suggestions for group interviews

a. Follow the suggestions for single interviews.
b. Mix interviewers and interviewees together. Don't put all interviewers at the head of a table.
c. Keep careful control of the meeting. Don't let two or three vocal people take over.
d. Don't rely on the results from group interviews exclusively.

8. Questionnaires. The questionnaire is so frequently used that it must be the most popular form of research method. It's also one of the most difficult research tools to use. It's difficult because language is a very complex medium; what one word will mean to one person is almost impossible to predict. Some people will be intimidated by formal language; others will be insulted by informal, conversational questions. There are so many problems involved in preparing a questionnaire that results should not be taken seriously unless they are *extreme*, unless respondents show real preference for one answer over another.

Advantages

a. You can reach a lot of people at once.
b. All people get exactly the same questions.
c. You do not have to worry about your behavior influencing the results.
d. You can tabulate results easily.

Disadvantages

a. You can't control for different interpretations of the same question.
b. It's costly in terms of time and material.
c. You can't tell why people who do not respond have taken this action. You end up with a biased sample and you don't know what the bias is.
d. You have no way of knowing what factors may have influenced respondents' answers.

Suggestions for questionnaires

a. Don't try to be fancy or cute; ask questions that require factual answers. For example, don't ask, "Do you think you would recommend brand X to a friend?" Ask "Have you recommended brand X to a friend?"

b. Within the limits of time and space for the questionnaire, try to ask the same question in several forms, using different phrases.

c. Make sure the people answering your questions are really qualified to give you an answer, that they have information about the subject. This will often mean that you have to ask questions that reveal such knowledge or lack of it.

11

PLANNING DATA INTERPRETATION

Once you have selected your methods, you begin the process of conducting your research. If the project involves more than a few hours' work, you'll collect data in bits and pieces, getting a little from here, a little from there. If you've planned your effort carefully, you should be able to keep pretty good control over this process, even though you can count on some delay and some problems getting everything you want to get.

As the data begin to pile up in your head and on your desk, you'll probably start thinking about it. You will probably start to think about what it means in relation to your purpose. You may even form some preliminary conclusions. Your object in doing so, of course, is to keep mental control over the whole process, to keep things sorted out in your brain. Besides, there is no way you can avoid doing this preliminary interpretation; it's a natural tendency.

THE PROBLEMS

Thinking about your results *as they come in* can cause some serious research problems. First, data tend to be collected rather haphazardly. You get the data from one source at a time, even though the data may be destined for use in answering six or seven separate questions. So, you're left with incomplete data to answer any one research question. If you start thinking about what the data mean at this point, you're quite likely to draw initial conclusions that aren't valid. Doing this can then color your thoughts about the data when you get it all collected.

Second, if you think about the data as it starts to come in, you may find yourself redesigning your research before you have all your results. This happens frequently in almost all research situations. If a series of interviews *starts* to suggest that the original research was just a bit off target, the interview questions will be changed. The problem is, of course, that preliminary results may not be valid, and any change based on them can invalidate the rest of the research.

Finally, there is a tendency to *build* interpretation, to take initial results and draw conclusions from them, and then to look for the same sort of results as more data come in. It's quite easy for this to get out of hand, and for you to unintentionally start trying to make results fit your preliminary conclusions.

None of these things happen because you want them to. None happen because you try to prejudice your interpretation. They happen because data collection just isn't orderly. Data don't accumulate in nice neat piles. It is thus quite easy to get confused by the data, to look at partial data and start thinking about it as if it were complete. Thus, there is a need to plan in order to control for this problem.

SOLUTION

The obvious solution to this problem is to *wait* until all data has been collected before you start interpreting it. That's the obvious answer. It doesn't work very often, because it's difficult to just shut down your brain for a month while you collect and sort through piles of data.

The other solution is to plan your interpretation, to organize it so that it can't get out of control. The procedure for this planning depends heavily on what you did during the last stages of the brainstorming process and during the first stages of the process of planning for actual research. The key to planning interpretation is the *data shell*.

If you have designed the tables, charts, and graphs you plan to use to present your data, you have also designed a marvelously effective tool for planning your interpretation and for controlling the flow of data into your brain. Here's how you can use the data shell to do these things:

1. For each chart, graph, or table, fill in what you *expect* to get in the way of results. On the basis of what you know about the subject, *guess*.
2. Look very carefully at your guess. Speculate on what it will mean if your guess is right and what it will mean if you're wrong.
3. Take your guess—your data shell filled in with tentative figures—to a statistician. Find out whether your guess represents anything significant; find out whether these figures *would* represent anything significant. Determine with the statistician how the data can be analyzed.
4. Think very carefully about your data collection methods and try to identify any element of methods that might bias the results, that might have the effect of making your guess come true—regardless of the true data.

This is a very simple procedure. What it does, though, is hardly simple:

1. It reveals, very precisely, just what your research bias is. By defining exactly what you expect, you gain a measure of control over your often unconscious biases.
2. It gives you a baseline against which to measure your real results. You define what you expect and what it would mean if you got your expected results. Any deviation from this forces you to think again—very carefully.

EXAMPLE

The process makes most sense in terms of an example.

Situation

You're working in personnel for a government agency. You have received some complaints about promotion policy and procedure. The complaints involve the agency promotional list (based on test scores) and the final promotions (based on the list rankings and an interview). The complaint is that high scores on the tests are being overridden by personal favoritism, which is evident in interview results. This would, it is said, violate the principle of promotion on the basis of merit.

Question to Be Answered

You want to answer a number of questions about the promotional procedures of the agency, but the first question is "Are the complaints *valid*?" Is there a consistent difference between promotional list rankings and actual promotions?

Data Shell

Using the simple line graph in Figure 11–1, you will plot the relationship between ranking on the promotional list and final promotion results.

Results Prediction

There are a number of ways the results *could* come out. Several are described here.

If the results looked like Figure 11–2, it would mean that there was a negative relationship between ranking on the promotional list and actual promotional opportunity. This could mean that the promotional test was simply no good. It could also mean that managers were, indeed, throwing out the results of the test and making

FIGURE 11-1/DATA SHELL FOR THE RELATIONSHIP BETWEEN PROMOTIONAL LIST RESULTS AND ACTUAL PROMOTIONS

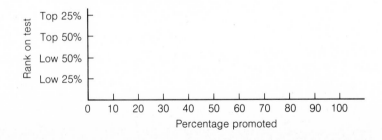

FIGURE 11-2/ONE POSSIBLE RESULT

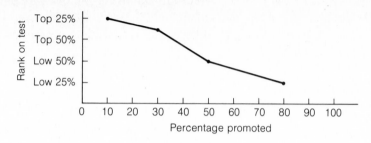

personal judgments on the basis of the interview alone—but it would mean that they were doing this *systematically*.

If the results looked like Figure 11-3, it would indicate that the complaints were substantially invalid, that test scores and final promotion were linked quite closely. It would probably also indicate that managers had confidence in the test and used the interview to *confirm* test results.

If the results looked like Figure 11-4, it would mean that the interview results were *sometimes* given precedence over the test results, that the complaints were *sometimes* valid. It would then be necessary to find out why this happened.

Implications

Having looked at several of the possible outcomes in concrete terms, it's possible to see what the results will mean—before they actually come in. If the results show up as in Figure 11-3, showing that the

FIGURE 11-3/ANOTHER POSSIBLE RESULT

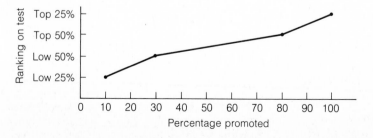

FIGURE 11-4/ANOTHER POSSIBLE RESULT

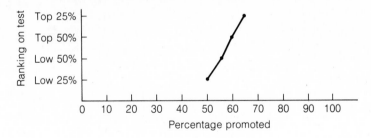

complaints are invalid, then the research effort can stop at this point. If any of the other results occur, then more research will be necessary to solve the problem.

By looking at possible results, then, you are able to anticipate and plan for second- and third-stage research. You can then set up contingency plans that you can have approved before you get started on the project, which may save you some trouble in convincing the boss that you simply have to have further information.

Tricks to the Procedure

The best way to do this is not to think about the business too deeply; instead, just *doodle*. Draw out a rough graph or chart or table and start drawing lines on it or filling in numbers. Ask yourself what these numbers would mean if they were found to be true representations of the situation. Jot down your answers and keep doodling. Then talk to a colleague about what you've done. After you get a response, go back and work a bit longer on your data shells. Refine them a bit. Then, break your research into phases—decide what, if any, further research will be required if you get X result and what would be required if you get Y result.

NOTES TO MANAGEMENT AND STAFF

To Management

If you take even a short look at the *expected* results of research, it can give you some real insight into the sort of problems you're going to run into when the results come in. You

To Staff

It's well known that research always takes unexpected turns during the data collection process. You can't anticipate everything. But you can anticipate a vast majority of the in-

To Management (continued)

can't make any decisions until the actual results are in, but at least there will be no real surprises, nothing will suddenly force you to take wholly unanticipated actions. All too often it's the suddenness of research findings that makes them troublesome. Dealing with expectations in this way will take a bit of the shock out of the final report.

To Staff (continued)

terpretation problems you're going to have by carefully designing all your data shells and then just playing around with possible results. It tends to make your thinking more systematic and to give concrete expression to vague thoughts about "What if . . . ."

It's also pretty well known that most researchers have some trouble with statistical analysis and data processing experts, the people who do all the calculations with the data you've gathered. If you give them data shells—even empty ones—much of this trouble can be avoided. I've worked with dozens of people in statistics and data processing who would be overjoyed to see this kind of device before they were given raw data to analyze. The reason is simple: The data shell sets forth the exact relationship you're after. It's a very precise description of the kind of analysis you want the statistician or data processor to perform. From it, the data processor can usually design the analysis program for your data in advance. This can significantly shorten the time required between gathering the data and writing the final report. It can save all parties a lot of frustration.

CHAPTER SUMMARY

So that you do not get lost during the actual data collection, and so you don't jump to conclusions, you should plan your data interpretation. The key step in this planning process is filling in your data shells with the results you expect to get and then analyzing what these results might mean. Doing this will give you a firm perspective on the data and will also permit you to plan the statistical analysis.

SECTION THREE SUMMARY AND THE ANSWERS TO SOME QUESTIONS YOU MAY STILL HAVE

Summary

The logical process of research is to identify the data you need, locate data sources, figure out how to get the data from the source, and plan your interpretation. As you do each of these steps, you think about overall considerations such as reliability, objectivity, measurability, and applicability, as well as cost and the nature of the political situation you're working in.

The process requires some innovative thinking. First, it often requires you to think of indirect measures. Second, it requires you to think of ways to quantify information about people, something which designing data shells can help you do. Third, you often have to make sure of your interpretation by establishing a baseline of expectations; you have to predict results and think about what they will mean before you get too deeply into the actual data collection process.

Answers to Some Questions I Always Get Asked at This Stage

1. Research has to be more complicated than this. There must be more tricks to it!?

   Exactly. I have presented nothing more than a general overview of the research process. As you get into any specific project, you'll need to learn and master specific research techniques. For example, if you conduct interviews, you'll have to learn the dozens of techniques for various interview situations. But as you look at each technique, you'll want to remember to evaluate it on the basis of the general principles in this section. Too often, people master techniques without fully evaluating them from a general research perspective. The bibliography at the end of this book contains references to a number of good books on specific aspects of social and economic research.

2. Don't political considerations affect the nature of the data you collect.

   Yes, but you've already taken care of this problem when you narrowed the focus of the report during assignment analysis and while you were dealing with the needs of various readers. You should actually be able to go out and collect objective information about your subject at this stage—and leave the interpretation to later.

SECTION FOUR

ANALYZING RESULTS

After you've done all this work to plan the research, you go out and get *results*. You get piles, stacks, file cabinets full of results. You fill up computer tapes and endless pages of tables and graphs. *Now, what do you do with all this information?*

The answer to this question has to be fairly general, because the problems of analysis and synthesis of data are too closely related to the nature of the data collected for any one specific rule to apply to all types of data. This section is, then, about the *mental set* you should adopt when dealing with *any* collection of information. The guidelines in it should give you a good mental framework for your analysis.

This section covers the three most important issues you will deal with during your analysis:

1. What results mean and what they don't mean
2. What you can and cannot do with statistics (and guidelines for sampling)
3. The cause–recommendation problem

WHAT RESULTS MEAN AND WHAT THEY DON'T MEAN

12

Politicians stand before audiences and spout statistics as though they had computer printouts in their heads. The newspapers publish "scientific" data as though it alone will solve the world's problems. Management information systems are being created at an alarming rate as managers look to information to solve the problem of plain bigness in government. In recent years, there has come to be a very strong *belief* in data. Because of this, there is more information available about more subjects than at any other time in history. The government knows, for example, who drinks how much coffee and where and when it's consumed. This information hasn't lowered the price, but I suppose it's comforting to know.

Having all this information, we suppose that it provides us with the answers to all our questions. Well, it does and it doesn't. Data about coffee drinkers, age and sex of highschool students, the turnover rate in any given unit of any given agency, and the amount of time children spend watching television after school *is useful*. In many cases, the results of research do provide us with the answers to basic governmental questions. But there are limits to the uses of data, limits that are too frequently ignored. Because of this, it's not unusual for studies to be done over and over and over again. The *office reorganization study* is a good example. It's done about once every 3 years, and over a period of 20 years different researchers play the endless game of finding fault with the previous research. Over a span of 20 years you can usually expect office reorganization research to complete a circle: The structure rejected 20 years ago will suddenly be the solution to all the problems in the office.

PROBLEMS

There are three problems concerning results—two of them are fundamental, one is merely procedural.

The Problem of Problems

Researchers are constantly trying to solve problems. They collect data about the current problem, analyze it, and suggest solutions. Their solutions are put into effect with great fanfare and hope. They fail, or don't succeed nearly as well as they *should have*. Everyone immediately condemns the solution and goes about trying to find a better one. They find it and it, too, fails.

The problem is that problems are inevitable. The world just can't be perfect. People will take a perfect system and make it less than perfect—just for the sake of change.

One of the best examples of this sort of thing occurs every time managers bring in a management analysis team to study the agency and make suggestions (the military is famous for this). This team goes about collecting data and inevitably finds problems. There is *no way they can avoid finding problems*. They collect piles of data about staff complaints. They find inefficiency. And they make recommendations to solve these problems. People get *fired* in these affairs, sometimes justifiably and sometimes not. The problem is that *research almost always proves that something is wrong. It's the researcher's job to interpret this research so that the normal, day-to-day problems aren't treated as if they were major problems.*

The Problem of Prediction

Unless you happen to be interested in results for their own sake, you don't collect data simply because you have nothing else to do. You collect it to provide a basis for decision making. The boss has a decision to make that will affect people; you supply the data that will help the boss make the decision.

The problem is that the data you collect is data about the past. You can't collect data about the future, because the future hasn't happened yet. You can measure past or present attitudes toward a subject, for example, with great accuracy, but this does not mean that you can use these data to *predict* what will happen tomorrow.

In recent years, there have been several good examples of this problem. In 1973, for example, many market predictions were bright and cheery; car sales were going to go up, up, up—they said. The consumer had a bright attitude. Big cars were selling like mad. The economy was going along quite nicely. On the basis of *past* evidence, businesses made billion dollar decisions about production and sales, and government agencies made hiring plans and plans for growth of services. Then the future became the present—and we had the Arab oil embargo and the 400 percent increase in the price of oil. Certainly no one could have predicted the embargo—or could they? If they could have predicted it, no one would have paid any attention, because the *mass* of economic data suggested that the world economy was healthy, and most people just pay attention to masses of data.

On a more common scale, in a normal bureaucratic situation, a training officer once surveyed agency staff to find out how many of them would like to see evening classes in public administration given at the agency. Hundreds replied that they would. Hundreds said they were interested in improving their skills. The program was set up, on the *prediction* that this attitude would be reflected in actual enrollments. The first classes met and were canceled because fewer than ten people came. The place was California; the time was June 1978—right after Proposition 13 (Jarvis–Gann) passed.

The point of this is simple. You're going to make predictions on the basis of the data you've gathered. You have no choice. Just remember that your predictions are subject to all sorts of random, unpredictable influences. *If conditions change, your research may turn out to be worthless.*

The Problem of Too Much Data

In most people's minds, having a lot of data is good. Logically, this has to be true; the more you know, the better your predictions are likely to be. Yet we often find the opposite is true. Most situations in government are very complicated; the more you know, the less you're sure of. The reason this is true is simple. The brain can only handle a finite amount of data at a time. Too much data confuses people; it gets in the way of the thinking process.

One of the best illustrations of this occurs everyday on crowded highways and city streets. After an hour of fighting traffic, most people have to take time to relax before they can get started on working. Their brains are just tired from having to deal with all the information and decisions that driving involves.

SOLUTIONS

To say there are solutions to these problems is a bit too strong a statement. But there are approaches to solving the problems.

The Problem of Problems

The necessary approach to this problem is to establish clear definitions of *significance* during your research and interpretation. For example, suppose you were looking at a supervisor's record, determining how well the supervisor was able to get work done *on schedule*. You're looking at data for 3 years and you find that the supervisor has failed to make deadlines (clearly set deadlines) in 27 percent of the cases you've looked at. The person has had some problems and has made some mistakes. The question is "How good or bad is 27 percent?" It certainly sounds bad; no one likes to fail that often. But it could be a very *good record*. In baseball, for example, it would be an absolutely magnificent record for a batter (a success rate of 73 percent at the plate would be astounding). In other fields, such as flying for an airline, it would be a very poor record. You have to know the context to be able to judge anything.

The data shell can play a big part in establishing a clear context for data. If you have done some careful thinking about what results you *expect* to get and have marked these expected results on the data shell, you'll find interpreting data easier. This often requires you to do some background research, but it's worth it.

For example, there is an old saying among military personnel that if a GI isn't complaining, something's wrong. In other words, the *norm* is for there to be a certain level of complaints. In graphic form, this might look like Figure 12–1. If you conducted a barracks survey to find out what complaints the GI's had about a number of subjects, you might get figures that looked like Figure 12–2. This figure makes things look pretty bad. There are a lot of complaints, particularly about the upper-level officers. But Figure 12–3 shows what the results look like when compared to what you *expected* to get.

FIGURE 12-1/NORMAL LEVEL OF COMPLAINTS

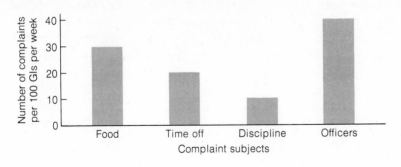

This is a hypothetical example. The data are not valid. The point is important, though. Only if you have a clear idea of what is normally expected, only if you're working with a knowledge that the *norm is imperfection,* can you draw valid conclusions from the data you collect.

The Problem of Prediction

There is no way to *guarantee* that data about the past will truly describe the future. There are some ways of thinking about data that will improve your ability to predict.

1. In general, pay more attention to data that tells you something about basic values or behavior than data about very specific situations. For example, after every political assassi-

FIGURE 12-2/ACTUAL COMPLAINTS

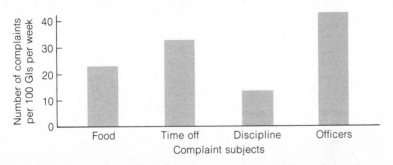

FIGURE 12-3/EXPECTED AND ACTUAL RESULTS TOGETHER

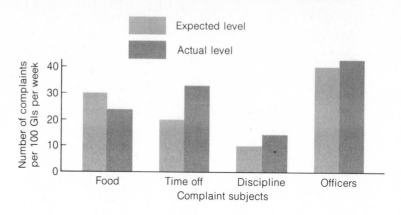

nation in this country, polls are taken that show that people
demand gun control. Three months later, the proposed legislation goes down to defeat in Congress. Why? Because the
polls reflect momentary outrage—not deep feeling. The
people don't want gun control enough to force the issue;
their feelings aren't strong enough. The data collected at
times of crisis just isn't a reliable indicator of real feeling.

2. In general, pay attention to *hard data* rather than to *soft data*
or opinion. On college campuses in the past several years
there has been a major increase in the numbers of *minority
group* students. Many polls have been taken to determine
how *majority* populations feel about these students. In general, the polls have shown that the groups get along reasonably well. In many cases, though, there is highly contradictory evidence, such as student groups formed on the
basis of ethnic or racial identity, separate student newspapers, visible conflicts between minority students and
majority faculty and staff, and a remarkable lack of socializ-
ing between groups. Which evidence do you believe? The
evidence of behavior—not opinion.

3. Look at trends, not individual data points. The data you collect is usually data about a single point in time. The problem
is that single points in time don't tell you anything. If you
can, collect data over a period of time. If you can't, be very
careful about making predictions on data taken over a short
term.

The Problem of Too Much Data

If you want to keep your head clear, you have to put the data somewhere else. If you want to be able to make sense out of data, you have to put it somewhere organized. The data shell provides you with a place to put all the data you collect. Here's an example of how the data shell, the graphic form, makes sense out of a mass of data.

In an audit of a check disbursing agency, an auditor found the following information about missing checks and put this information into a neat list:

1. July 17, 1967, two checks (2390-15, 2390-65)
2. January 15, 1967, one check (2080-22)
3. June 16, 1967, one check (2280-16)
4. September 14, 1967, two checks (2750-36, 2750-90)
5. April 12, 1967, one check (2110-25)
6. October 14, 1967, two checks (2950-13, 2960-17)
7. February 15, 1967, one check (2100-10)
8. May 12, 1967, one check (2210-37)
9. August 17, 1967, two checks (2550-13, 2550-17)
10. December 20, 1967, twelve checks (3126-17—3216-28)
11. November 15, 1967, three checks (3014-16, 3014-18, 3015-20)

Putting the data in the form of a graph, as shown in Figure 12–4, reveals something interesting. The data shell provides a structure for all the data and reveals a trend toward more and more checks disappearing! The list didn't show this.

FIGURE 12-4/CHECKS MISSING

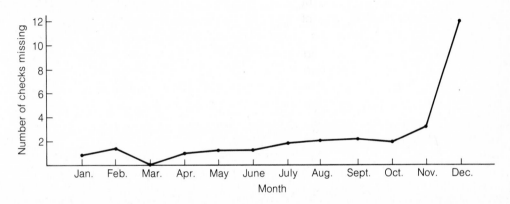

EXAMPLE

A management consultant took a very sophisticated survey of the management and staff of a large state agency to determine whether the managers were giving staff an adequate opportunity to participate in management decisions. The survey was designed to show two things: how staff presently viewed the management style of the agency and what they would *prefer*. Staff were asked a number of questions about how they were involved in management decisions, how they communicated with management, and how they felt the organization should be run.

The results were rather complicated in raw data form, so they were tabulated in a complex comparison, as shown in Figure 12–5. Looking at these *profiles*, as they are called, it is easy to come to the conclusion that staff would like to be more deeply involved in the management decision-making process, that they would like communication in the office to be more open, and that they often dis-

FIGURE 12-5/A PROFILE OF STAFF PARTICIPATION AND DESIRED PARTICIPATION IN SELECTED MANAGEMENT FUNCTIONS

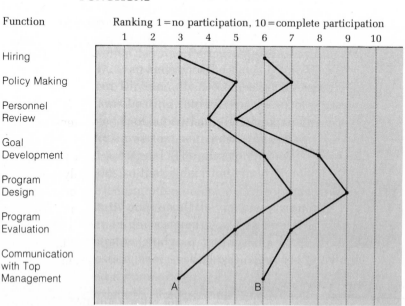

The Gap between Line A and line B indicates the difference between where staff feel they now are (line A) and where they would like to be (line B)

agreed with management on matters of policy. You could quite easily draw these conclusions and begin to make recommendations for office reorganization. You might even change some managers.

A more cautious look at these figures might produce different conclusions and different recommendations. First, if you think about the *normal* problems you expect to find in such a survey, the results don't look all that bad. I've seen at least a dozen such surveys and I've never seen one that didn't indicate that staff wanted to play a greater role in management decisions. If the gap between the present situation and the desired situation were really *broad*, I'd pay attention to the data. If not, I'd be cautious before overturning a functional office.

The second caution I'd advise here is simply that some hard data should be gathered to confirm these findings. You could, for example, try a simple experiment. Bring several people, or a whole group, into the management process. Let them spend a few hours after work on a no-pay basis. Let them take some decisions home to think about for a week. Let them make or help make a few hiring and firing decisions. You might find that they did well, and that they really did want to be a part of management. You might confirm the survey results. Then again, you might not.

Finally, I would examine the overall history of management in the agency by looking at minutes of policy meetings, previous reports on management, etc. I'd see what other results from other studies indicated. If there seemed to be a long-term desire to participate in management decision making, then I would add this finding to the current one and start to move in that direction. However, if I found evidence that staff had previously complained about not getting enough direction from the top, or that general meetings between management and staff were poorly participated in, I'd tend to question the *new* data.

The point of this example is not to suggest that a manager or researcher should not pay attention to results. It is merely to suggest that the results of a study must be dealt with in the context of the general trends in society and in the agency. No decision should be made on the basis of data collected during a single study alone. The data from a study must be weighed carefully along with the data from other studies, along with good managerial judgment.

NOTES TO MANAGEMENT AND STAFF

In trying to arrive at a valid interpretation of data, it's important not to take either a management or a staff perspective. For example, after finding that there is inefficiency in office operations, it's important for managers not to merely resolve to crack the whip a bit harder. It's equally important that staff don't immediately start to place blame on lack of direction. A lot of this sort of self-serving interpretation goes on, with management and staff both looking at data merely to support a predefined position. What's really needed is a lowering of ego profiles and a complete and objective view of the data. Both manager and staff ultimately benefit from the research being looked at from as broad a perspective as possible.

To Management

Keeping a study in perspective is one of the primary responsibilities of managers. The staff involved in research will almost always have a tendency to get wrapped up in the details of what they're doing. Even the best researcher will do this. The manager has to take steps to remind research staff not to get so involved in the particulars of their study that they forget the rest of history and the rest of the world.

One way to *help* staff keep a reasonable, broad, perspective on the research effort and on the data collected is to assign at least one *generalist* to each effort. If you're doing a study of public reaction to a new regulation, for example, don't select a staff of lawyers and sociologists only. Put someone with a background in some wholly unrelated field onto the the project—a person with a mathematics background, a biologist, or an auditor or an ex-English major. Balance the research team if you can. A crew of ten experts in the field will likely forget to establish and maintain a sense of context.

To Staff

It is no discredit to your ability that management needs to help you keep a broad sense of context. The reason it's necessary is simply because anyone capable of good research is also capable of intense concentration; you just can't do research if you don't have this ability. It gets you through the long process of brainstorming and designing the research, it carries you through the days of collecting data, and it then betrays you at the end—unless you do something deliberately to break it. You really do need to stop everything, take a deep breath, and start the whole interpretation process with "Well, let's take a look at what we have found out—as if we were looking at it as outsiders." One of the functions of a consultant is to provide this sort of outside view, to restore overall perspective to the research. It's a role I've had to play often in taking a rough report and making it into a polished effort.

You don't need a consultant, though, if you select one member of your research group, or find someone in the office who knows nothing of the project, to take a consultant's role at the end of the research project—during interpretation of results. This person can ask all the simple, general, questions that have to be re-asked after the intense effort to collect data is over.

Whether you get someone else to help you maintain perspective while you're interpreting results or not, you can help yourself if you do two simple things. First, always make sure you give a complete picture of your results to the people you're working for:

To Staff *(continued)*

Incomplete:	"We found 15 cases of possible fraud in the operations of _____ Division."
Complete:	"Out of 7890 cases surveyed, we found 15 cases of possible fraud in the operations of _____ Division."

Always present your facts in the context of the overall research effort. In this way, you can permit the readers (the users) to draw valid conclusions. You maintain objectivity this way.

Second, when you're getting ready to pull your research together into a report, look over your notes and mark each item in them with either *fact* or *opinion*. Just skim down the pages of rough notes or outline and make this distinction clearly in the margin. Then when you get into writing, you won't get carried away with your argument and discussion; you won't lose sight of where you stand on firm ground and where you are on quicksand. You separate objective research and subjective politics in this way.

The validity of your interpretation depends so much on taking steps such as these that you ought to schedule them as a formal part of your research effort.

CHAPTER SUMMARY

Data must be interpreted within the context of the general situation that caused the need to collect it. Having great quantities of data isn't the end of the research. The data must still be interpreted. There are three good rules to remember during this interpretation process:

1. *The natural state of things is to be imperfect. Make sure the problem you've decided to solve is really a problem.*
2. *The past is the past. Use data about the past to predict the future very carefully.*
3. *Don't try to interpret great quantities of data until you have expressed the relationships among the data graphically (or mathematically, if you are so inclined).*

WHAT YOU CAN AND CANNOT DO WITH STATISTICS (AND GUIDELINES FOR SAMPLING)

13

To be accurate in your interpretations of data, you have to make sure that the data are significant, that the problems you've uncovered aren't just the result of normal human imperfection or that the results aren't merely due to some accident. You use statistical analytical methods to do this.

There are a number of general uses for statistical analysis. In many cases, you will have two sets of numbers—different numbers—and will want to find out if the differences are *significant*. In other cases, you'll notice that when one thing changes, another thing changes; you may wish to know whether there is some valid connection between these two things. In other cases, you may have collected data and you may simply want to know if what you have is the result of chance or the result of something else. You can get *approximate* answers to these questions through various statistical tests.

Statistical analysis is often confusing in its details. There are numerous ways to test results in order to discover connections among items or to show significant differences between items. You need about a year of statistical training and practice before the mystery of all the methods is gone. But you don't need a year to gain a basic understanding of what statistical analysis is all about and when it is and is not useful. This basic understanding is what this chapter is about. For texts covering the details of statistical tests, see the bibliography at the end of this book.

Statistical analysis is based on a simple assumption—that unless something acts to influence events, they are governed by chance. Chance can be dealt with numerically; if you know all the possible events, you can figure out how often each event will occur—*on the average.* For example, there are only two possible events that can occur when you flip a two-sided coin—heads or tails. Since there is nothing about the coin that can influence the result, you can *predict* that when you toss the coin you'll get heads 50 percent of the time and tails 50 percent of the time—on the average. Knowing this, suppose you threw tails ten times in a row. You would suspect that something was influencing the events, that somehow your toss was making the coins come out all tails. You would *suspect* this; the statistician would give you an estimate of whether your suspicion was valid or not. The statistician could never say for sure that something had influenced the results; the statistician could only say that it was likely that the ten tails in a row were *not* due to chance.

Statistical analysis is, then, the practice of giving a numerical value to our suspicions about whether things have happened by chance or because someone or something *made* them happen. *All the statistician can do is make a vague suspicion into a numerical probability.* Because statistics are misused so often, it's a good idea to imprint this simple rule on your mind:

YOU CANNOT PROVE OR CONFIRM ANYTHING STATISTICALLY; YOU CAN ONLY GIVE A NUMERICAL VALUE TO YOUR SUSPICIONS THAT SOMETHING OTHER THAN CHANCE IS RESPONSIBLE FOR YOUR RESULTS.

PROBLEMS

A number of general problems must be dealt with whenever you do *any* form of statistical analysis, from the simplest form of averages to the most complex multivariate analyses.

The Problem of the Unknown

The basic assumption behind statistical analysis is that you can identify possible influences on your results—all of them. You must be able to do this or else you can't calculate the numerical influence of any one factor. For example, in criminal behavior studies, researchers have found that there is a probable connection between coming from a broken home and juvenile delinquency. They say that more children from broken homes become juvenile delinquents than do children from stable families. But, there are numerous exceptions to this rule—and there is no good explanation of why there are so many exceptions. What this means is that there are other unidentified factors that influence the end result—delinquency. Until these factors are identified, the conclusion about "broken homes leading to delinquency" isn't valid enough to take action.

In short, when you're analyzing a situation, an event, you must make sure that you have identified all parts of the event and all factors contributing to the event before you make any conclusions on the basis of statistical analysis.

The Problem of Poor Data

The most exquisite analysis is absolutely useless if the data it is used on are "bad" in any way. If the collection method has biased the data or if the data don't really represent the event being analyzed, then the analysis is worthless.

For example, in an audit of a state agency not long ago, the auditor found that every cash transaction checked was handled perfectly, absolutely according to regulations. He checked with a statistician to determine whether his sampling method was correct from a statistical point of view. It was. He didn't even need a statistical analysis to say that this was a significant finding: The odds against things being perfect are astounding. But he was also wrong. He had announced his audit by telephone two days before he arrived at the office. The office responded to this announcement by preparing a set of perfect records and hiding all the mistakes. The statistician should have smelled a rat when everything came out so perfectly; it's statistically unlikely that this will happen.

In short, if your research methods aren't good, the results you get shouldn't be subjected to analysis—statistically or otherwise.

The Problem of Small Numbers

If you toss a coin *once*, you cannot hope to be able to analyze the results statistically. Your result will be a 100 percent result—either a head or a tail. You won't be able to say whether or not you've done anything to influence the result because the probability of getting a 100 percent result is absolute. If, however, you toss the coin 100,000 times and still get a 100 percent result (100,000 heads or 100,000 tails), you can analyze the probability that you've done something to influence the result.

In dealing with statistics, you have to have a fairly large number of *events* to compare before you can start to make any probability statements. Very often in research, you won't have an opportunity to collect information about enough events to be able to use any form of statistical analysis. For example, suppose you're a personnel officer. You've been asked to look into the case of an employee who has been dismissed because he has been rude to three people who have called the office. The three people happen to be aides to members of Congress. Of course, it was mere chance that these three callers were powerful people—you can't hold that against the employee. What you have to do is determine whether this rudeness is (1) normal for the person, (2) excessive in terms of what other employees are doing, and (3) not the result of some outside influence. With only three cases to deal with, there is no way you can find out these things. You cannot, for example, say that this is a pattern of behavior; nor can you say that it isn't a pattern. You just have to ignore these statistical conclusions or get more data.

In short, you can't analyze unless you have an adequate number of cases. What's adequate? This depends on what you're trying to do with the numbers and on how confident you want to be in drawing conclusions from the numbers. Determining what's adequate is what you do when you and the office statistician sit down before research and analyze your data shells.

The Problem of Chance

In a class on research methods, I once tossed a coin 100 times to prove a point about statistics. I got:

66 heads   34 tails

Nearly everyone in the class recognized that the difference between these numbers and a 50–50 chance was *significant*, even without doing any statistical analysis. They also drew the conclusion that I had somehow influenced the results. I objected to this because:

1. I had tossed the coin in a number of different ways—even just throwing it against the wall.
2. It was a new coin and therefore not worn out on one side or another.
3. I'm not dextrous enough to cheat.

The class insisted that something had happened to influence the results. I insisted that it was simply chance.

We have, as a people, become so fascinated by statistics that we have forgotten something important about life—it's a very chancy affair. Individual events are not governed by statistical probability. Things often happen by chance. Over the long run, and on the average, you can expect statistical probabilities to hold up. In any individual case, they may not.

This point needs to be stressed because in the United States many people seem to have lost all sense of chance—the accidental. If something goes wrong, they immediately look for someone to sue, to blame. They assume that something has influenced the event. They assume that there is something behind every action affecting their lives.

A common example of this feeling occurs everyday in offices around the country—when promotions are handed out. People work very hard to impress their superiors; they stay late at work, they try to speak out at meetings, they try to get their work done well. Then, they expect the boss to promote on the basis of a careful analysis of their work. When they don't get promoted, they get very upset (understandably). They may go through months of soul searching trying to figure out why someone else was chosen. There are often good reasons for these decisions. But often, when it comes down to two pretty good people, it's just luck. I even know of cases where it's been *pure luck*—the promotion was decided on the basis of a coin toss.

In short, it's a good idea to remember that while a statistician can tell you that something probably happened because of something else, the statistician cannot and will not rule out *chance* as the cause of the event.

SOLUTIONS

There are no solutions to these problems, except to remember that they are problems and to take some actions to avoid them. The specific things you can do include:

1. Plan your analysis before you get the data. Sit down with a statistician before you start to collect the data, explain what you are planning, what data you plan to collect, and what you intend to show with the data. The statistician can then suggest how to set up the research to ensure reasonable reliability and that you have enough data to be able to analyze it statistically.

2. Always make sure that the data you collect can be expressed in very precise numerical terms. There is no way a statistician can judge the significance of figures if the figures represent something vague, such as opinions or values. The statistician cannot work with data that can't be dealt with in clearly defined numerical terms.

3. Do not estimate. When you're taking data, measure as accurately as possible.

4. When in doubt, don't rely on statistical analysis. If you are even vaguely concerned that your data aren't good, don't resort to the statistician to make something out of nothing. There are many ways to misuse statistical analysis—don't do it.

EXAMPLE

The United States economy provides a good example of the misuse of statistical analysis. In analyzing economic trends, economists have found a very significant relationship between increases in interest rates and decreases in economic activity and inflationary pressure on the market. This relationship has been studied over a long period of time, in great detail, and by a number of observers who have differing biases on the subject.

On the basis of this statistical correlation between high interest rates and a slowing of inflation, some very high level policies are put into effect whenever there is an inflationary period. The Federal Reserve Board tightens credit, interest rates go up, and the amount of money available to consumers of goods goes down. This brings prices down—according to the law of supply and demand.

In the years following the 1974 Arab oil embargo, this tactic was used extensively to combat the inflation caused by rising oil prices. It failed. It failed for a number of reasons. The analysis shows a correlation between interest rates and prices, but it does not account for the factors that influence prices directly. These factors are, in some cases, simply unknown. Others were not taken into account when the correlation was first established. There certainly was no way of taking a monopolistic oil cartel's arbitrary pricing increase into account when the statistical correlation was established. So, the data base for the correlation has changed, but the analysts have not taken this into account. The correlation is thus no longer a valid one, and the increasing inflation of the mid- and late 1970s (in the face of high interest rates) was the result.

The reason for this error is simply that the people making the decisions forgot that the statistician does not make *laws*. Every bit of statistical analysis is subject to change as the conditions change. The Arab oil embargo was a chance occurrence that was not predicted or predictable by any form of statistical analysis.

NOTES TO MANAGEMENT AND STAFF

To Management

I'm not really suggesting that you fire the agency statistical staff or throw away your computer. I am suggesting that you treat these people as you would any other group of experts. Listen to what they have to say, but remember that they're only able to help you improve your chances of *guessing right* in any situation.

To Staff

I can think of no more important advice to give at this point than to suggest again that you plan your statistical analysis before you collect data. Every computer programmer and statistician that I've worked with over a period of 6 years has made this suggestion. Doing this will save you an immense amount of time and trouble.

CHAPTER SUMMARY

The function of statistical analysis is to give you a numerical way of turning a guess or suspicion into a statement of probability. There are no such things as statistical laws. It's all just a way of improving your ability to see relationships in data and to draw conclusions from the data.

APPENDIX

GUIDELINES FOR SAMPLING

With all the problems involved gathering data and analyzing it, your research effort becomes less a search for absolute truth than a search for indications that if you make one decision the results will be generally positive and if you make another decision the results will be less positive—or even negative. Even the best-designed research cannot ensure absolute reliability. Without research, the decision maker may have about a 50–50 chance of making the right decision. With research, the chance can be improved to 60–40 or even 90–10. Of course, if the research is not reliable, the chance may actually be reversed.

Sampling is a part of the research game, a part that can cut the cost of research without significantly altering the reliability. It can help you limit the amount of data you have to collect to get a reasonably good answer.

The game of sampling is really quite simple. Suppose you wanted to find out how many unemployment insurance claims had been improperly calculated in a particular state over a period of two years. Unless you already had all the data in a computer storage facility, it would take you a decade or so to sort through the millions of claims involved to find out *exactly* how many were miscalculated. If you were willing to take a *close estimate,* you could *sample,* that is, look at a *representative number of claims.* Your final calculation of the total number of improperly calculated claims would look like this:

$$\frac{\text{Number of claims sampled}}{\text{Total number of claims}^{\cdot}} = \frac{\text{Number of improper claims found}}{\text{Total number of improper claims}}$$

Knowing three of the elements of this equation, you can easily calculate the fourth—Total number of improper claims.

The game of sampling begins with a simple, analytical step. To start, you have to know *how good an estimate is necessary for your purpose.* Do you have to be within 1 percent of the actual? Will 10 or 20 percent do as well? The answer to the question is essential. It will tell you how large a sample you'll have to take.

The presidential election polls provide a good example of why this first question is so important. Before the pollsters take a sample, they *guess* what the outcome is likely to be (or they take a quick, small sample). If they think that the election is going to be very close, they take a fairly large sample. If they think the election is a shoe-in for a candidate, they take a small sample; if they're off by 5 percent in an election that's going to end up 64 percent to 36 percent, they aren't really concerned. The same margin of error in a close election would be intolerable. If it looks like the race is going to be very, very close (say 50.5 percent to 49.5 percent), they may even decide that a sample isn't worth the effort. They may just wait until election day. This is what the networks mean when they say a race is "too close to call."

Once you have established the degree of precision with which you want to estimate, you have a number of things to consider before you can select a sample number and a sampling method.

1. *The size of the universe being measured.* The universe is the total number of things you're dealing with—all the claims filed for unemployment insurance, or whatever. The smaller the universe is, the less reliable a sample will be. For example, suppose you wanted to find out why people drive the cars they do, and you further narrowed this down to a question about why some people drive exotic cars such as Porsches and other people drive more ordinary cars such as standard-sized American sedans. You cannot interview all the car owners—it would take centuries. You must sample. But you have two completely different universes. The number of Porsche drivers is rather limited; the number of standard sedan drivers is very large. If you took the same *percentage* sample of each group, you might end up with the following sample sizes:

	Universe size	Percentage	Sample size
Porsche drivers	75,000	0.5	375
Sedan drivers	30,000,000	0.5	60,000

Clearly, you need to sample more of the Porsche drivers to reach a representative number; the chance of getting a high proportion of "oddballs" in a sample as small as 375 is pretty high. But you would not need to sample as many as 0.5 percent of the sedan drivers in order to get a representative sample.

The reason for the larger *proportionate* sample for the smaller universe is that the smaller the universe, the more likely it is that its elements are not randomly distributed. For example, toss a coin 100 times and record your results at 1 toss, 2 tosses, 10 tosses, 50 tosses, and 100 tosses. Here are the results of one such set of tosses:

	Heads	Tails	Percentage of heads	Percentage of tails
1 toss	1	0	100	0
2 tosses	1	1	50	50
10 tosses	4	6	40	60
50 tosses	24	26	48	52
100 tosses	51	49	51	49

As you go through the tossing process, you'll notice runs of heads and tails—short periods in which you'll toss three or four heads or tails in a row. But over the long run, you see a more random distribution.

Just as importantly, you may have noticed that for 1 toss there is no chance of random distribution. For 2 tosses you have an almost equal chance of throwing two heads or two tails as you have of throwing a head and a tail. The larger the universe, the more likely its elements are to be distributed randomly. Because of this, it is almost impossible to sample small groups successfully. If, for example, you wanted to find out how many Americans were born on July 4, a universe of all people working in your office wouldn't be big enough to ensure your finding a representative sample.

2. *The randomness of the universe.* Before you can sample any universe, you have to establish that the elements of it are, indeed, randomly distributed throughout the universe—that there are no groupings. You have to make sure the deck isn't *stacked.* For example, in sampling unemployment insurance claims, you might find that the claims were not randomly distributed within the file cabinets; they might be filed in

order of value, or in order of date and then in order of value. If, then, you took the one-hundredth claim, then the two-hundredth, then the three-hundredth, and so forth, you might very well select claims that did not actually represent the universe. You might get all claims over $100 or all under $100. In short, before you sample, you have to make sure the deck you're working with has not been stacked—that it's shuffled.

3. *The randomness of the sampling.* Before you actually start taking a sample, you want to make sure that you aren't going to do anything to bias it by your collection method. The problem here is that what most people think of as *random*, really isn't. Closing your eyes and reaching into a file cabinet isn't random enough; in fact, it can prove to be quite biased. Without knowing that you're doing it, you will tend to select files from the same part of the file cabinet—and this could bias your results. True random sampling must be achieved mathematically. An effort must be made to ensure that every item in the universe has exactly the same chance of being selected as every other item. This can get quite complicated. Suppose, for example, you were drawing names from a fishbowl. You are going to select 500 names out of 5000. The first name you select will have exactly one chance in 5000 to be selected. The second, though, will have a better chance—one in 4999. The chances slowly improve so that pretty soon the chance is one in 4501, about a 10 percent improvement. To avoid this, you have to put the already chosen names back in the fishbowl, so that every time you choose, you're taking one out of 5000.

   The business of keeping your sampling procedure random can be handled with a computer programmed to generate a random set of numbers, or with any large enough random number table (often found in the back of technical books on statistics). See the bibliography at the end of this book for several sources of random number tables.

Sampling Procedure

With these things in mind, you can design a sampling procedure fairly easily by using the following steps:

1. Determine how accurate you need to be. Decide what your margin of error can be before the results cease to suit your purpose. Do you want to be within 1 percent or 30 percent?

2. Determine the approximate size of your universe. You can deal in approximations as long as the universe is fairly large; a universe of 100,000 isn't really much different from a universe of 200,000. At lower levels, precision may be quite important. The difference between a universe of forty and one of eighty is significant.

3. Decide how precise you want to be. Precision is different from accuracy. Precision involves thoughts about how closely you want to measure something. Accuracy involves thoughts about how sure you want to be of your measurement. You can measure a table top, for example, with great precision, reading your ruler down to thirty-seconds of an inch. Your measurement may not be accurate, though, if the ruler is no good. In sampling, precision boils down to a simple question of whether or not your sample size is large enough so that if you repreated the sample over and over again, you'd always get the same result (plus or minus some factor). Decide how big a plus or minus factor you're willing to put up with.

4. On the basis of these three items, calculate your sample size, or get sample size from a table. The actual calculation is complex enough to be beyond the scope of this book. See Herbert Arkin's *A Handbook of Sampling for Auditing and Accounting* (McGraw-Hill Book Company, New York, 1974) for sample size tables, or see your office statistician.

5. Assign a number to all individuals in the universe. You don't have to do this in writing, just find out how many items are in the universe and give each a hypothetical number. Make sure, though, that you assign these numbers in the sequence in which you'll encounter the items.

6. From the random number table (in Arkin and other references listed in the bibliography at the end of this book), take as many random numbers as your sample size permits. Assign these numbers to various items in your universe. These are the items you will look at.

7. Pull the items you're going to sample and examine them.

EXAMPLE

Suppose you are trying to determine the extent of fraud in welfare payments in your city. First, for your purpose, you do not need to find every case; you only want a reasonable estimate so that you can discuss the effect of fraud on city expenses. You decide you're willing to be within 10 percent. Second, you find that you have a total universe of 3.5 million welfare payments during the year in question; they are filed according to the time at which they were processed. Third, you decide you'd like to be reasonably confident that your sample was accurate. You decide that you'd like a 95 percent chance of being able to get the same result if you repeated the sample with different items selected. Fourth, you go to the tables and find that you need to sample about 520 payments. Next, you set up a sequence for sampling; you number the 3.5 million payments from 1 to 3,500,000. You wouldn't actually mark the numbers, but as you went through your sample, you'd count your way through. Sound awful? Then you would have to find another, more convenient numbering system, perhaps selecting items by day of issue. Once you had a convenient numbering system that would allow you to work your way through the items, you would then go to a random number table, take the first 520 numbers from it, and select the items in the universe with the corresponding numbers. You would examine these payments.

NOTES TO MANAGEMENT AND STAFF

To Both

This brief section is really intended as an introduction to sampling. It should give you a reasonable sense of what sampling is all about, so that the technical details are easier to follow. Some things to remember about sampling:

1. It reduces the precision of the data collected. It thus adds a known factor of uncertainty to the data collection process.
2. It must be carried out in a random fashion unless you have a great deal of money to spend on establishing a representative sampling program based on population characteristics (such as those used by some pollsters).

14

THE CAUSE-RECOMMENDATION PROBLEM

Reports are written to help people make decisions. Very frequently they're written to help people solve problems. Thus, most reports involve some form of recommendation. This part of the report is one of the most difficult to handle, and one of the portions people spend the least time on. Recommendations often get added to almost as afterthoughts, not as important portions of the report. And yet, this is what the whole report leads up to.

At the end of the report the reader wants the researcher to answer three simple questions:

1. What does all the data mean?
2. What caused this to happen?
3. If it's bad, what can we do about it?

If you spend 3 months gathering information about a situation and then only spend 3 hours deciding what to do about it, you've really let your reader down—as much as if you had collected the wrong data in the first place.

PROBLEMS

Before you can make a worthwhile recommendation, you have to know the cause of the problem you're dealing with. The recommendation must eliminate the cause, or else 3 years later someone will be doing your study all over again.

Making a recommendation without knowing the real cause of the problem is something that happens so frequently in everyday life that many people have begun to find it hard to distinguish between *cause* and *blame*. For example, when a baseball team has a really bad season, sportswriters, fans, and owners often call for the team's manager to be fired. After all, they reason, the boss is always responsible for poor performance. True, but the boss isn't always the *cause* of the poor performance. Unless this cause is dealt with, nothing will change. Replacing the manager on a team with no pitching will get you nothing more than a new manager on a team with no pitching—the team will still lose.

This same sort of recommendation is often made in administrative research efforts. A study team will find that the staff of an agency have a lot of complaints about the work, and they'll recommend that the director of the agency be replaced. But a pep talk can't solve the problems of long hours, boring work, too much paperwork, etc. In short, the recommendation made is an attempt to solve the problem without dealing with the *cause* of the problem.

Determining the cause of anything is, of course, very difficult. That's why it's so easy to simply place blame and make a quick recommendation. Sports provide another good example of this. When a team wins, sportswriters frequently spend hours talking about the *key* play in the game. They look for and find *turning points*. The cause of the victory, they say, is this one key play. In most cases this is just so much hogwash. You don't win a game on the basis of one play. You win because you're a better team; your players play consistently better than the other players and thus they don't allow the other team any *key plays*.

The same sort of *causes* are often found by researchers who simply haven't bothered to go through a thorough analysis of cause. For example, when a group of employees was found to score differently on written and oral portions of a promotional test, researchers concluded in a report that the people giving the oral test were trying to raise the scores of those who had done poorly on the written test. Here are the test scores they were working with:

Employee	Written test score	Oral test score	Total score
1	60	37	97
2	58	38	96
3	60	29	89
4	60	27	87
5	55	27	82
6	40	40	80
7	38	40	78
8	39	39	78
9	37	40	77
10	30	25	55

There are some interesting differences in scores here. The oral scores do not appear to be consistent with the written scores. But this does not mean that there was any deliberate action taken to raise scores of those who had done poorly on the written test. In fact, there are a number of possible causes for the data:

1. The written and oral tests could have been tests of different kinds of skills.
2. The employees who took the tests could have different abilities to take different kinds of tests.
3. One of the tests could have been invalid.
4. Both tests could be invalid.
5. Oral test results could have been deliberately inflated to make those who did poorly on the written test feel better.
6. The employees who failed the written test could have tried harder on the oral test; employees who did well on the written test could have gotten complacent.
7. The results could have been the result of mere chance.
8. The results could reflect the real abilities of those taking the tests.
9. The employees could have faked the results in order to get the tests thrown out by the research team.

Some of these possible causes are a bit far-fetched. Others are as logical as the conclusion drawn by the original research team. Which is the true cause? There is no way to tell, because the research team just jumped to a conclusion and never bothered to find out.

Establishing cause is also difficult because there are many cases in which there isn't just one cause to a problem. The results above could very well have been caused by any combination of the nine possible causes listed. Some of the employees who scored high on the written test could have gotten complacent and thus scored low on the oral test. Some of those who did poorly on the written test could have tried harder on the oral test. In one or two cases, the oral examiners could have raised the score to make the employees feel better. Any or all of these things could have occurred in any combination to produce the results shown. Figuring out the exact combination would be quite difficult. But no recommendation can be made until this has been done.

Another reason why cause is difficult to establish is that some problems don't have any cause except chance. This is, of course, extremely difficult to accept, and it's pretty difficult to justify to a boss who's looking for some way of solving the problem. You will find it hard to say "The solution to this problem is for us to be lucky next time." The reason for this is that people are always dissatisfied with chance as a reason for anything. When there's an automobile accident and someone gets hurt, the immediate response is "Why me?"—as if there had to be a reason. If a doctor happens to have to sneeze during an operation and someone dies because of it, the same question gets asked. But who can say what caused the doctor to have to sneeze at just that moment? It's just a random, chance thing. No recommendation will ever eliminate the chance that it could happen again, because there's no cause to eliminate.

The final major difficulty in establishing a cause is that it's often quite difficult to distinguish between *cause* and *excuse*. Parents know this better than anyone else. You ask your child, "Why did you hit Jimmy?" and you get the excuse "'Cause he hit me first." That's not the cause, though. The cause is deeper, and you may have to do some lengthy questioning to get to it.

Since so much of government work involves dealing with people, it's extremely important to sort out excuses from causes. Here are some examples of what you may end up with if you do this thoughtfully:

Excuse	*Cause* (possible causes)
I didn't see the light, officer	The light wasn't visible. The driver wasn't looking.
I didn't have time.	I didn't place a high enough priority on this to make time to do it.

Excuse (continued)	*Cause (continued)*
The program is ahead of its time.	We haven't convinced anyone that the program is worthwhile. The program isn't popular. The program doesn't do what it's supposed to do. No one cares about doing what the program was set up to do.
I got stuck in traffic.	I didn't bother to leave enough time to allow for traffic.
The program is doomed.	I haven't got the guts to fight the governor (boss) on this issue.
The boss doesn't like me.	The boss doesn't like you. You aren't good at the job.

Excuses are offered so frequently to hide a real cause that it's quite difficult to distinguish one from the other unless you make a real effort to do so.

SOLUTIONS

The only solution to this problem is to adopt a very cautious and systematic approach to establishing cause. You can avoid the problem of jumping to conclusions by establishing a mental procedure for this portion of your interpretation.

> *Step 1:* Identify all the possible causes for the data you have collected. Spend considerable time on this step. Make a formal list.
>
> *Step 2:* Don't try to prove one cause. Instead, work to eliminate causes. The rule is: *eliminate the impossible, and whatever remains must be the truth—no matter how strange it may seem.*
>
> *Step 3:* If you can, test your conclusion about cause. You can do this mentally by repeatedly asking yourself the question: "What caused this cause?" In doing this, you will force yourself to avoid excuses.

EXAMPLE

In an audit of a state government office, an auditor once found that forty checks, worth up to $200 each, were missing from the drawer of the clerk responsible for them. After a complete check to make sure that she was correct about the checks being gone, the auditor tried to determine the cause and make recommendations so this problem couldn't happen again.

The list of causes she developed follows, along with the results of her analysis of whether the possible cause was indeed possible:

Cause	Analysis
1. Checks were stolen by an outsider.	1. Impossible. Office locked at night. Desk locked at night. No break-in evidence. And no evidence that any of the checks had been cashed.
2. Checks were stolen by staff.	2. Not possible. Desk clearly visible to all in office. Desk locked during day.
3. Checks were given out but not recorded.	3. No checks cashed, so this isn't possible.
4. Checks weren't in the shipment in the first place.	4. Impossible. Records signed by four people indicate these checks were in the shipment.
5. Clerk stole checks.	5. Impossible. No checks cashed, and date for cashing has expired.
6. Clerk lost checks.	6. Possible, if checks fell into trash can just below drawer in which checks were stored. Check could then have gone out with the trash.

After considering several other possible causes, the auditor concluded that the checks had fallen into the trash and been disposed of harmlessly. Next, she turned to the problem of writing a recommendation. Could the recommendation possibly be "Don't drop checks into trash," or "Move trash can"? No supervisor would accept such a recommendation, because it just wouldn't eliminate the cause. "They fell into the trash can" is the excuse for the missing checks. A little retrospective questioning leads to some interesting conclusions about the real cause.

Question	*Answer*
1. How did the checks end up missing?	1. They fell into the trash and were taken out in the evening.
2. Why was this allowed to happen?	2. No one noticed that they were gone.
3. Why didn't someone notice?	3. Because they were not paying attention.
4. Why weren't they paying attention?	4. The clerk in charge of the checks doesn't have a *balancing* or *cashing out* procedure that forces him to pay attention.
5. Why don't they have such a logical procedure? Every business does.	5. The office closes at 4:30 P.M., at the same time the other clerks close check disbursement windows. The undisbursed checks are returned to the central storage area at that time. Everyone goes home at 4:30, so the checks aren't balanced until the next day. Thus, the loss was not noticed until the next morning when it was too late to do anything.
6. Why doesn't the clerk stay after hours to balance everything?	6. No overtime is authorized.
7. Why isn't overtime authorized for this one person?	7. It's a bad neighborhood and keeping one person late might result in danger to that person.
8. Oh, then why don't you close office windows a bit early so that there's still time for balancing accounts?	8. "I never thought of that."

Recommendation: Close all check disbursement windows except one so that the control clerk has plenty of time to cash out at the end of each day. Make sure at least one or two other employees stays with this person if the cashing out runs late. Allow these employees to come in a little late the next morning to avoid having to pay over-time.

Note in this very simple example how the questioning process almost automatically leads to the recommendation. Note how the answers to the questions begin to get more specific as the questioning proceeds. The excuses are soon eliminated and the causes begin to be explored.

NOTES TO MANAGEMENT AND STAFF

To Management

The quality of your solution to a problem depends on how carefully staff have worked to search out the cause. You can help staff do this by insisting that they *budget research time* for it. In the research plan, make sure that there is time for interpreting, as well as gathering, data. Make sure that staff take this on as a formal task—with meeting times and the whole works.

To Staff

If you go back to the lists of reader questions in Chapter 5, you'll find that many of these questions involve cause and recommendations for dealing with cause. You know well in advance of the research effort that these are questions you're going to have to answer. And, since the object of anticipating the readers' questions is to help you plan your research effort, *you should consider the process of finding cause and making recommendations to solve the problem a part of the research effort—not just something you do at the end*. You should thus be prepared to do some research to answer these questions about cause and what to do about cause(s) you find.

CHAPTER SUMMMARY

Establishing the cause of a problem is essential to making a useful recommendation to solve the problem. To make sure you have thoroughly analyzed your data to establish cause, follow a rigid procedure when you're thinking about cause. Start by identifying all possible causes. Next, eliminate causes that are impossible. Finally, make sure that what's left over isn't mere excuse by asking yourself (or someone else) why this happened.

SECTION FOUR SUMMARY AND THE ANSWERS TO SOME QUESTIONS YOU MAY STILL HAVE

Summary

It is important to plan your interpretation, just as it is important to plan your research methods carefully. In fact, the whole process of gathering, validating, and interpreting data should be seen as a systematic extension of the initial brainstorming process. From your initial outline, you take a series of carefully planned steps to answer the questions your reader wants and needs answered, and to cover the subject you have been assigned.

Answers to Some Questions I Frequently Get Asked at This Stage

1. It isn't really possible to plan for everything, so why bother?

   This is a legitimate question. The answer is simply that you can plan for about 80–90 percent of everything. I know one researcher in public health who planned a 20-year research project knowing that there were minor adjustments to be made along the way but that there would be no opportunity to make any major adjustments without ruining the effort. She did it. She spent a long time planning. And she got her results. She had only minor adjustments to make over a period of 20 years! So, you do this extensive planning, first, because it is actually possible to do it, and second, because doing it keeps you from getting lost, permits you to know what adjustments you do have to make along the way, and keeps you from having to panic at the end of the whole affair.

2. When I get results, what if they're not politically acceptable? What do I do then?

   We come back to political issues, which were only briefly explored in the early chapters, because they always surface during the interpretation process. There is no question that in many cases the boss will simply not like the results you get—no one likes to be told that something is wrong. No one likes to find out that decisions made a few years ago were wrong and must now be corrected. So, what do you do if you find out things you're sure the boss won't like? You report them. You have no choice; if you want to be of some help, you have to give the boss the answers to the questions asked.

If you don't, at some time in the future someone else will discover the same things you have—and then it may be really unpleasant for you.

This answer still doesn't get you over the problem of dealing with the immediate possible negative response of anyone to criticism, whether it's your boss or someone else who's the subject of the report. To solve this problem, you have to adopt a very simple strategy; you have to remember that the person who asked for the report did ask for the report. You are not the enemy. You are working for the person who will read the final report. Even if you're working in one agency and investigating another, your purpose is to help, not attack. Working from this positive strategic position, you can make recommendations which, in almost all cases, will be taken positively. This will require some special attention during the writing process.

The other answer to this question about results that are unpleasant is "You don't have all that much to worry about in the first place. If you have been stopping at recommended places in your brainstorming and research planning, there aren't going to be any surprises." It's unpleasant surprises that get you in trouble most of the time. No political person likes to think that everything's OK only to find out that everything's not OK. So, if you have taken the steps already covered in early chapters of this book, you're going to find yourself with few problems of this nature. Those you do face, you can write your way out of.

3. If I've followed every step suggested so far, what have I got at this point?

You have, written down in at least rough form, almost an entire report. Specifically, you have:

a. *An assignment analysis, which provides you with the information that usually goes into an introduction*

b. *A complete outline of the report—all the questions you have to answer for the report to satisfy the reader and all the subject headings for each section of the report*

c. *Everything organized*

d. *All of the tables, charts, and graphs you're going to use to present your information*

e. *A firm idea of what the data means, as it is collected*

f. *Strategies for analyzing the data, statistically and in terms of finding cause*

This leaves you with one task: to phrase your final report carefully and effectively. You do not have to organize your report; that has been done. You don't have to think about how you're going to treat the data; that has been done. Instead of facing a blank piece of paper and wondering what the final report should look like, you only have to fill in the blank spaces with good prose. All your planning effort pays off at this point; you can just sit down and write up the report—quickly and efficiently.

SECTION FIVE

ASSEMBLING THE FINAL PAPER

The unfortunate truth about research is that it is absolutely worthless if it isn't described and explained well. The final report is the only tangible product of the entire research effort. It must be good.

You're halfway to the point of having a good report at this stage, because you're working from a complete outline that has been reviewed and approved by the person who asked you to do the report in the first place. But you can still wreck the whole project if you don't write well, if you don't phrase your ideas carefully and effectively.

Writing, like research, is a skill that takes some time to master—through practice. But, there is still no reason why someone intelligent enough to do research, and capable of holding a reasonably coherent conversation, can't write a pretty good *first draft*. And this first draft should need only careful *editing* to make it into a final draft.

Writing is difficult. You'll never get every word and phrase exactly right, but you can produce a good, clear, understandable report in a very short time. To do so, you need to go into the process with a full knowledge of the problems you face, a general strategy for solving them, and a set of specific procedures to follow while writing and editing.

WHY WRITING IS A PROBLEM

15

Writing is the process of filling in your outline with prose. You begin
with an organized, complete, idea of what you want to say. The
outline you've prepared may even be so detailed that each heading is
limited to covering a mere paragraph. You also have a very complete
picture of who your readers are at this stage, so you should find it
reasonably easy to write at a level that is appropriate to them. In
short, writing the report should be a breeze. After all, you know
English phrasing by heart—you speak the language everyday, dealing with adults and children, professionals and the general public.
You're good enough with the language to adapt your speaking style
to the needs of these people. The process of phrasing sentences
should be no problem.

Knowing this, you pull out a pad of paper, get out your outline and
your data shells, all filled in with the information you've collected,
and you begin to write. If you're normal, here's what happens:
(1) You do just fine for a few sentences. (2) In midparagraph you

remember that you should have said something in the first sentence. (3) You realize that you can't quite get this additional bit of information into the first sentence because of the way you originally phrased it. (4) You put it into a new sentence and tie it back to the first sentence with a long transition. (5) The transition gets in the way of the phrasing of the next sentence, so you have to change what you had planned to say slightly. (6) The change in plans makes you forget what you were going to end up with. (7) You get lost and start the whole paragraph over again. (8) In starting over again, you change a phrase in the first sentence. (9) This change in phrase means you have to adjust your second sentence. (10) You decide it's time for a coffee break—you get up after half an hour and quit, with nothing done.

Writing doesn't always happen this way, but people *write themselves into a bind* frequently enough for the process to be really worth trying to solve.

PROBLEMS

Although there are some writers who are able to write almost *naturally* and without seeming difficulty, many writers find it hard to overcome the difficulties inherent in the writing process. Writing is a skill that requires a particular kind of disciplined mind if it is to be done naturally. If you don't happen to have one of these 1 in 10,000 minds, you have to work *artificially* to achieve the same effect. To do this, you have to overcome several serious problems.

The Cumulative Problem

In writing anything, you make decisions about wording and sentence construction cumulatively—the decisions you make during the first few minutes exert a powerful influence on the decisions you *can* make later on. If you plan on writing consistently, you have to be very careful every step of the way.

The cumulative problem affects your freedom to make decisions in very subtle ways. For example, if you begin a paper with a sentence about the background to the report, the tone of this sentence will affect the tone of your conclusions and recommendations. Thus, if you begin by saying:

> "In an effort to improve the general efficiency of her office procedures, the Assistant Director of _____ suggested that we review all aspects of the office's operations. . . ."

you're going to have trouble writing anything *negative* about the assistant director. You've too firmly established the general cooperativeness and openness of this person to be able to criticize her strongly in the end. There's nothing particularly wrong with this; it's just that the phrasing at the beginning should be completely consistent with the phrasing at the end. If you did have some criticism to make, you'd be hard-pressed to make it sound serious after such a nice opening.

The Thinking-While-You-Write Problem

You think as you write. There's no way to avoid doing this. But it does cause problems, because you don't think and write at the same *speed*. If you handwrite your work, you probably manage about 12–18 words per minute. If you type, it's probably 35 words per minute. If you dictate, you may go as high as 120 words per minute. You think faster; on a word-by-word basis, you can probably handle 600–1000 words per minute (this is good, fast, phrase-by-phrase reading speed).

The problem with thinking faster than you write is that you can often get the two processes out of synchrony; your thinking can get far ahead of your phrasing, and you can get confused.

Suppose, for example, that you start out the writing of a sentence with the sequence of ideas represented by the letters

ABCDEFGHIJKLM.

You want to write out this idea, dealing with these things in this order. So, you start. You write down

ABC.

In the time it has taken you to do this, your thoughts have jumped far ahead. You may be *thinking* about M. So, you write

ABCM.

Now you really have a problem, not only are you slightly out of synchrony, but you have the elements of the sentence out of the order you originally wanted them to be in—you're thinking of two things at once: the subject and how you're going to get out of this bind without starting over. So, you write

ABCMLKJIG.

Now you're in real trouble. You have half the sentence backwards, and you've left some elements out. To solve this problem, you write another sentence to include the missing elements,

DEF.

But this doesn't make sense on its own, so you add half of your next idea onto this,

DEFNOPQR.

You have now effectively written yourself into a bind. You've lost control of the phrasing process.

This sort of thinking–writing problem happens to everyone not blessed with superhuman concentration. Here's what it looks like in terms of writing a single sentence:

Phrasing process	*Thinking process*
Under the circumstances,	There are a number of troublesome circumstances in this case and I really do feel hesitant to write about the problem because of its political nature . . .
particularly considering the political nature of the problem,	The politics of this thing make me wonder just what to do about the problem. . . .
we may consider,	But having considered all the possibilities I think I may be safe in considering. . . . The solution does seem to be the best one, but perhaps I ought to mention the fact that there are others and give the reader the true picture of the whole process we went through. . . .
among other things,	Maybe I'd better get to the point here. . . .
the problem actually being considered here is	It boils down to a political problem we had to deal with in order to get this business done. . . .
political in nature	And it was this politics thing that gave us all the trouble in this project and makes a recommendation

Phrasing process (continued)	Thinking process (continued)
and therefore difficult to solve.	hard to arrive at. . . . This is getting to be a long sentence; maybe I'd better end it here.

Out of a process like this, you get sentences like this:

> "Under the circumstances, particularly considering the political nature of the problem, we may consider, among other things, the problem actually being considered here is political in nature and therefore difficult to solve."

Every year there are dozens of articles in the newspapers attacking government people for writing bad prose. Many insult the writer by suggesting that this sort of bad writing is deliberate. Maybe some of it is, but the vast majority of the problem stems from the thinking–writing mix-up. With simple ideas, this isn't a problem. With anything complicated to write about, it is. That's one reason why journalists write so easily—they have simple things to say. You don't have the luxury of easy generalizations and one-sided arguments. Your work has to be complex, as complex as the political situations you have to deal with. And given this, you have to solve this thinking–writing mix-up problem.

The Problem of Style

While you're thinking about content, about getting things down clearly, you've also got to be making style decisions, decisions about what word to use and what sentence structure to select. You have to decide which *style* will appeal to your various readers. These style decisions complicate the whole writing process, particularly when you have several audiences.

The Problem of Words

There are thousands of ways to write down any given idea. Most variations in style are the result of there being so many words to choose from. English has about 800,000 words (about 300,000 of them are technical terms). There's a lot of words you can choose that mean the same thing or something very close. For example,

see   perceive   observe   sight   spot

You could use all these close equivalents at any given point.

Because there are so many word-choice decisions to make, many writers focus almost all their attention on these. But there are other kinds of style decisions to be made, decisions about what sentence structures to use, about prepositional phrases and where to put them, about subordinate and coordinate clauses. These decisions are, in many cases, much more important than those concerning words. One decision about sentence structure will affect the word choice in an entire sentence. If it isn't made carefully, you may not be able to use the words you want to use.

The problem here is to find a way of overcoming the natural tendency to focus attention on word choice, to develop a writing procedure that makes word-choice decisions secondary to the more important overall sentence-structure decisions.

SOLUTIONS

Some general strategies for writing that you can adopt will help you overcome these problems. They are the basis for the detailed writing procedure described in the next chapter.

Work One Sentence at a Time

You're filling in an outline, so you really shouldn't have to think too far ahead of yourself. You can concentrate on answering one reader question at a time. Forget that you have twenty pages to write, concentrate on the particular sentence and paragraph facing you. Get it done right. Be completely satisfied with each sentence and paragraph before you venture on to the next.

This is not normal writing advice. Most writing teachers suggest that you just go ahead and write—get something down. I think they're wrong, particularly when you have a good outline to follow. Under these circumstances, anything less than careful writing of each sentence on a sentence-by-sentence basis is just wasting time. You don't want to write ten drafts. You want one or two.

So, before you sit down to compose, decide to write slowly and carefully. Decide that you're not going to let a bad sentence slip by. Decide that you're just not going to write yourself into a bind.

Decide on a Style and Stick to It

Before you start each section of the report, take some time to think about who will be reading this particular section. Decide what level audience you're dealing with. Consciously decide on a style—on how long you want sentences to be, on what kinds of sentence structure you think will be most clear, and on what kinds of words you'll use. Write down your decision in very brief note form and keep the note on your desk. When in doubt, check your note. This will give you a bit more chance to focus on the content of your sentences. You get style considerations out of the way, and then just write.

When Making Style Decisions, Focus on Sentence Structure

The relative importance of sentence structure over words can be illustrated simply. Here are four words and the various sentences you get when you restructure them:

Words	Sentences
Car	1. The car hit John.
Hit	2. John hit the car.
The	3. Hit the car, John!
John	4. John hit the car?

Even with simple sentences such as this, the structure is the real determinate of meaning. If you find yourself having a problem while you're trying to get a sentence down on paper, don't change the words, play around with the structure. Move phrases and clauses around.

THE NEXT CHAPTER

You can develop your own specific approach to putting these strategies to work, or you can look at the next chapter, which deals with one logical and practical way of building sentences.

16

BUILDING SENTENCES AND PARAGRAPHS

The mental processes that go into writing a paper are hardly simple. You may make 100,000 decisions while writing a paper of twenty or thirty pages. You can try to make all these decisions consistently in the first place, or you can try to edit them into consistency after you've done several drafts. There are problems involved in both approaches.

PROBLEMS

Whatever process for writing you choose must not in any way interfere with your thinking about the *subject*. While you're writing you must be able to concentrate on each sentence without losing sight of the whole.

SOLUTION

A logical approach to building sentences begins with an analysis of what a sentence is. A sentence is an idea.

SENTENCE = IDEA

This is an old cliché, but a useful one to explore. If a sentence and an idea are the same thing, then a logical approach to building sentences would be to build them in the same way you build ideas. If this can be done, then the writing process itself will not in any way interfere with your thinking about the subject. But how do you build an idea?

The thought process is probably considerably more complex than anyone can describe, but computer scientists have imitated it in its basic form. The process by which a computer takes data and makes sense out of it is at least similar to the human thinking process. And this process is orderly, exactly what you want in a *writing* process.

The computer handles data in roughly the following manner: All data is put into the computer, *coded* so the computer can recognize what it is, and then stored. As a new piece of data comes in, it is identified and stored along with similar pieces of data. To *do* anything with the data, the programmer starts by defining basic functions—expressed in many cases as *verbs*. An instruction to do something with the data, to think, looks like this:

COMPARE _____ AND _____
Function   Data   Data

The end result of this instruction is that the computer pulls the bits of data from memory and generates an idea, for example:

THING A IS BIGGER THAN THING B

The computer may make this comparison numerically, rather than with the words BIGGER THAN, but the function is the same. The computer has built an idea, a very simple idea, but an idea nonetheless.

Something like this process probably goes on in the human brain at a speed that makes it seem that thinking is considerably more complicated. The brain is so fast that to the thinker, the whole process seems simultaneous. If you think about it, though, your thinking probably does follow this pattern. For example, suppose you are driving in the slow lane of a highway. You suddenly see an expensive, fast, sedan go past you at about 90 miles per hour. You take this fact in, identify the car, and probably say something nasty under your breath. Next, you see the familiar highway patrol car go past you at 95 miles per hour. You record this fact. Then your brain goes looking for a connection betweeen the two events and you come up with:

Highway patrol car chases speeding XZ450

You have just made a thought, and I have just written that thought as a sentence.

This is, of course, just barely a sentence. It's almost a newspaper headline. But you can make it into a larger sentence by simply adding the subsidiary details you noticed while you were observing the main event.

> "When I was driving past the I-70 interchange, just before reaching the bridge, a *highway patrol car* with two officers in it *chased down* a *speeding* yellow and purple 1977 XZ450, which was driven at least 90 miles an hour by a middle-aged man."

Notice how the "headline" portion of this sentence has not changed, except for a small change in the form of the verb (*chases→chased down*).

If you listen carefully to newscasters, you'll find that this is the way they build a story. The initial segment of a radio news broadcast begins with a sequence of simple headlines. Then, each headline is expanded into a single long sentence, followed by shorter sentences to add details that couldn't be fit into the headline sentence. *The newscaster can get an amazing amount of information into a short span of time, because he or she builds the detail of the sentence around a single, very simple, clear, main idea.*

The process for doing this is really very easy to learn. You begin with your headline sentence—the simplest form of your main idea that you can think of. You write this down on a piece of scratch paper. Then, on a clean piece of paper, you fill in the whole sentence, referring to the headline any time you get even vaguely lost. What do you do to make sure you fill in the sentence completely? You answer the normal questions anyone has about any thing or event, questions that newspeople have memorized:

—Who?   What?   When?   Where?   Why?   How?

—Who says so?   Under what conditions?   So what?

—How big?   How fast?   What color?   What kind of?

As you fill in the headline sentence, you answer as many of these questions as you think need to be answered in order to fill in the idea sufficiently for the reader. You use the questions as a checklist.

This simple procedure keeps your mind focused on the subject—the main idea—of your sentence. It helps you keep the main idea simple so that the reader will understand it. It allows you to gain real control over the complex thoughts government work requires you to explain. Here's an example of how a simple statement about taxes becomes a clear, complete, but complex statement of policy. It starts with a headline sentence, "Taxes are due."

Sentence	Question
Taxes are due.	What kind of taxes?
Corporation taxes are due.	When?
Corporation taxes are due within sixty days of fiscal closing.	Why?
Because of a new regulation governing the timing of tax payments, corporation taxes are now due within sixty days of fiscal closing.	Under what conditions?
Because of a new regulation governing the timing of tax payments, corporation taxes are now due within sixty days of fiscal closing, unless an exception has been secured prior to the fiscal closing date.	

Note that in this now complex sentence the main idea retains its integrity. It's sitting right in the middle of the sentence, with all the modifying words and phrases around it. But it has not been changed.

Building sentences in this simple manner requires you to take one careful step—you have to take each outline heading and prepare a quick, rough, suboutline for it. You have to jot down all the main ideas you are going to deal with under the particular outline heading. For example, suppose you were writing a report for a park service. The subject of the report is "The Influence of Backpackers on Deer in Yosemite Park." Suppose you were ready to write the abstract or executive summary of the report. You might end up writing down these headline sentences:

1. Deer respond to backpackers.
2. Deer repond to influx.
3. Food reserves were exhausted.
4. Herd reproduction was suppressed.

5. Situation is serious.
6. Backpackers' access to deer must be limited.

You've almost written a telegram; the ideas need not be expressed in any more detail for you to begin working on them.

First, you look carefully at the list of headline sentences and make sure that they're in the order you want them to be in. You can see the basic logic of your thoughts very clearly when they're in such simple form. If you decide to leave them in this order, you can begin writing. Here's what you might end up with working from these six headline sentences (provided you knew the subject):

> "During the peak vacation months, red-tailed deer in the Yosemite high country respond to the large numbers of backpackers entering the area by moving from summer feeding grounds to higher elevations. In 1969, for example, deer in the Tilden Valley responded to the influx of hundreds of backpackers by moving to the Tower Peak range. Because this range has quite limited food sources, the food reserves available were exhausted before early August. The herd's reproduction potential was suppressed and those fawns which were born the next season were feeble and sickly. Because the influx of backpackers grows as the sport becomes more popular, the situation facing the red-tailed deer herds is serious, with some herds facing complete elimination unless something is done about the problem. To save these herds, backpackers' access to deer areas must be limited, perhaps by limiting the number of camping and fire permits allowed during peak summer seasons."

Note that you end up with six sentences. All the detail of the abstract has been added to the headline sentences. And there's a lot of detail included in this simple paragraph.

Advantages to Writing from Headline Sentences

Aside from the fact that this simple method allows you to keep general control over your writing, there are a number of specific advantages to this approach.

1. *You cannot get lost.* Once you have written down your main ideas as headline sentences, once you have made sure that these are in the order you want them in, you will not be able to forget what you're doing. You can, for example, leave off in the middle of a sentence, take a flight to Europe, spend two weeks having a good time, return, sit down at your desk, and finish the sentence. All you have to do is look at the headline sentence and jog your memory so that you can fill in the details the reader still needs. You won't lose your train of

thought while writing—if you write it down in the first place.

2. *You can write fairly long, complex sentences without fear that you're getting in over your head.* The simple headline sentence acts as a focal point for the reader, allowing the reader to see the main idea and the detail in their proper relationship. The reader won't get lost; neither will you. If you have trouble with a phrase, you simply cross it out and try another one. The headline sentence remains untouched, and so your *idea* stays firmly in your head.

3. *You can edit.* If you decide after two or three days that you don't like a phrase, all you have to do is cross that phrase out of your draft. You don't rewrite whole sentences, you just take out or change the subsidiary portions.

4. *Once you learn this approach, it becomes second nature.* It takes a good news copywriter a while to learn how to turn out stories this way, but once the skill is learned, writing gets to be reasonably quick and easy. It's never something you want to try without thinking, but writing can become almost a *mechanical* skill using this approach. You can, for instance, learn to dictate in this manner. You take a piece of scratch paper, jot down your headline sentences, and then fill in the detail as you dictate. You can also type your drafts this way, being pretty sure that if you have thought out the headline sentences quite clearly the first typed draft will be substantially OK.

5. *You can make consistent style decisions as you build the full sentence.* Since the headline sentence is simple (almost to a fault) and since all the headline sentences are going to be this way, you can add to them all in consistent ways, thus giving your writing a consistent style. For example, suppose you have a subject that requires you to use official jargon, but you still want to write so that the reader gets the basic message. You can build your sentences so that all the difficult stuff is placed in phrases after you've stated the simple main idea. Schematically, your sentences would look like this:

Main idea + Modifying phrases + Modifying phrases

The general reader would be satisfied to read the main idea, and the expert reader would be able to get all the detail. Among the other kinds of style decisions you can make as you build a sentence around a headline sentence are:

   a. Decisions about whether to use phrases or adjectives to describe something ("the building process" or "the process of building") *b.* Decisions about where to put long clauses (before or after the main idea, or in the middle)

    c. Decisions about passive or active voice ("We did it." or "It was done.")

    d. Decisions about level of vocabulary ("use" or "usage" or "utilization")

Guidelines for many of the most common style decisions are found at the end of the next chapter.

6. The final advantage of this approach is that it is something you can do with any kind of writing. I've used it in just about every field, from physics to business administration. It allows you consciously to adjust your writing to the demands of any audience, just as newspeople adjust to the demands of radio, television, newspapers, or magazines.

EXAMPLE

To give you a good idea of what kind of writing you can do using this simple approach, here are several examples of prose from government work—all bad. Following each example is the *headline* sentence the writer ought to have used. Following this is the revised sentence.

Original

"In appraising tangible personal property, the assessor shall give recognition to the trade level at which the property is situated and to the principle that property normally increases in value as it progresses through production and distribution channels. Such property normally attains its maximum value as it reaches the consumer level [Rule 10, *California Administrative Code,* Trade Level for Tangible Personal Property]."

Headline sentence

"Property should be appraised at different values."

Revision

"Tangible personal property should be appraised at different values, depending on where in the production–distribution–consumption process it is. Raw materials have generally less value than the same materials in finished product form; goods held for wholesale are generally less valuable to the holder than goods held for retail; goods attain maximum value when *purchased* at retail."

Note here that the original and revised sentences are about the same length, but the revision gave specific examples.

Original

"Unless an agency obtains an exception from Accounting Systems Branch, Audits Division, Department of Finance, all expenditures of less than $150 that, with respect to an item of nonexpendable property, (a) add to it or (b) improve, better, or as an extraordinary repair and maintenance item extend its originally estimated life will be considered to be a revenue expenditure which benefits the current period [State Administration Manual, California]."

Headline sentence

This is a procedure statement, so the headline sentence should be an instruction to *do* something.

"Charge expenditures to current year's account."

Revision

"When you spend less than $150 to add to, improve, or otherwise extend the originally estimated life of a piece of nonexpendable property, charge this expenditure to your current fiscal year's account, not to your account for capital expenditures."

Note that in this sentence you still need to know what an item of nonexpendable property is—you can't get away from jargon in all cases. But the sentence is clearer. (I checked it with a budget officer who said, "Right, that's what we mean.") Note also that the exception statement is left out. It would go in a detail sentence following this one.

NOTES TO MANAGEMENT AND STAFF

To Management

If you want to help staff write clearly, you can do so by encouraging them to prepare complete outlines. This will help them write

To Staff

It takes a lot of discipline to learn to write this way, but it soon begins to pay off. I've seen journalists dash off 500 words in less

To Management *(continued)*

more clearly because the outline provides headline sentences, or at least parts of headline sentences. When you encourage staff to prepare a complete contract for the final report, you are actually having them write out a portion of the final report in rough form. You thus get a chance to review the phrasing for the final draft well before any of the research has been done.

To Staff *(continued)*

than half an hour—and the writing was good, too. I've taught this method to a number of scientists, one of whom learned it so well he wrote a final draft for a thesis for a masters degree in two days. But you have to work at this process consciously. You have to do it systematically—no shortcuts.

If you decide to try it, you're likely to find it rather slow going at first. It may take you ten or twenty minutes to figure out what the headline sentences should be for a paragraph. It may take you half an hour to write that paragraph. As you practice, though, you'll find you get faster. Finally, you'll get so that you can jot down the headline sentences very quickly, check them over to make sure they're what you really want to say, and then fill them in in a few minutes.

While you're learning this approach, you'll have some minor problems. First, you'll probably find it difficult to simplify your thoughts down to a headline sentence. You start out with a head full of complicated ideas, and reducing these to a bunch of simple sentences is difficult. You may not feel very good about what you do write down; it will look childish. It always does at first. Until you start filling in the details, you will think that you've oversimplified. In the end, this is rarely true. To help you get used to thinking in these simple terms, you might think about writing as the process of elaborating on a rash statement, the kind you make in arguments.

Boss: "Well, Bosley, what in all of this miserable gobbledegook is it that you want to say? Does the damn thing work or doesn't it!?"

You: "No, for crying out loud, *it doesn't work!*"

The italic portion is your headline sentence, perhaps translated a bit to read

> "Proposed procedure won't work"

and turned into a full sentence

> "Because there is general employee resistance to any change in the way in which we handle checks in this office,

To Staff *(continued)*

the *proposed procedure* to have all checks initialed by the chief clerk *won't work,* in spite of the advantage it could give us in terms of being able to spot any check errors immediately."

The second difficulty you may encounter is in deciding which of your thoughts constitutes a headline sentence and which should go into the phrases and clauses you add on. There isn't any quick solution to this problem; it will take you some time and practice to get to recognize what your headline sentences really are. There is a way of telling whether you're making too many sentences, though. As you're working, look at what you've written and see if you are *repeating* words—particularly nouns and verbs. If you are, you're using two or three sentences where one would do. Here's a simple example:

"In doing this study, we found a number of important factors involved in the failure of staff to respond to management directives. They fail to respond, for example, because directives are not given in written form. They also don't respond because they hate the assistant director. The main reason for their failure to respond is, though, that they're just pigheaded."

Note that words *respond* and *failure* are repeated. This doesn't mean that you should go running to a Thesaurus to find substitute words. It means that you should combine all sentences into one, with the repeated words in the *headline* portion of the sentence:

"Staff fail to respond to management directives because the directives aren't in written form, staff hate the assistant director, and—most importantly—staff are just plain pigheaded."

This is a silly example, but it does illustrate how repetition is an indication of too many sentences, an indication that too much material is going into separate sentences that could go into modifying phrases to support one headline sentence.

CHAPTER SUMMARY

To gain control of the writing process, build sentences the way you build ideas. Start with a simple headline sentence and add detail to this main idea. To write a paragraph, start by listing out all the headline sentences you will use in the whole paragraph, make sure these are in proper order, and then fill in details—one sentence at a time.

EDITING AND REVIEW

17

No matter how good a researcher and writer you are, you are not perfect; you will have to edit and review your work. And, your work will be edited and reviewed by others who read it—your boss, other people in the office, perhaps even someone from the outside. For many researchers, this is the least pleasant part of the entire assignment-to-report process. No one likes to make mistakes, and there are few people who like to have mistakes pointed out. The human ego is delicate; it doesn't stand up well under criticism—even under self-criticism.

But you must review and edit. Only in review can you hope to catch all the mistakes you will make. And other people have to review your work or else the work will likely reflect only your thinking, not the thinking of the agency you work for. After all, it's an *agency report—not your report.*

Review also has a number of positive functions. First, it's a good training tool. Whether you're training yourself by reviewing yourself, or your boss is training you, or you're training the boss, review is essential. People learn best by trial and error in many situations, and the review process makes you aware of the errors you have made. If review is done constructively and carefully, you can learn what you've done right (so you can repeat it) and what you've done wrong (so you can avoid it). Review can also be a team-building tool in the office. If you and others in the office can go over each other's work in an objective and constructive manner, you will find that the experience is good for all concerned. It builds a sense of trust among all in the office. It breaks down the barriers of ego; when you review openly and honestly, you begin to see how important it is to get other peoples' opinions. Nothing is better for developing a sense of cooperativeness than for everyone in the office to realize that for work to get done well everyone should make some contribution.

The ideal review—self and cooperative—is very complex, difficult to achieve, and immensely worthwhile. But there are a number of things that stand in the way of achieving it.

PROBLEMS

Nearly every human emotion can be generated by the review process. Thus, nearly every human problem can be generated by review. For the sake of simplicity, and because this is not a psychology book, we'll stick to the major problems of review.

The Winners/Losers Problem

It's terribly difficult to criticize anyone's work without seeming to criticize the person, and without seeming to place yourself above the other person. It's terribly difficult to take criticism without feeling "put down." But, if review is to be successful, this sense of there being winners and losers has to be overcome. If you're reviewing and editing your own work, you have to be able to spot errors and correct them without feeling that you are somehow utterly stupid; if you're criticizing someone else's work, you have to do so without making this person feel utterly stupid.

The Problem of Mistakes

In any effort involving, perhaps, 50,000–100,000 decisions, *mistakes will happen.* You just can't make every decision correctly, nor can you expect to be able to correct every mistake. You just have to learn to live with some of them. You can hope that the mistakes will be minor ones, but you have to expect major errors of judgment.

The problem of most reviews is that the reviewer works from just the opposite assumption—the assumption of zero errors. Staff egos may get so involved in the work that they just refuse to admit to any errors; they fight every suggestion that there could be a mistake in the project. Managers often reinforce this feeling by making a big deal over a simple misspelling, something you can expect to happen to almost any person writing twenty pages of prose.

Of course, there's a contradiction implied in talking about review from the point of view of expecting mistakes. How can you maintain high standards if you go around admitting that you expect mistakes? How can you be sure that if you set a standard *low* you won't find yourself aiming at the low standard—and falling predictably short?

The Problem of Blame

The person who has conducted the research and written the report is responsible for the contents of the report—responsible but not necessarily to blame. Separating these two normally closely linked concepts is important.

Responsibility is a professional, social concept. If you are *responsible* for something and something goes wrong, it is your job to make amends, to fix things up—if you can. This doesn't mean that the responsible party is actually *to blame* for what went wrong; it could easily be quite beyond control. For example, suppose your staff does a poor job during a research project you're responsible for. Unless you selected the staff, and unless you were able to get money and time enough to do the work properly, you can't be blamed for the failure, but you'll have to take responsibility for it. You have to *fix* whatever went wrong.

The distinction is critical to a good review. If you blame people for mistakes, you run the risk of being just plain *wrong*. If you ignore blame and concentrate on simply getting the thing repaired, you may actually get people to take responsibility and to do the job over again—the right way.

The Problem of Standards

There are two kinds of standards—personal and objective. We all have both kinds. I, for example, cannot abide the idea of getting information from a questionnaire; I think this device is a disaster. Professionally, though, I have to admit that I have seen well-done questionnaires; good, reliable data can be obtained from them if they're carefully designed. Which standard do I apply? In my own work, I apply the personal standard; I seldom use questionnaires. Looking at others' work, I apply the objective standard; if the questionnaire is well-designed, I accept the results.

These sorts of dual-standard issues arise at all levels of research and writing. In some cases, it will be a question of a word or phrase. In other cases, it will be a question of basic content or methods. It doesn't much matter what the subject is, personal standards cause problems.

The trouble with personal standards is that they change with the mood of the person holding them, and people's moods do not remain constant over any length of time. Thus, a personal standard expressed at the very beginning of a research effort is likely to be completely revised by the end. A report that "isn't all that important" can suddenly become "the most important thing we've got to do in this office." And the opposite can also happen.

Professional standards, though, remain constant—if you have the ability to state them and state them clearly. Objective standards keep all involved in the report process from getting too deeply involved in issues of "like" and "dislike."

The Problem of Defensiveness

When you are hurt, you attack, you fight back at the person or thing that hurt you. When you are criticized, you criticize back. These things happen unless you recognize that the attack isn't really an attack, that it's really a helping hand.

The reviewer's job is to extend this sort of helping hand, to point out weaknesses and strengths so that the person with them can develop the strengths and eliminate the weaknesses. That's the theory. To most people who have written reports, it's just hogwash. They've been hurt in review often enough to know that there's no helping hand being extended. And they've told everyone in the office how unfair the review was. But in most cases they're *wrong*. The review was neither unfair nor an attack. It just wasn't very well handled by the reviewer.

The problem lies in finding a way to point out weakness without generating a counterattack. It's a problem of diplomacy and its solution is a diplomatic one.

The Problem of Momentum

Unless yours is a brand new office filled with new people, you've developed an office momentum, especially where reports are concerned. If it's a positive one, great. If it's a negative one, you have to break this momentum before you're going to have any chance of getting good work done. If, for example, the boss has a reputation (earned or just invented) for being a nasty critic, the boss is going to have to do something significant to get rid of the reputation. If staff have a reputation (again earned or just invented) for doing shoddy reports, staff are going to have to exert a considerable amount of energy to change this momentum. It doesn't just go away.

In an agency I worked for in the mid-1970s, this momentum problem was responsible for incredible inefficiency and hard feelings between management and staff. A pattern of harsh criticism from managers and pouting defensiveness from staff had been established. No one in the office could remember when it was established. It turned out that the pattern had been established before the present manager had been brought on, and that staff had almost completely changed since the old manager had gone. But the pattern remained. It took five months of weekly meetings before everyone in the office realized that the pattern could be broken, before the momentum was finally broken. Thereafter, the new manager could go about doing things properly without generating unnecessary trouble every time she made critical comments.

This is an extreme example, but if you look around your own office, you'll probably find similar examples. The problem is that in most offices the pattern of review is and has always been a negative pattern. I have never worked in an agency where there has been a sense that the reviewer and the research/writer were just members of the same team.

SOLUTIONS

Since review is troublesome in so many ways, it's not an easy problem to solve. In addition, any solution must be a solution to review problems at all levels—from review of wording to review of context.

Have a Review Policy

If you look through office policy and procedure manuals, you'll find policies on almost everything—but very few policies regarding review. This function seems to be left entirely up to the people in charge of review, as though it were a matter of personal prerogative. And in most offices it's treated in just this manner. The boss or reviewer jealously guards his or her review policy. Why this is true, I do not know. But it is true in many, many offices.

The problems outlined cannot be solved until the office has a review policy. As long as review is a power held in secret by the reviewer, there can be no sense of teamwork, and there can be no assurance that objective standards will be applied to work. Staff will take criticism personally. They will be defensive. And self-review will be almost impossible, because no one will know what standards to use to conduct a self-review.

Generate a Review Policy Cooperatively

When you're dealing with people who are capable of doing research and preparing a pretty complete report, you're dealing with people who are quite able to think on their own. And these people have good ideas about what a research report ought to look like. So, if you're the boss, make sure you bring a representative group of people from the staff into any review policy deliberations. And, if you're staff, make sure that when you get together to set up a self-review policy you include the boss in your deliberations.

Much has been said in recent years about the need for *participative management* and *management by objectives*. It goes double for management of research and review processes.

Admit the Problems You're Having

When you sit down to talk out a review policy, begin by admitting whatever problems are prevalent in the office. If you're the boss, it wouldn't hurt to admit that review isn't easy for you. If you're staff, it wouldn't hurt to admit that you're just not sure of what the office standards are. If you can start out in this way to identify problem areas, you'll find the policy easier to develop.

Create a Complete and Specific Review Policy

Don't set up a two-page review policy filled with vague statements such as "Research should be thorough." This would give everyone the impression that something concrete had been done, but you really wouldn't be any better off than before. If you're going to go to the trouble of making a policy, have it cover the subject. Here's a suggested scope.

A review policy should cover:

1. Who reviews what? Cover who is responsible for each level of review and exactly what the responsibilities are.

2. When does review take place? There has to be a timetable for review; otherwise it will get delayed. Staff need to know when they're expected to get their part done. Managers should know that they have to get things done in reasonable time, too.

3. How should a review be conducted? What items should be covered first, second, etc.? What's most important? How should review comments be communicated?

4. What are the reviewer's responsibilities to upper management and to the staff people being reviewed?

5. What should be done if the reviewer and the person being reviewed disagree on a major issue of either content or style?

6. What standards should be applied to the review process for content, organization, and style.

A policy that really covers these questions will make it possible for staff to work with a sense of security, knowing what they have to do and whom they have to report to.

Every office will have different answers to most of these questions; nevertheless, some of them can be answered in a general way. Here, then, are some suggestions for an office policy on review:

1. Who reviews what? Anything that leaves the office must be reviewed. A single letter that gives the reader a false impression can cause an immense amount of trouble. Review of all material is primarily a responsibility of the *writer*, not of managers. No manager has the time to review every letter or even to read every page of every report prepared in an office. The writer and the writer's immediate supervisor should review all reports for

   —Accuracy of content
   —Organization
   —Clarity
   —Internal consistency
   —Consistency with the assignment

   Reviewers at a higher level should not have to do this sort of review. There is nothing sillier than an agency director reviewing a report for style. It's just a waste of time. Higher-level review should concentrate on making sure the report is appropriate to release to the readers who will eventually use the information—and to the public if this is an issue (and it is since the Freedom of Information Act). Reviewers at a higher level should deal with questions of wording or punctuation very quickly—by sending the report back. They should not have to deal with nit-picking issues.

2. When does review take place? The best form of quality control is continuous quality control. It's a good idea to provide a schedule for review during the actual research, to specify checkpoints in the research effort and conduct a thorough review at these points. The worst time to review is at the end—after all the mistakes have built up, after the cumulative effect of early mistakes makes an effort to correct them a major undertaking.

3. How should review be conducted? Systematically! The reviewer should not just pick up a report and start reading. The first review step should be to review the original assignment and the original report outline. Then, proceed in a logical fashion to determine whether the report satisfies the initial contract made between researcher and manager. Do this in the following order:

   a. Make sure the report content satisfies the contract. If it does not, send the report back to be redone. Make no comments about style at this time, because style will change anyway when the content is adjusted.

   b. If the content is OK, look at the organization. If the report is difficult to follow because it is disorganized, send it back to be reorganized. Don't comment about style at this stage either. Style will change when the organization changes.

   c. Third, check to make sure that all the data are clearly presented in graphic forms the reader can understand quickly. If it isn't, then the reader is going to have trouble understanding the prose explaining the data, so send it back to have it redone.

   d. Finally, examine the report for style. Generally, as long as the report is clear and does not give any false impressions, its style should be approved. But, you may wish to look at style in terms of *tone* as well. Changes in tone are difficult to make without a complete revision of the report, so it's always best to set a tone before review takes place, before the report is prepared.

It is possible, following this procedure, to have to prepare a report *four times*, but it's highly unlikely. In most cases, when content or organization are fixed, the style is fixed at the same time. Style is often bad because the content is weak, so fixing one fixes the other.

4. What are the reviewer's responsibilities? To upper management, the reviewer has the responsibility of keeping the report constructive; no report should be allowed to sound negative. Improvements are one thing; bitchiness and negative, complaining tone are quite another. This does not mean that facts should be altered in any way. The reviewer has the responsibility of maintaining the integrity of the research effort. But conclusions and recommendations should not be made in such a way that they indicate an adversary relationship between those doing the research and those being studied. The reviewer has a responsibility to keep reports from degenerating into a we–they complaint session. But the reviewer also has the responsibility of transmitting truth, even if it is unpleasant. To the person whose work is being reviewed, the reviewer has a more specific responsibility. If criticism is made, the criticism should be explicit, careful, and thoughtful. Anything less is going to create problems, not solve them. A critical statement should contain:

   a. Statement of what the problem is
   b. Statement about the seriousness of the problem
   c. Statement of what the writer should do about the error

   Anything short of this is going to *sound* nasty and arbitrary.

5. What should be done about disagreements? The reviewer obviously has the *power* to demand changes. Exercising this power is destructive in almost all cases. Because of this, the reviewer and the person whose work is being reviewed should *discuss* any serious problems. If there is anything seriously wrong with a report, this should be handled verbally—not in a set of curt notes or comments on the side of the report pages. Nothing divides reviewer and writer more unpleasantly than not *talking out problems*. And the reviewer has a responsibility to listen, as well as talk.

6. What standards should be applied to the review process? Every report will have different standards for content, organization, and style. At the end of this chapter is a brief outline of some general standards that can be applied to almost all reports.

EXAMPLE

Since the review process is as much a process of interpersonal relations as it is a process of finding and correcting mistakes, it's impossible to illustrate completely. It is possible to take a look at a brief piece of writing and suggest what ought to be done about it. The example here is adapted from a memo written in a California agency, but it could have come from any government agency, anywhere.

> "Subject: Fair Labor Standards Act
>
> As announced at a meeting last week, this new Act will impact primarily in the area of overtime compensation. Under its provisions, all employees not now specifically exempt from the Act must henceforth be paid for all overtime worked at the rate of time and one-half for all overtime worked. It will not be permitted to give such employees compensating time off in lieu of this cash payment.
>
> Although managers must determine whether an employee is covered by this Act and its provisions on an employee-by-employee basis, the Personnel Office has reviewed the job descriptions and classifications for agency employees and determined that all employees with a classification of 75B, 65A, and 75C are covered by the Act. It is incumbent upon all supervisors to consider the consequences which may accrue due to overtime authorized for these persons.
>
> If you have any questions regarding the Act or its implementation, please contact _____ in the Personnel Office."

There is so much wrong with this memo that it's difficult for a reviewer to know where to start. It's a real temptation to really take the writer to task for the obvious bureaucratic style—it's awful. I would resist this temptation, though, because the primary problem is a content problem. The memo doesn't answer half the questions that should be answered in any memo regarding policy changes. It does not explain the act, does not deal with the act's implications for the office, and does not tell the reader what actions to take. I would send this memo back to the writer to be completely redone, along with a copy of policy memo questions (page 55). That's all I'd do—not a word about style.

I would, though, bring the writer into the office to talk about the memo. It's so bad that I wouldn't trust myself to communicate my criticism in writing.

NOTES TO MANAGEMENT AND STAFF

To Management

If you have felt a bit ill at ease while reading this chapter, you should have. This chapter is really aimed at managers, because managers have the responsibility for review. The responsibility is a real burden, because if the review process isn't handled well, the report

To Staff

Review is perhaps the most difficult thing to do—from a personal, emotional standpoint. It is difficult to tell someone who has worked for months that the final product has real flaws and must be done over again.

If you want management to be professional

turns out poorly—and the manager who reviewed it gets the blame. Review is also extremely difficult to do well. For these reasons, it's important to be very blunt about the subject:

THE MANAGER IS RESPONSIBLE FOR REVIEW AND FOR THE CONSEQUENCES OF THE REVIEW PROCESS. REVIEW CAN BE A CONSTRUCTIVE PROCESS, BUT ONLY IF THE MANAGER TAKES IT ON AS A PROFESSIONAL RESPONSIBILITY, NOT AS A PERSONAL TASK. STANDARDS USED IN REVIEW MUST BE OBJECTIVE, WELL KNOWN, AND APPLIED WITH UNIFORMITY. ANYTHING SHORT OF THIS WILL DESTROY THE USEFULNESS OF RESEARCH EFFORTS IN THE OFFICE.

In short, staff are on the spot at every stage in the research process. Management is on the spot during review. *If you want staff to do a professional job of getting the information you need to make decisions, you have to do a professional job of review.*

about review, you have to make this possible. You have to seek out criticism. You have to accept criticism with grace and recognize that it is meant to be helpful. You have to realize how difficult it is for the boss to come right out and say that something is really wrong. Try doing this yourself with someone you supervise. It's difficult to do.

So, although the primary burden for review lies with the manager, you ought to share some of it. Specifically, you should review your own work carefully using the standards you think the boss would use. You should note potential problems and *ask* about them during review. If you plan to be working in an office for a long time, you'll want to establish a positive working relationship with reviewers.

I know that all this sounds quite idealistic. It is. But it also possible—and necessary.

CHAPTER SUMMARY

Review is a necessary final step in the research process. To be effective, it must be based on objective standards applied to work in an even-handed manner. Critical to this is that the office have a well-known rview policy, so that self-review and review by others can be carried out in a consistent manner.

APPENDIX

SOME GENERAL GUIDELINES FOR REVIEW

Content

Content is specific to the individual report, so there are no general rules that would apply to every report. But there are a few principles:

1. The report should satisfy the contract and should be consistent with the initial outline formulated during brainstorming. If it isn't, there is a good chance that the content will not satisfy the needs of the people who are going to read the report.
2. The report should answer the questions of all readers, even if it has to be broken into separate sections to do so.
3. The report should deliver what the title promises.
4. There should always be a clear distinction between facts and interpretations of facts. For the most part, data should be presented graphically, with interpretation in prose. If necessary, headings should be used to separate the two.

Organization

The first rule of organization is that the readers' questions should be answered in the order in which they're likely to be asked. There is no need to structure a report in any other fashion.

The second rule is that the answer to any question should be organized to fit the purpose of the answer. The purpose–organization connection described in Chapter 7 should be strictly considered.

Style

There are two basic style issues—clarity and tone. Tone is the most important of the two and should be taken care of first.

Tone Rules The tone of government reports should be positive. There is nothing to be gained, either in terms of getting things to work the way they should or in terms of personal goals, in writing with a negative tone. The writer should always focus on what can be done to solve a problem rather than what the problem is. Some good specific rules to follow to achieve a positive tone are the following:

1. Keep personalities out of the report. Don't attack someone who's trying to do a job and has just made a number of mistakes. It may be necessary to replace someone; this may be your recommendation. But there is no need to get personal.

2. Make all recommendations very specific. Don't just recommend that "actions be taken to solve the problem." This sort of thing almost guarantees that the problem will be waiting when the next study is done. Instead, make recommendations that will actually solve the problem: "The problem of uneven distribution of workload in this office can be solved by assigning six of the staff to a work pool."

3. Remember that you're a part of the problem—government. Your job is to improve, not attack. Make your language reflect this commitment to improvement. For example, say:

"An improvement in performance is important if the agency is to meet the goal of _____ by _____. To achieve this, _____ should be done in the following manner: _____."

rather than

"The agency will not meet its goals under the present management. If it is to correct this failure, it must _____ by _____ in the following manner _____."

The recommendation in both these cases may be the same, but in one case you'll encourage cooperativeness and in the other you'll generate defensiveness. There is no sacrifice in integrity in taking the positive stance. The data still reveal the problems. The recommendations still require action. But there is a better sense of cooperation with the positive approach. There will be times, of course, when the carrot will not work. *In general,* it does quite nicely. Only use the stick when you've found a case of *repeated* problems.

Clarity This term is overused and generally undefined. It is vague, but it doesn't have to be vague. There are a number of things you can look for in your writing that will tell you whether your sentences are clear or not on an objective basis. Rather than take the negative approach and tell you what the errors are, here are a set of guidelines for making sure your style is clear.

Wording. Although word choice isn't the most important factor that influences the clarity of your writing, it's the easiest to deal with. There's one rule: Always choose the most common term that says *exactly* what you want to say. When you have a choice between terms that mean the same thing, choose the simplest term. When you mean "review," say so; don't say "reexamine critically."

This doesn't mean that you should simplify everything to the point of idiocy. When you can use a simple word, do so. When a simple word isn't exactly what you mean, don't use it. Use the specific word, the technical term, that you need. Thus, when you mean "regulation," say so; don't try to simplify this to "law." Or, when you mean "unauthorized," don't try to simplify to "illegal." Don't use simple terms when they're imprecise. Do use them when they are precise.

Sentence sense. Make sure that your headline sentence, your main idea, makes sense *on its own.* Even if the headline sentence sounds a bit stiff and stilted, it should still make sense without anything added. Here's an example of one that doesn't:

> "Notice is hereby given that a *deficiency is proposed* to be assessed."

If you look at the headline sentence alone, "Deficiency is proposed," you can see why the sentence sounds awkward. The headline sentence doesn't make any sense—you can't propose deficiencies. You need a whole new headline sentence:

> "Deficiency has been found."

This gives you a new sentence:

> "Notice is hereby given that a deficiency has been found in your recent tax payment. An additional assessment of _____ is proposed."

If you wanted to make the headline sentence even more precise and make the idea clearer, you could start with:

> "Your recent tax payment was deficient."

And you would get:

> "Notice is hereby given that your recent tax payment appears to be deficient. An additional tax of _____ is proposed."

Notice that as you change the headline sentence, you change the sense of the whole idea without substantially changing the phrases and words used to add to the headline sentence.

If you want your writing to make sense, make sure that the headline sentence is clear. Then you can build on it without creating a lot of awkward phrases.

Verbs for action. When you want to talk about an action, put the word describing this action in *verb form.* This may sound like a very simple rule. Everyone knows that the verb is used to describe the action of the sentence. But many people violate it by turning the verb of the sentence into a noun. Here's a simple example:

"*Approval* of requests for transfer by the department director is necessary."

Note here that the action of the sentence is *approve*, but that this word has been made into a noun and put at the beginning of the sentence. This makes it necessary for the writer to find another verb, *is necessary*. Not only that, it makes the sentence ambiguous. You really can't tell if the director is approving requests for transfer or if there is someone else who has to approve the director's requests.

We tend to do a lot of this kind of thing in writing formal prose; it's unnecessary and it leads to longer, more complex sentences. If you find that you do it often, that you begin a lot of your sentences with actions stated in noun form, try restating your headline sentences with these words restated in verb form. Then rebuild your sentence. You'll find that the sentences get easier to read and to write.

To recognize this problem, look at the beginning of your sentences for words that end in:

Suffix	Example
–al	Denial for deny, refusal for refused
–ion	Construction for constructed, examination for examined
–ment	Employment for employed
–ance	Compliance for complied, reliance for relied
–ence	Dependence for depended
–ity	Specificity for specified

It isn't absolutely necessary to eliminate all these constructions, but if you construct sentences in this form all the time, it will make your work hard to follow. Here's what it might sound like:

"Specificity of the regulations is a cause for their commendation by the public."

This means:

"The public commends these regulations because they are specific."

Or

"Because the regulations specify what needs to be done, the public commends them."

In general, the idea becomes clearer as you switch from the noun form to the verb form.

Keep headline sentence intact. The headline sentence contains the main idea of the sentence in its simplest, clearest form. If the reader can *find* this portion of the overall sentence, the reader is likely to be able to understand—at least to get the basic idea. If this is to happen, you have to keep the parts of the headline sentence intact. This means that as a general rule, the additional information you put around the headline sentence should be *put around* it, not mixed in with it. Diagrammed, your sentences should look like this:

> Additional information—HEADLINE SENTENCE—Additional information.

Not like this:

> HEAD—Additional information—LINE—Additional information—SENTENCE.

In an actual sentence, the effect is almost the same. Here's an example from a fund-raising campaign memo:

> "Your responses expressing concern for those not able to contribute at the level of $750–1000 over a three-year period, which would be the amount necessary for us to reach the $250,000 mark, is well taken."

The sentence here was written haphazardly, without a thought for whether the headline sentence could be found or whether it made any sense. It doesn't, and the writer didn't even recognize the problem. Put together, the elements of the headline sentence read:

> "Your responses is well taken."

With the headline portion of the sentence intact, you can *see* it better, and so the error is easier to spot. The rewrite begins with a new headline sentence:

> "Your concern is valid."

This leads to the following sentence, with modifying phrases kept out of the headline construction:

> "Your concern is valid because many may not be able to contribute at the level of $750–1000 over a three-year period, even though this would be the amount necessary for us to reach the $250,000 mark."

Prefer simple modifier forms. You have two choices when you want to add information to a headline sentence. You can add single words or you can add phrases. In general, your writing will be clearer and easier to read if you choose the single words.

"A matter of importance"   becomes   "An important matter"

"At a level of $300"   becomes   "At the $300 level"

"It is obvious that"   becomes   "Obviously"

"Each of these examples"   becomes   "Each example

It's almost always possible to find a single word to substitute for a long phrase, and it's often worth looking for one. A lot of phrases strung out after part of the main idea can confuse the reader.

CHAPTER SUMMARY

This is a very general set of standards, probably not specific enough for you to use as the basis for review of any particular report. But you may find these useful as a basic guide when you start to prepare an office review policy and you begin to deal with the question of standards. I have found that these standards are a good foundation to any review policy; I've used them as a starting point in a number of offices.

APPENDIX

WHAT TO DO WHEN YOU'RE REVIEWING AND YOU CAN'T FIGURE OUT HOW TO FIX A PASSAGE

Having standards is only part of an effective review. You also have to have a procedure that helps you figure out what's wrong with a particular sentence and what to do to fix it. Many people just keep writing the sentence over and over and over again until they get it right by accident. 1 think you can do better.

The key to correcting mistakes is to start over again. You can get so wrapped up trying to fix a sentence that you can even forget to think about it. So the best thing to do is analyze the sentence in much the same way that you analyzed the assignment.

1. First, underline all the key words in the sentence.
2. String the key words out in the order in which they ought to occur (chronological order for processes, comparison order for comparisons, etc.).
3. Fit all the words together with connecting phrases.

You only go through this kind of process when you're really stuck on a sentence. Most of the time you can write pretty easily just by concentrating on your subject. But when you have a real problem, this method works. Here's what it looks like in practice on a *really difficult sentence,* from a scientific report:

> "Among commercial bean varieties, moths showed no ovipositional preference between bush beans and lima beans when presented with other plant hosts, each variety receiving slightly different but statistically significant like numbers of eggs."

The writer of this sentence played around with it for considerable time before giving up and starting from scratch. If you begin with a list of the key words in the sentence, you get:

—bean varieties
—moths
—preference (a verb made into a noun)
—bush beans
—lima beans
—other plant hosts
—eggs

This is obviously going to be a complex sentence. So we have to organize the elements carefully. The sentence describes something that *happened*—a process. Thus, we put the elements in chronological order:

> Moths/bush beans, lima beans, other plant hosts/eggs/prefer/ bean varieties

Connecting these, we get:

> "When moths are placed in a chamber with bush beans, lima beans, and other plant hosts, they lay about the same number of eggs on each of the commercial bean varieties, indicating that they do not prefer either bush beans or lima beans for ovipositioning."

Only the writer of the original sentence can do this sort of editing, because only the writer can know exactly what connections should be made between the items in the key word list.

Perhaps the most important point to make about this simple editing procedure is that *the same process that helps you understand the assignment—what someone else said—can help you understand your own work.* In fact, this sentence could sum up this entire book. You conduct research by breaking the project into its parts and then assembling them, along with the data you've collected, in the same logical order.

SECTION FIVE SUMMARY AND THE ANSWERS TO SOME QUESTIONS YOU MAY STILL HAVE

Summary

Writing and review are both processes that can be done in an orderly manner. To write, you need an outline and you have to have the information you're going to write about clearly organized. From this point, it's pretty easy to build good sentences by starting with headline sentences jotted down for each paragraph. When editing and reviewing, you can deal with the report in an orderly manner, provided you have a clear office policy to guide you. Without such a policy, review tends to be a merely personal affair, which can and does degenerate into bickering and mumbling behind each other's backs. It is possible to establish viable, objective standards for reports, but they must be done carefully. They're best done cooperatively.

Answers to Questions I Frequently Get Asked at This Stage

The writing process described in these chapters is the best way I know to solve writing problems. It works for me and has worked for dozens of other people who have had the discipline to try it. But these chapters have been designed to demonstrate this process, and in doing so, I've left a number of common questions about writing unanswered.

1. How about introductions? How do I go about getting a paper started?

   There are a million "best" ways, and one sure, efficient way that almost never fails is to just start right off and answer the first question on your reader question list. Don't bother trying for a cute introduction; just get into the subject. For example, if you're doing a paper that requires you to answer the question "What's the problem?", you'll find it quite acceptable to start off "The problem we were given was . . . ." There is no need to beat around the bush. Get to it.

2. Won't that get boring?

   No. Your reader will get bored if you spend two paragraphs just getting to the subject. After all, this report writing isn't likely to win you any awards for suspense and mystery writing. If the reader cares about the subject, your report will get read.

3. Can I use "I" in the report? What else should I try?

   There's a lot of talk about making government reports more "human" and "personal" these days, and yet most people don't feel it is appropriate to use "I" in a report. They feel this way because the report really represents the whole office, the agency, in which it is prepared. The author may not even get any credit for the report. So "I" is logically frowned upon. What can you use as a substitute? You can always say "we" when it's necessary. But you should avoid things like "the author" or "the researcher." Instead, try eliminating the personal reference entirely. Instead of "I think the staff should collect . . . ," say "Staff should collect . . . ." In short, avoid all the lead-ins to sentences that require you to say "I." This doesn't mean that the use of "I" is strictly forbidden. Sometimes you will want to make a point very strongly, and will want to emphasize that this is personal opinion. I've done this many times in this book. Under these circumstances, it's usually OK. The only question you should ask yourself is "Why am I expressing personal opinion in an official report?"

4. What about passive voice?

There is nothing wrong with passive voice. Sometimes it's even more efficient than active voice. And it's just as clear. You wouldn't get confused by:

> *"The project was completed."*

Or

> *"The data were collected."*

These are passive, and there is nothing troublesome about the phrases at all. What most people find troublesome isn't the passive voice but the practice of turning verbs into nouns, which happens to generate a passive verb at the end of the sentence. People will object to:

> *"Completion of the project was accomplished."*
> Real verb   Passive

Instead of:

> *"The project was completed."*

Or

> *"Collection of the data was conducted."*
> Real verb   Passive

Instead of:

> *"The data were collected."*

It isn't the passive form that causes the problem, it's the verb turned into the noun that makes the sentence seem stilted.

5. What about long sentences?

There are so-called rules that say sentences over some arbitrary length are "bad." The long sentence is usually thought of as something over twenty to twenty-five words. This is just hogwash. You can write clear long sentences as easily as clear short sentences. In some cases, breaking a single, unified, complex idea into three short, choppy sentences destroys clarity rather than adding to it. The key to clear sentences is the simplicity, sense, and positioning of the headline sentence. If you write a good headline sentence and build on it carefully, it doesn't matter how long the sentence gets—up to about fifty or sixty words. At this point length does become important, because it gets difficult to fit phrases into the sentence. However, there is no valid, arbitrary length standard worth paying any attention to. Pay attention to the sense of your headline sentence and how carefully you add information to this basic sentence core. Write systematically and you won't have any problem writing perfectly clear, long sentences.

6. What if the boss wants me to use a word I don't like? What if the boss has favorite phrases?

   Why fight it? As long as the changes don't really affect clarity, why not just give in? After all, the report reflects some of the boss's thinking too. In short, it is silly for professionals to worry about this issue—which is raised during nearly every research project. When I write for an agency, I often read over several reports just to find out what the boss's key words and phrases are. They tell me something about the way the boss thinks, and they help me provide convenient guideposts for at least one important reader.

7. What about the length of the report?

   There are a lot of myths about short reports and long reports and how much a report weighs, etc. They're all just the result of egos clashing. If you actually answer the questions the boss wants answered in a short report, you can be reasonably sure the boss will accept the report. The reason that some reports keep getting rejected until they reach 200 pages is that it takes the writer that long to get around to answering the real questions behind the report. Most of the time, I work anonymously—the person reading the final report never knows that a consultant has been involved in it. I never worry about the stories I hear about how long or short the report should be. I just concentrate on quality, and I haven't had a report sent back in a long time.

SOME NOTES ON MANAGEMENT PARTICIPATION IN RESEARCH

The manager's job is to make sure things get done—not to do them. In normal office situations, the manager doesn't actually work; the manager just coordinates the work of others.

Research is not normal work. It requires special staff skills and it requires special management policy. It is, after all, an almost pure mental skill. The manager can't go around and inspect work in progress, because the work is in the researcher's brain. Managing research successfully thus requires some unusual efforts, both from staff and from management.

Research also places the manager in the awkward position of not knowing as much about the subject as the researcher does. The boss does not have the clear advantage of superior experience or superior knowledge to back up decrees. The boss is in the weakest position—from an authoritarian standpoint—during any research effort.

STAFFING AND QUALITY CONTROL IN RESEARCH

18

Because research isn't normal work in most agencies, it places some special demands on all involved. It just doesn't fit into the normal office patterns. Most people who have done research projects in government agencies recognize the symptoms of this special nature of research. When a research project is underway, schedules have to be adjusted, roles of those involved in research change dramatically as they take on the authority that goes with a demand that they get data, and priorities in the office shift. This is usually most evident at the very end—when the report is being written, edited, and typed. If it's a major report, the whole office changes. Everything gets cooperative, and traditional relationships break down. The boss's private secretary may be called into service to help edit and type the final draft, and junior staff will suddenly find themselves taking calls in private offices. Things get pretty strange.

During this process, the manager is under particular strain. To manage, you must keep control of things. You must know who is doing what—where, how, and why. This is the reason for having lines of authority, for having different roles in the office, and for maintaining formal relationships. When these begin to break down in research—and it is inevitable that they will—the manager is faced with a number of problems to solve. Every manager will deal with these problems in his or her own way, but it's useful to look at them in a general manner and to discuss general approaches to solving them.

PROBLEMS

Replacing Traditional Authority with Intellectual Authority

Implicit in any request for a report is a certain *humility*. You do not ask for a report if you already know what the report is going to contain (unless you're playing games or using the report as a training tool). In most cases, the report request is an admission that you need help. Even if you treat the whole business in an authoritarian manner and demand a report, you're still implying a need for help. You need the data and you don't have the time to get it yourself.

Staff perceives this, and it often changes their attitudes toward their roles in the office. Few self-respecting staff cynics will openly admit that they feel more important when asked to do a report, but the evidence that they *do* is overwhelming. Slowly their conversation shifts from day-to-day concerns to talk of overall agency concerns. They tend to get detached from the regular work of the office, and they often begin to demand—and get—special treatment. They become an extension of management, not just ordinary workers.

There is a conflict between the *reality* of this feeling and the *old reality* of the traditional lines of authority in the office. *The old lines of authority break down in the face of the real need for research staff to have free access to all the resources in the office.* Rules are put aside. Research staff are encouraged to break routines so that the report can get done. The researcher will slowly take on a new identity in the office. It's inevitable.

As the traditional lines of authority break down, as the researcher becomes exempt from normal operating rules, you have to find new sources of authority. You have to replace the authority of *boss* with the authority of *advisor*. You have to establish your intellectual authority.

Doing this isn't difficult for any good manager, but it does require some different management approaches. It mostly requires a turn toward *participative management*. Much has been written about how to manage participatively, and I don't intend to repeat the theory here. In practice what this means is that in a research effort, you exert your authority by controlling and guiding the research *process*. Instead of concentrating on review of results, you take a part in and guide the research process. You do this by talking and asking questions.

In the very beginning of a research effort, for example, staff will be thinking about what direction to pursue. There will be a lot of very casual conversation about what the project should cover and about what questions need to be answered. You should probably let this go on for a while; then call in your researcher (or researchers) and simply ask questions. Ask about what they've done. Ask them if they've considered all the users of the report. Discuss with them the direction they've taken and how this direction will lead them to answers that will or will not serve the needs of the agency. In short, take a broad managerial perspective in your discussions and simply make sure that staff are keeping that perspective in mind as they work. In doing this, you will exert the influence you need to without imposing rigid rules on an essentially creative process.

The Staffing Problem

When you ask for a report, you're most often asking for staff to give you information that will help you solve a problem. You may actually want something innovative. To get this, you'll have to have someone innovative working on the report. But, at the same time, you don't want a bunch of half-baked ideas from some person who has no real appreciation for the workings of government.

Your initial tendency may be to put someone creative and energetic on the project; your second thought may be to put some "old reliable" on the project. Your final tendency may be to wonder which you really want. You want both. Research requires both creative, quick-thinking people and disciplined, reliable, level-headed people. If you can't find one person with these qualities in combination, get two. But there is a more creative approach to solving this problem that works well in some offices. First, identify those people in the office who are both creative and reliable. You'll find a lot of them in the managerial ranks. Many very good workers end up as managers—whether they enjoy managing or not. They have to be reliable; you don't promote people who let you down (except in rare cases where you promote to get rid of the person). And they have to be relatively creative, because management has required them to shift perspectives—from a staff perspective to an overview. If you take a little time to observe these people, you'll find some of them who just *love* projects and who are quite good at them. Others will just *hate* projects.

In one office I have worked in, the agency director saw these tendencies in her managers. She adjusted her staff accordingly. She gave the project-oriented managers very strong, reliable administrative assistants—people who could take over an office for a month or two if necessary. And she thus created a staff of very experienced researchers for the *major* studies done by the agency.

In another office, an upper-level manager solved the creativity–discipline problem in a similar fashion. He found those managers in the office who were good at and liked research, and made them *resident advisors*. For every study done in the office, these people performed the task of listening to research staff problems and suggesting solutions. They gave staff someone to talk to—someone high enough to be a reliable indicator of management philosophy in the agency and low enough to be "unthreatening." After about three years, these advisors became real experts at directing studies, and the general level of information that upper management could expect from a staff study improved considerably.

The Clout Problem

Often, the staff assigned to do research are junior staff. Many will be new *staff analysts*. These people don't have the official clout to do effective research if that research involves gaining access to records and meeting with other agency representatives. Yet, often, they're the only staff who can be spared for a study.

The manager who wants effective research has to figure out some way of transferring to junior staff the authority and official presence to be able to cut through red tape to get to information. In addition, management may have to deal with the problem of inexperienced research staff getting hoodwinked by older, more politically wise staff.

GENERAL SOLUTIONS

No single action can solve all these managerial problems. But a solution can be found. It begins with a general strategy. *To establish control over a research effort, you have to work to control the re-*

search process—not the product. Instead of trying to tell the re-searcher exactly what you want (how can you possibly know what recommendation you want?), just make sure the researcher does all the steps in the process carefully. Make sure the assignment is analyzed thoroughly. Make sure the researcher takes time to consider all readers' interests. Make sure the data collection is planned. And so forth. Control the process of research; the results will then be valid. Don't try to get too deeply involved in any one step. Don't try to argue about the results or to fight over interpretation. Instead, just sit back and ask questions about how staff have done or are planning to do each research step. You'll force staff to think this way without seeming to force answers on them.

You can actually manage a research process this way, and you have a great advantage if you stick to this *process management.* The advantage is that you don't get lost in all the detail of the research; you keep your general perspective on the whole project. In doing so, you provide staff with the firm, basic guidelines they need during this complicated process. When they get too high in the clouds, you bring them back to earth by reminding them of the basic thinking process, by asking them simple procedural questions. Staff will recognize the value of this sort of advice, and you will get good research results without the danger of alienating your staff by trying to do the work for them.

Treat Research Efforts as a Special Class of Work

There ought to be an open and frank relationship established between management and research staff at the very beginning of the research effort. Staff ought to be told that the old rules are temporarily suspended, that for the time being this is a participative effort. Roles should be dealt with specifically, and staff should be told that after the project is over there will be a return to the old lines of authority. In short, admit that you're all going to have to work as a team, that every opinion is valuable to the research effort. Carefully define the role you'll play in the research process, and then stick to this role. Set forth clear lines of responsibility. In short, reorganize your entire research group along new, functional lines. Make sure you explain that this new structure will disappear when the project is done.

Schedule Plenty of Your Time for Participation

After you've gone over the initial assignment, set up a firm schedule of meetings. Make sure you know when portions of the study will be completed; make sure you participate at every critical point in the development of research plans. Don't expect to be invited to the really important work sessions—invite yourself.

One good way of doing this is to ask staff for a schedule of their own work group meetings. Then, just drop in. Don't make it a formal visit, just drop in, talk freely, answer questions, and settle disputes. Your influence will be appreciated and won't seem intrusive.

Select Staff Carefully

Try to find staff members who can actually do the job you're asking for. If you want data to use in an office reorganization, pick someone in the office with some managerial experience as well as someone fresh and new to the job. Spend some time in this process of selecting staff, and consider seriously taking someone off other, routine jobs to take on research. Don't just take the people who happen to be available.

Perhaps the best staffing advice I can give takes the form of an example. I remember working in one agency on a number of reports. One of the reports I revised concerned the coordination of one unit with another—both in the same agency. The staff who had prepared the report (after about three months of work) had suggested a clearly unworkable change in administrative procedure. The report was rejected, and I was called in to fix it. I read the report, walked down the hall to the office of someone I had worked with before, and talked about the report for about three hours. We figured out a better coordination procedure, and I went back and rewrote the report. The problem? The fellow who knew the most about the subject hadn't been assigned to the research effort. Why? He was too busy doing routine, day-to-day stuff. His supervisor had refused to allow him to be taken off the day-to-day work. The manager who wanted the study had thus assigned two relatively new people to the job, and they had wasted three months. They were bright people, but government organization is a complex business; they just didn't have the experience. They collected good data, but didn't know how to interpret it.

A good general staffing rule to follow is:

CHOOSE THE BEST PEOPLE YOU CAN FIND IN THE OFFICE FOR RESEARCH EFFORTS. YOU WILL MAKE DECISIONS ON THE BASIS OF THE RESULTS, AND THESE DECISIONS WILL OFTEN BE FAR MORE IMPORTANT TO THE OFFICE THAN A FEW WEEKS OF PRODUCTIVITY LOST. PULL GOOD PEOPLE OFF ROUTINE WORK. LET JUNIOR STAFF REPLACE THEM TEMPORARILY.

Keep an Open Office

The manager's most important role in research is to provide a managerial perspective whenever staff have a dispute. Keep your door open; let it be known that you want to help settle disputes.

Act on Recommendations

There are times when results will not be to your liking. Expect this; you've asked for a study because you suspect that something needs to be changed. When you get results you don't like, accept them. Once you determine that they're *valid*, act on them. Don't ignore recommendations merely because they're unpleasant. Don't get defensive.

Research depends on the creative energy and interest of the researcher. Nothing kills this energy and interest faster than to have a report buried. If you want to establish an atmosphere that promotes good research, so that you can have good data on which to base decisions, you'll have to treat results with integrity.

CHAPTER SUMMARY

All this advice really boils down to this: It's the manager's job to guide research, to see to it that staff have the resources to do a good job of getting data, and to then act on the basis of the research. *The manager is responsible for maintaining the integrity of the research effort. The manager must take steps to make sure the research can and will be done well; otherwise, research is just a waste of time, effort, and money.*

In managing research, the best approach is to concentrate on making sure staff do all the steps properly. Keep the processes of research under control, and you ensure good results.

THE END

This has been a book about mental processes, about steps in the thinking that goes into a research effort. If you added up all the steps discussed, you'd probably find about eighty or ninety distinct, important procedures, beginning with the initial assignment analysis and ending with editing and review procedures.

Since there are so many steps, it is unlikely that you can remember all of them in exactly the right order—I can't. In addition, there is a danger of getting lost in the slow progress of research, of forgetting where you're going and how you're planning on getting there. This isn't a problem peculiar to this process; it happens whenever you get involved in something that takes a lot of steps.

A good friend and I once decided to take on another process with a long and detailed series of unknown steps. We had a Porsche engine to rebuild, something a lot of people would shy away from. We didn't; we decided that it was, after all, just a matter of doing every step in order and doing every step carefully. It took three months to get the thing apart and to get parts and reassemble it. During this time, there were moments when we were sure the thing just wasn't going to work. We would stare at the workbench littered with parts and we'd just know that it wasn't going to run. But we kept cleaning parts, attaching bits and pieces together, fitting one assembly to another. Without any real sense of getting things done, without being able to see that the engine was going together right, we just kept doing steps described in the manual. Then, one afternoon, we looked at the workbench and saw no more parts—just a complete engine.

Doing anything that takes a lot of steps always makes you wonder about whether you've done one step wrong—somewhere in the past. We looked at the engine and were not sure that it would run. We had done everything by the book, had taken every step carefully, but we weren't sure it would fire up. We installed it and it looked like what an engine should look like. All the proper lights went on when we turned the key. And, of course, the thing ran.

In following the procedures outlined in this book, you're likely to have a similar experience. You'll work along for a while, particularly in the very beginning, and wonder if these steps will really get you where you want to go. You'll have all the parts of the research effort spread out before you and wonder if you'll ever get the whole business back together. It will take some real patience before you'll find out. You'll just have to keep following steps, one step after another. Then, all of a sudden, the whole report will be staring you in the face. One sentence after another you'll have put the thing together. And, if you have done all the steps carefully, it will be good.

The most important thing that will happen at this point is that you'll realize what my friend and I realized after we got the Porsche engine running: If you do all the steps right, you get professional results. There is no mystery to good research. It's a function of orderly, disciplined, careful thinking—thinking in steps. If you do the steps, your thinking is probably going to be as good as that of any professional researcher.

It took us three months to put the Porsche engine together. A professional would have done it in three days. We took that long merely because it was new to us; the professional would have known all the steps by heart—from practice. The same thing is going to be true the first time you try some of these methods. It took me about a month to get quick at analyzing assignments. It took me several years to learn all the little tricks to analyzing the readers' interests and predicting readers' questions. It will take you some time, too. But as you repeat the processes, they will get easier, and you'll begin to get a sense of how they all fit together. After a while, they'll become second nature.

Will it ever get easy? No. I still skin my knuckles when I put an engine together. And I still have to work through these steps carefully and thoughtfully when I work on a research process. I get really tired doing it; research wears you out. But I enjoy the process, because in the end I've found that it works. I follow all the steps, and it works. And it works not because I'm brighter than the next guy or because I've got some mysterious abilities; it works because the process of doing research has been pretty clearly established over several hundred years. When you force yourself to do all the tried-and-true steps, the result is good research.

And, will the boss "buy" the report? Yes. Oh, you'll get a few suggestions, and you'll have to change a few words here and there, but the boss really just wants a good report and will recognize one when you present it.

BIBLIOGRAPHY

Research

Freedman, Paul. *The Principles of Scientific Research.* New York: Pergamon Press, 1960.

Gorden, Raymond L. *Interviewing: Strategy, Techniques, and Tactics.* Homewood, Ill.: Dorsey Press, 1975.

Hillway, Tyrus. *Introduction to Research.* Boston: Houghton Mifflin, 1964.

Kahn, R. L. *The Dynamics of Interviewing: Theory, Technique, and Cases.* New York: Wiley, 1957.

Nagi, Saad Z., and Ronald G. Corwin. *The Social Contexts of Research.* London: Wiley, 1972.

Scribner, Richard A., and Rosemary A. Chalk. *Adapting Science to Social Needs: Knowledge, Institutions, People into Action.* Washington, D.C.: American Association for the Advancement of Science, 1977.

Warwick, Donald. *The Sample Survey: Theory and Practice.* New York: McGraw-Hill, 1975.

Sampling and Statistics

Arkin, Herbert. *A Handbook of Sampling for Auditing and Accounting,* 2d ed. New York: McGraw-Hill, 1974.

Burstein, Herman. *Attribute Sampling.* New York: McGraw-Hill, 1971.

Caulcott, Evelyn. *Significance Tests.* Boston: Routledge and Kegan Paul, 1973.

Ford, Julienne. *Paradigms and Fairy Tales: An Introduction to the Science of Meanings.* Boston: Routledge and Kegan Paul, 1975.

Slocum, M. J. *Sampling: A Quick, Reliable Guide to Practical Statistics.* New York: Simon and Schuster, 1960.

Spence, J. T., *et al. Elementary Statistics.* New York: Appleton-Century-Crofts, 1968.

Tippet, L. H. C. *Random Sampling Numbers.* Cambridge, England: University Press, 1959.

Weiss, C. H. *An Introduction to Sample Surveys for Government Managers.* Washington, D.C.: The Urban Institute, 1971.

INDEX

INDEX

Alternatives:
    organizing analysis of, 110–111
    question list for, 73
Analysis, 193–227
    basic process defined, 34–36
    form for outline of, 120
    of poor data, 207
    of readers, 53
Assignments, 9–43
    ability to remember, 10, 34
    analysis of, 46
    how to clarify, 29–30
    how to give, 29–30, 68
    initial thoughts about, 21
    narrowing scope of, 30, 38, 40–41
    questions to ask about, 38
    reading between the lines, 37–39, 43
    vagueness of, 9–11, 30
Audits, definition of, 97
Authority, during research, 274

Bias:
    controlling for, 163
    in research, 165–183
Brainstorming, 19–97
    basic steps, 26, 31, 118
    objectives of, 22
    summary of process, 118

Case analysis, pattern for, 77–78, 119
Causation, 218–228
    different from excuse, 219–222
    different from responsibility, 251
    in problem studies, 75
    organizing cause-effect statements,
        119
    procedure for determining, 222
Checklists:
    assignment elements, 36
    assignment questions, 38
    data sources, 157–158

Checklists (continued):
    organization patterns, 118–122
    questions to answer when asking for
        data, 151
    reader questions, 70–82
    steps in planning data collection,
        167–168
Contingency planning, in research, 187
Contract for report, 22–125
    basic contract process, 22–23
    example, 24
    management review, 44, 99–125
Cost/Benefit Analysis, questions for, 61
Credibility, in research, 5–7, 45

Data collection, 127–181
    interpretation and, 183
    secondary and primary, 149, 160
    sources of data, 150
    when to start, 65–66
Data Shells, 136–141
    interpretation and, 183–186, 199
Decision making, and
    recommendations, 73
Definitions:
    audit, 97
    data processing, 104
    design, 89
    effect, 97
    efficiency, 97
    job, 92
    letter, 93
    management, 87
    procedure, 96
    programs, 98
Design, defined, 89

Effect, defined, 97
Effectiveness, defined, 109
    organizing for evaluation of, 119

Index

Efficiency, definition of, 97
  in research, 44
Environmental Impact Reports, 77–81
Existing data, 162–170
  sources, 150
  uses of, 164

Feasibility studies, 77–73
Feedback:
  on assignment, 13
  on project design, 64
Focus of study, and title, 100–106
Frustration, in report process, 49

Graphic forms, 142–147
Group projects, staffing, 64, 273–279

Implementation, questions about, 76
Interviews, 178–181
Introductions:
  how to start, 268
  questions to answer in, 6 –81
IRAC pattern, 119

Job, defined, 92
Job descriptions, 70
Job letter, 116

Key words:
  in assignment, 13, 36, 37, 83
  report outline and, 105
  subject of report and, 83
  thinking and, 12
  title and, 100–103

Management, defined, 87
Manuals, organizing for, 107, 118
Measurement of results:
  direct, 133
  indirect, 133, 189
  numerical, 132

Objectivity in research, 132
  and politics, 4–7
Office reorganization, studies, 194
Organization, 99–123
  basic patterns, 108
  purpose and, 107
Outlines, 99–123
  readers' questions and, 54–56
  writing from, 229–231

Passive voice, 269
Paragraphing, 241–242
Personal pronouns, use in reports, 268
Personnel recommendations, 71
Planning in research, 226

Policy memos, 55–57
Politics in report process, 3–8, 46,
  85, 189, 226
Predictive research, 194–195, 210
Problem analysis:
  organization of, 119
  questions for, 74–75
Procedure, defined, 96
Professionalism in research, 7
Program, defined, 98
Program justifications, 58–63
Progress reports, 45
Proposals, 81–82

Questionnaires, 180–181

Readers, 46–81
  analysis of, 53
  defined, 50–51
  of job letters, 112
  satisfying, 52–56
Regulations, explaining, 70
Reliability, defined, 132
Reports:
  environmental impact assessment,
    77–81
  explaining a rule, 70
  feasibility studies, 71–73
  giving assignments, 68
  job descriptions, 70
  length of, 270
  multi-audience, 58–63, 77–81
  policy memos, 55–57
  program justifications, 58–63
  progress, 45
  proposals, 81–82
  public, different from in-house, 14
  recommendations of personnel, 71
  response to complaints, 69
  studies of a problem, 74–75
Research:
  as a cause of problems, 174, 201, 273
  conditions, and interpretation of, 195,
    211
  difficulty of, 122
  experimental, 176–177
  interactive, 163–164
  measuring results of, 130
  observational, 176
  passive, 164
  plan for, 55
  pyramiding in secondary, 151
  quantifying concepts in, 88, 130, 138
  scope of, 93
  secondary and primary, 129
Research methods, 127–191
Research process, control of, 277

Review, 249–259
    as a training function, 249–250
    attitudes towards, 250–252
    policy, 254–255
    procedure for, 266–267
    standards for, 252, 260–265

Sampling, 212–217
Scope of assignment and report, 33, 52
Sentences:
    basic structure, 243
    building, 239–242
    length of, 269
Statisticians, working with, 141, 208
Style, 243–244
    guidelines for, 262–265
    strategies for, 16–17, 236–237, 243
Systems analysis, 121

Tests, 177–178
Thinking process:
    control of, 12, 24–25, 183
    simple is best, 91
    step-by-step, 280
Title, and research scope, 103–105

Wording, 261
    in title, 105
    loaded, in assignment, 42–43
    tone, 45, 64, 261
Writing, 229–265
    and subject analysis, 85
    and thinking, 232–233
    process for, 238–244